# Texts and Monographs in Computer Science

# Texts and Monographs in Computer Science

*continued after index*

W. Bischofberger  G. Pomberger

# Prototyping-Oriented Software Development

## Concepts and Tools

With 89 Figures

Springer-Verlag

Berlin Heidelberg New York London Paris
Tokyo Hong Kong Barcelona Budapest

*Authors*

Walter R. Bischofberger
Schweizerische Bankgesellschaft
Abt. UBILAB, Postfach
CH-8021 Zürich, Switzerland

Gustav Pomberger
Institut für Wirtschaftsinformatik
und Organisationsforschung
Johannes-Kepler-Universität
Altenbergerstraße 69
A-4040 Linz, Austria

*Series Editor*

David Gries
Department of Computer Science
Cornell University
Upson Hall
Ithaca, NY 14853-7501, USA

ISBN-13:978-3-642-84762-2     e-ISBN-13:978-3-642-84760-8
DOI: 10.1007/978-3-642-84760-8

Library of Congress Cataloging-in-Publication Data
Pomberger, Gustav, 1949– Prototyping-oriented software development: concepts and tools/
G. Pomberger, W. Bischofberger. p. cm. – (Text and monographs in computer science) Includes biblio-
graphical references and index. ISBN-13:978-3-642-84762-2
1. Computer software – Develop-
ment. I. Bischofberger, W. (Walter), 1962–. II. Title III. Series QA76.76.D47P66  1992  005.1 –
dc20  92-18009

© Springer-Verlag Berlin Heidelberg 1992
Softcover reprint of the hardcover 1st edition  1992

Typesetting: Camera ready by author
33/3140 – 5 4 3 2 1 0 – Printed on acid-free paper

# Preface

This book is intended for anyone who plans, designs and implements software systems, for anyone who is involved with quality assurance, and hence for anyone who is interested in the practicability of modern concepts, methods and tools in the software development process. The book aims at software engineers and at students with specialized interests in the area of software engineering. The reader is expected to be familiar with the fundamental concepts of software engineering. In writing the book, the authors tap years of experience in industrial projects and research work in the development of methods and tools that support the software development process.

Perhaps now more than ever, the buzzword "software crisis" serves to alert us that software systems are often error-prone, that significant difficulties arise in mastering complexity in the production of software systems, and that the acceptance and adequacy of software products is significantly lower than is the case with other technical products. The following goals have been suggested for the improvement of the software development process:

- exact fulfillment of user requirements
- increased reliability and robustness
- greater modularity of both the development process and the product
- simple and adequate operation, i.e., better ergonomics
- easy maintainability and extensibility
- cost-effective portability
- increased reusability of software components
- reduced costs for production, operation and maintenance

Research and development work in the area of software engineering has increased dramatically in recent years. Research results that have been known for some time have been made feasible in practice due to technological advances, and thus new methods and tools have been made available to practitioners. Such methods and tools are no longer used individually, but are imbedded in a coordinated development strategy and supported by integrated development tools.

More and more scientists and practitioners agree that the classical sequential software life-cycle model and its associated tools no longer suffice, or are even unsuitable, for handling problems that arise during software development.

As Brooks reminds us: "We must take it as given that the user does not and cannot know what he wants with respect to artifacts as complex as those we now build. The mind of man cannot imagine all the ramifications of such artifacts. There must be an iterative cycle in which the professional works with the user to define the requirements; demonstrates their consequences in human factors, cost, and performance; then in a prototyping phase iterates with the user to develop a product that is, in fact, satisfactory [Bro87]."

While implementation is as late as possible in the classical sequential life-cycle model (only after the specification phase has been completed), here we take the opposite approach and implement a prototype as soon as possible. We need new implementation techniques and tools for the implementation of the prototype. The same applies to the design of the system architecture. It is practically impossible to attain an adequate system architecture on the first try. Here again we are better served if the design is iterative and the products of the development phases are verified by means of architecture prototypes. Thus is why exploratory and incremental design and implementation techniques are growing in importance. Using these techniques changes the structure of the life-cycle model and how it runs its course, as well as the tools needed.

The book strives to identify concepts and tools that support the prototyping-oriented development of software products. Technical aspects are emphasized over purely organizational ones; the latter are treated to some extent, but not in detail. The reader is introduced to well-known concepts and tools as well as to new ones developed by the authors.

## Acknowledgements

It is impossible to name all the people who influenced the writing of this book. Particular gratitude is due to Siemens AG Munich, who generously funded our research activities and the development of TOPOS (a TOolset for Prototyping-Oriented Software development), upon whose foundation this book could be written. We do want to mention by name M. Gonauser, W. Remmele, H. Schlemm, D. Kolb, and D. Klugmann of Siemens AG Munich.

We also owe a debt to E. Gamma, R. Marty, R. Keller, W. Pree, B. Schäffer, D. Schmidt, A.Weinand and R. Weinreich for valuable ideas and much discussion, and for availing software components. For conscientiously reading the rough draft and contributing valuable suggestions for improvements, we express our thanks to M. Dürst. In addition we are grateful to Springer-Verlag for the harmonious cooperation. Last but not least, we owe special thanks to our language specialist, R. Bach, for his patience and support in the formulation of the manuscript.

*W. Bischofberger*                                         *G. Pomberger*
*Zürich, Switzerland*                                        *Linz,*
*Austria*

December 1991

# Table of Contents

## Part II TOPOS A Toolset for Prototyping-Oriented Software Development

# Introduction

Computer science is a rapidly evolving field. The speed of advances in hardware and software technology is unprecedented in other areas. In spite of these advances the requirements of computer users grow faster than they can be satisfied by the development of new applications. It even seems that with every advance in software technology the gap between supply and demand grows.

At the end of the Sixties the software crisis became more and more obvious. It was recognized that methods and tools supporting a systematic software development process were lacking. For this reason the idea emerged that software should not be developed in an ad hoc manner, but that it should be engineered like other technical products. As a logical consequence of these thoughts the term *software engineering* was coined for the field doing research in methods and tools for developing software systems.

The first progress was made in structuring algorithms, which is frequently called programming in the small. This progress encompassed stepwise refinement, structured programming and supporting programming languages, as well as tools for programming in the small.

In the Seventies the structuring of software systems, known as programming in the large, was explored. Various abstraction mechanisms for structuring large software systems were suggested, such as modules, abstract data types, genericity, and inheritance.

Parallel to these developments the software life-cycle model emerged as a model of the software development process (e.g., Figure 1). All approaches based on this model have one thing in common: they prescribe the activities to be carried out, their results, and their sequence. First the requirements are specified, then the structure of the software system is designed, and finally the application is implemented and tested.

In order to support such a development process, structured analysis and design methods and CASE tools were developed. When these methods and tools are used, the requirements are frequently described with data flow diagrams and entity/relationship diagrams. From these documents the structure of the software system is derived methodically using structured design. These methods therefore help to ensure that the final implementation does, in fact, adhere to the specification in a controlled fashion.

Growing size and complexity of software systems makes it increasingly difficult—if not impossible—to obtain an exact, complete requirements definition from a client. Even if clients know exactly what they need, they usually do not know what is feasible and cannot anticipate future requirements. When a sequential approach is used, errors and problems in the requirements definition frequently do not emerge before the final product is used by clients. The implementation team then has to rework the system to satisfy new requirements. That puts them into a situation that is not considered by conventional sequential methods.

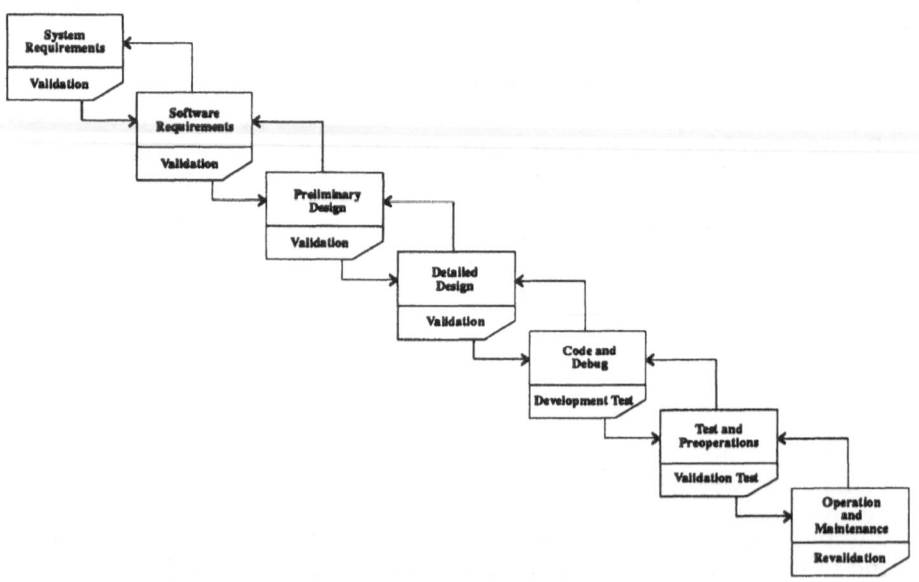

Figure 1. Conventional software life-cycle model (waterfall model) from [Boe76]

Research in the Eighties, therefore, concentrated on improving the specification of the initial requirements and the successive evolution of software systems. In order to solve these problems, two new concepts were developed: *prototyping* and *exploratory programming*. Applying one or both of these concepts leads to an iterative, cyclical development process as described, for example, by Boehm in his paper about the spiral model for software development [Boe88] (see Figure 2).

Prototyping helps to reduce the risks of incomplete and erroneous requirements definitions. Prototyping methods base on the idea that many misunderstandings between developers and clients as well as many errors can be eliminated during the requirements definition process if working software prototypes of the planned applications are built and examined. Today methods and tools supporting prototyping-oriented requirements definition are used, as described, for example, in [Con89], [Kel89], [Spi89], [Mar86a], and [Mar86b]. Unfortunately, prototyping methods are only useful if they are supported by tools that radically abbreviate the development time of a prototype.

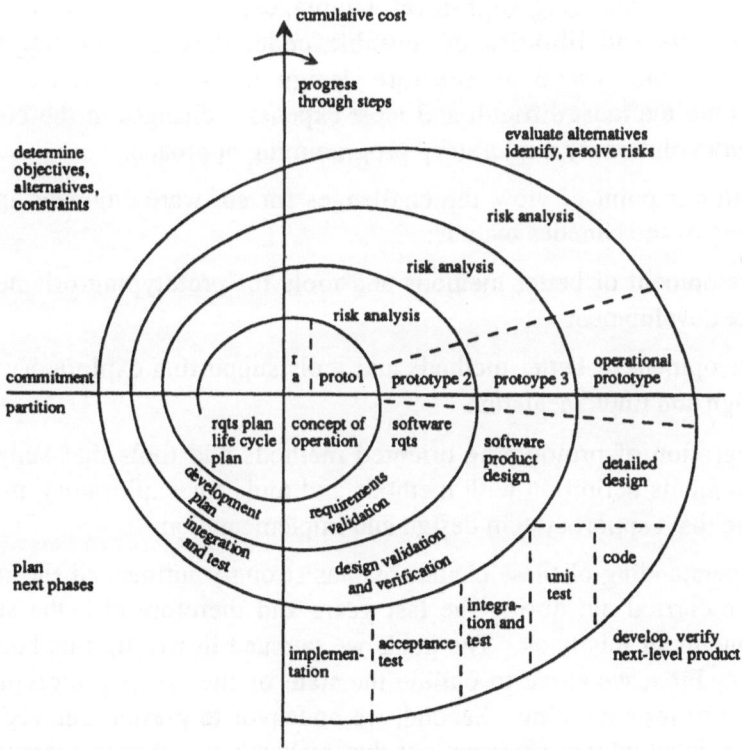

Figure 2. Iterative, cyclical software life cycle of Boehm (spiral model) [Boe88]

Researchers working in the field of artificial intelligence have to deal almost exclusively with novel, complex applications. Because of the novelty and complexity of their research area, it is in most cases difficult to find tools suited to quickly prototyping a new application.

For this reason it is not surprising that the paradigm of exploratory programming as well as many programming environments for exploratory programming were developed in the artificial intelligence community. Both exploratory programming and prototyping techniques are used to explore various solutions to a given problem. The difference is that prototyping is mostly applied during the requirements definition process, while exploratory programming, as its name indicates, is applied during system design and implementation.

Both exploratory programming and prototyping need tool support in order to realize and evaluate different solutions. Tools for exploratory programming, therefore, have to support fast development and modification of software systems.

While today's environments for exploratory programming support fast development with very high-level languages, interpretive development environments and libraries of reusable code, they do not support fast changes on the system architecture design level. Unfortunately these changes are the most difficult and most expensive changes in the course of using an evolutionary exploratory programming approach.

From our point of view the challenges for software engineering at the beginning of the Nineties include:

- development of better methods and tools for prototyping-oriented software development

- development of better methods and tools supporting exploratory system design and implementation

- integration of prototyping-oriented methods and tools that support requirements definition with methods and tools for exploratory programming that support system design and implementation

Our understanding of these challenges has strongly influenced the research we have carried out during the last years and therefore also the structure and contents of this book. The goals we pursued in writing this book were twofold. First, we strive to outline the state of the art in prototyping and exploratory programming. Second, we endeavor to present our vision of a software development environment that makes it possible to incrementally and evolutionarily apply both prototyping and exploratory programming. These goals have lead to a division of this book into two parts.

## Part I: Prototyping-Oriented Software Development—Concepts and Tools

- Chapter 1 gives an overview of various software development paradigms known today. First the sequential life-cycle paradigm is discussed. On the basis of this discussion, newer paradigms are explained and compared with the sequential paradigm.

- Chapter 2 gives an overview of the state of the art of prototyping by discussing various aspects of prototyping and a set of exemplary approaches and tools. The discussed approaches are user interface prototyping, prototyping of modular and concurrent software architectures, and prototyping of information systems.

- Chapter 3 presents concepts and tools that build the foundation for the successful application of exploratory programming. This chapter emphasizes programming environments as well as concepts and tools for the reuse of design information and code.

- Chapter 4 presents additional considerations about prototyping in a question-and-answer format.

## Part II: TOPOS—A Toolset for Prototyping-Oriented Software Development

- Chapter 5 starts with a discussion of a prototyping-oriented software life cycle, which consists of overlapping prototyping and exploratory programming processes. Then it presents the basic ideas underlying TOPOS, the tool set we have chosen as the vehicle to illustrate our idea of a prototyping-oriented software development environment. Finally, it explains the overall structure of TOPOS, i.e., its component tools and their interaction.

- Chapter 6 presents CMT, the TOPOS component management tool. CMT supports the management of the various documents that are produced during the prototyping-oriented software development process. Furthermore, it comprises the heart of the user interface of TOPOS by providing means to integrate, invoke, and coordinate other tools of TOPOS.

- Chapter 7 presents DICE, the TOPOS user interface prototyping tool. DICE supports WYSIWYG specification of the layout and parts of the functionality of modern user interfaces, as well as the immediate interpretive execution of the resulting specifications. DICE also provides an interprocess communication interface that makes it possible to connect it with other tools in order to flexibly add functionality to a prototype which cannot be expressed in terms of the user interface.

- Chapter 8 presents SCT, the exploratory design and programming environment of TOPOS. SCT is an interpretive exploratory programming environment for Modula-2. It makes it possible to interpret modules that are still being implemented as well as to compile and directly execute implemented and tested modules. Besides the features expected from an exploratory programming environment, SCT supports prototyping-oriented system architecture validation. This is achieved by making it possible to simulate modules and application parts that have been designed but not yet implemented, while all existing application parts such as prototypes and already implemented modules are executed. Since SCT consists of several tools, their underlying concepts and application is described in subsections.

- Chapter 9 explains and illustrates how other tools can be integrated into TOPOS.

- Chapter 10 starts with a discussion of how TOPOS can be applied in a prototyping-oriented incremental software development process and presents a comprehensive scenario that illustrates the process model.

- Chapter 11 relates experience with the concepts and tools embodied in TOPOS, assesses their implications, and considers further developments which could be undertaken based on the new concepts.

# Part I

# Prototyping-Oriented Software Development

## Paradigms, Concepts, and Tools

Careful planning is the key to safe and swift travel.

Ulysses[1]

---

[1] in [Asp78]

# 1 Paradigms for Software Development

Whenever people are confronted with the need to solve a complex task, they attempt to systematically decompose the task, i.e., to define an approach model. Such an approach model regulates how the process of solving the task is to proceed. It decomposes the solving process into manageable steps and is intended to enable a stepwise planning, decision and realization process.

This basic idea of systems engineering lends itself well to the development of software products. As with other projects, software development projects are divided into individual phases. Phases are chronologically and functionally separate parts of a project. These phases as a whole and their chronological sequence are known as the *software life cycle*, which has become a classical term in computer science.

Many different versions of the *software life-cycle paradigm* evolved during the Seventies. All these were developed with the goal of defining methods allowing for a rigid, sequential progression throughout the software development process. The application of these rigid, sequential methods was intended to allow organizing and managing the development process like other well-understood production processes. Unfortunately, this goal was not reached. It was recognized that the *sequential* life-cycle paradigm is only an ideal approach model that, although it incorporates the basic aspects of the software development process, is seldom if ever applicable in practice in its pure form. The search for new, more practical paradigms began and led to the prototyping, the exploratory programming, and the operational paradigms. This chapter treats all of them in order to give an overview of currently relevant software development paradigms and to provide the basis needed for the discussion of concepts and tools in succeeding chapters.

# 1.1 The Sequential Life-Cycle Paradigm

The software life-cycle paradigm has been described in countless variations (e.g., [Pre87], [Pom86], [Fai85], [Som85]). In brief, it postulates the following phases (see Figure 1.1) for the software development process: requirements analysis, requirements definition, system and component design, implementation and component test, system test, and operation and maintenance.

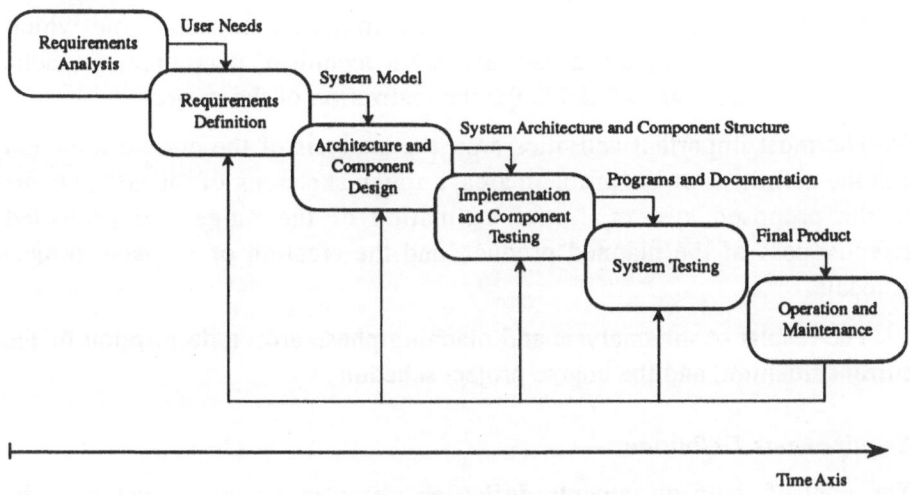

Figure 1.1. The software life cycle

Numerous proposals for further division of the phases into subphases can be found in the literature. However, there is consensus on neither the number nor even the content or nomenclature of such subphases. Such a detailed phase approach depends on the application area, the degree of complexity of the project, the size and qualification of the project team, etc. Fairley [Fai85] recommends that a division based on the complexity of a specific project be selected and explicitly recorded in the requirements definition.

In the following subsections we describe the content, range and results of the individual phases. We then examine the thought model that forms the basis of the sequential software life-cycle paradigm to derive its advantages and drawbacks.

## 1.1.1 The Phases of the Sequential Software Life Cycle

This section describes the software life cycle in terms of its goals, its most important activities, and the results of each phase. It does not discuss the kinds of methods and tools that can be used in order to achieve the goals; later chapters of this book deal with methods and tools in detail.

*Requirements Analysis*

For the particular problem area for which the development of a software product is proposed, the goal of the analysis and planning phase is to establish and document the activities that are to be carried out, along with their various interactions. It is therefore important to determine which activities can be computer-aided, and what technical, personnel, financial and time resources are available for the realization of the project.

The most important activities are: the analysis of the current situation and the definition of the problem area, a rough sketching of the components of the proposed system, initial estimation of the range and projected effectiveness of the planned product, and the creation of a coarse project schedule.

The results of the analysis and planning phase are: a description of the current situation, and the coarse project schedule.

*Requirements Definition*

The goal of the requirements definition phase is a contract between the client and the software producer. This contract defines the requirements on the proposed software system, the premises for its realization, and the project schedule.

The most important activities are: the definition of the requirements, the establishment of a detailed project schedule, and the validation of the requirements definition (i.e., testing the requirements for completeness and consistency and testing the technical feasibility and economic justification of the project).

The results of this phase are the contract between the client and the software producer and a detailed project schedule.

*Architecture and Component Design*

The goal of the design phase is to determine which system components are to be used and how they need to interact to meet the defined requirements.

The most important activities are: the design of the system architecture (i.e., the definition of the system components by means of the specification of their interfaces and interaction) and, if required, the specification of the underlying logical data model, the design of the algorithmic structure of the system components, and the verification of the architecture design.

The results of the design phase are: the description of the system architecture and the structure of the system components, as well as the documentation of the important design decisions.

*Implementation and Component Testing*

The goal of the implementation phase is to transform the concepts that were established in the design phase in such a way that the individual system components are executable on a computer.

The most important activities are: the refinement of the algorithms in the individual system components, the translation of the algorithms into a programming language (coding), the compilation and syntax-checking of the coded algorithms, the testing of the semantic correctness of the algorithms, and the correction of syntactic and semantic errors.

The results of the implementation phase are the source code of the various system components and the logs of the component tests.

*System Testing*

The goal of the test phase is the validation of the interaction of the system components, the detection of as many errors as possible in the software system, and the assurance that the system implementation meets the requirements definition.

*Operation and Maintenance*

Upon completion of the test phase the software product is released for the later user. The task of software maintenance is to correct errors that occur during actual use and to carry out system modifications and extensions. Normally this is the phase of longest duration and greatest expense in the software life cycle.

*Documentation and Quality Assurance*

In addition to the phases that characterize sequential life cycle-oriented software development as described above, two further activities need to be highlighted: documentation and quality assurance. The individual tasks that comprise these activities do not form actual project phases; instead they accompany all phases of the project.

Documentation serves to facilitate communication between developers during the development phases; thereafter it supports the operation and the maintenance of the software product. Furthermore, documentation serves the purpose of monitoring the progress of the project for the calculation of production costs and for the improvement of the planning of future projects.

Quality assurance includes measures for quality planning and for the achievement of quality attributes such as correctness, reliability, user friendliness, maintainability, efficiency and portability.

## 1.1.2 The Thought Model behind the Sequential Life-Cycle Paradigm

The sequential software life-cycle paradigm is based on the idea of *top-down decomposition* of black boxes, which leads to a stepwise refinement approach as illustrated in Figure 1.2.

The start of each phase requires well-defined input (usually in the form of documentation). This input passes through phase-specific processes—for which software engineering recommends certain methods and tools—and the results are passed on to the next phase. Each phase is clearly delimited and is to be left only when its results have been accepted in a verification and validation step.

The main idea is to start with a description of the system from the outside, i.e., a description of what the system has to do. In the requirements definition phase the system is viewed as a black box whose outward effect is precisely defined and whose inner structure remains hidden. During the design phase the process remains a top-down decomposition. Designing the system architecture concentrates on a decomposition of the system into tangible components. In order to master the complexity, these system components are viewed as black boxes. The main task of the architecture design process is the specification of the interfaces of the system components and the description of their mutual interaction. The inner structure of the system components remains hidden. Once the interfaces of all system components have been defined, the developers need only to concentrate on the component specifications while they design the algorithmic structure of the system components. Then in the implementation phase the algorithms can be independently translated into a programming language and tested individually. This decomposition process is followed by a synthesis of the system components. The interaction is verified in the test phase. This approach leads to a successive reduction in the complexity of both the development process and the system itself.

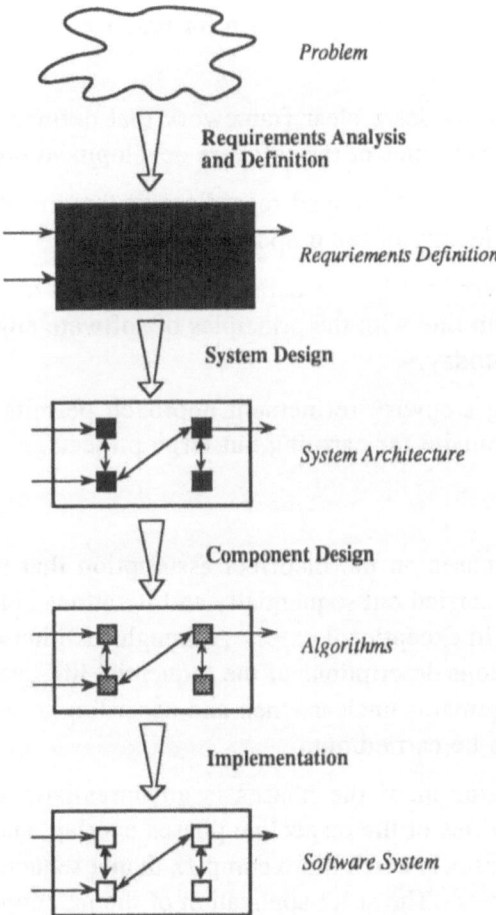

Figure 1.2. Stepwise refinement according to the sequential life-cycle paradigm (compare [Zav84])

### 1.1.3 Advantages and Disadvantages of the Sequential Life-Cycle Paradigm

Studies by Boehm have shown that the sequential life-cycle development approach is the most widespread software development approach and that it has in general proven itself [Boe81]. On the other hand, practice also shows the limits and the weaknesses of this approach. The following enumeration of the advantages and disadvantages is intended to assist the reader in evaluating the suitability of this approach for practice.

*Advantages*

- The paradigm provides a clear framework that defines and delimits the most important activities of the software development process.

- The paradigm can be employed regardless of the area of application or the size or complexity of the proposed project.

- The structure provided by the paradigm encourages a structuring of the product that is in line with the principles of software engineering as they are recognized today.

- The underlying stepwise refinement approach permits the division of labor—a prerequisite for carrying out large projects.

*Disadvantages*

- The paradigm bases on the incorrect assumption that the development process can be carried out sequentially and iterations between phases are only necessary in exceptional cases. Although such iterations are always included in various descriptions of the sequential life-cycle approach (see Figure 1.1), it remains unclear when and according to what criteria such iterations are to be carried out.

- The strict separation of the phases is an unrealistic idealization. In reality the activities of the respective phases overlap, and the interaction between the phases is much more complex than a sequential input/output model can express. The strict application of the paradigm requires that a phase can only begin when the preceding phase is fully completed. However, reality has shown that very few cases permit a complete requirements definition or an error-free architecture design right off the bat. Often only succeeding phases provide information necessary for the completion of a given phase.

- The strictly sequential approach results in tangible products or product components being available only at a very late stage. However, experience has shown that validation (especially of the requirements definition) is not usually possible without experiments close to reality—yet this is exactly what is prevented by the sequential life-cycle development approach. This means that modification requests on the part of the later user can only be made very late and thus their incorporation often involves high overhead.

The sequential life-cycle paradigm therefore certainly provides a basis for an engineering approach, although with significant drawbacks. It describes both the activities and the order of their execution, as well as the nature of the results of the phases. The activities defined by the paradigm are certainly necessary—although possibly not adequate—and cannot be circumvented by any ingenious methodology. Practice has taught us, however, that as a rule the goal of development of a system is not completely independent of the type of solution that is selected, as assumed in the sequential life-cycle paradigm. In order to avoid this dilemma, the interaction between the goal and the means must be more strongly incorporated in the development. The strict sequentiality with which the individual phases are carried out and the nature of the phase results are the weak points of this approach and need to be improved.

It is often assumed—and current reports from research and practice confirm the assumption—that a prototyping-oriented development approach has the potential to resolve some (perhaps even all) of the weaknesses of the sequential life-cycle paradigm that were listed above. The following section treats this subject in detail and shows the differences between the two approaches.

# 1.2 The Prototyping Paradigm

Reports about software projects in which prototypes have been used to explore user requirements and to overcome development problems have been being published for more than a decade. An analysis of publications shows that there is a lack of consensus in software engineering on the meaning of the terms *prototype* and *prototyping*. The same is true of the prototyping-oriented development approach. While various forms of the sequential software life-cycle paradigm differ only marginally, the proposals for prototyping-oriented system development vary considerably.

There seems to be agreement that software prototypes need to be *operational*, but the extent to which this operationality can be simulated remains controversial. There is near consensus that software prototypes, contrary to prototypes in other engineering disciplines, need to be produced *quickly* and *cheaply*. Some authors propose developing *real prototypes* in the sense of patterns that have all the significant attributes of the planned system and using these as specifications for the actual product development process. Other authors believe that software prototyping should be a bottom-up process: several simple basic functions are implemented quickly, the later user tests them, improvements are made, additional user requirements are implemented, and so on until the product is finished. For some authors, prototyping is nothing more than resolving the communication gap between the developer and the later user, i.e., a requirements definition methodology; other authors see both a requirements definition and an implementation methodology.

Before we look more closely at the prototyping-oriented development approach that builds on the life-cycle paradigm, let us examine the general goals and the types of prototyping.

## 1.2.1 Approaches to Prototyping

First we describe various approaches to prototyping and the ideas on which they are based. From there we derive definitions for the terms prototype and prototyping. From an abstract point of view prototyping is nothing more than a basic idea; however, its transformation into practice has lead to a multitude of approaches. We distinguish:

- various types of prototyping
- various types of prototypes

In the literature we find the following classification of prototyping (compare [Flo84]):

- exploratory prototyping
- experimental prototyping
- evolutionary prototyping

*Exploratory Prototyping*

The goal of exploratory prototyping is to obtain a requirements definition that is as complete as possible and can be verified by the later user on the basis of realistic examples. Its purpose is to permit the developers an insight into the application area, to allow them to discuss various approaches to a solution, and to clarify the feasibility of the proposed system in a given organizational environment.

Beginning with initial conceptions of the proposed system, a prototype (of at least the user interface) is developed that makes it possible to test these conceptions on the basis of concrete examples and to successively (re)define the desired functionality. The important factors are not the quality of the prototype implementation, but the functionality, the ease of modification, and the speed of development.

The realization of an exploratory prototype is therefore an effort carried out by a team consisting of software engineers and later users. Exploratory prototyping is an approach that supports requirement analysis and requirements definition.

*Experimental Prototyping*

The goal of experimental prototyping is to achieve a concise specification of the components which form the system architecture. Its purpose is to experimentally validate the suitability of system component specifications, architecture models, and ideas for solutions for individual system components.

Starting with the initial conceptions of the decomposition of the system, a prototype is developed to permit the simulation of the interaction of the designed system components. Based on concrete examples, the adequacy of the interfaces of the individual system components and the flexibility of the system architecture with respect to extensibility are experimentally examined. The quality of the prototype implementation, as with exploratory prototyping, is secondary.

Activities toward the realization of prototypes of a planned system or parts thereof are primarily carried out by the software developers, not by later users. Experimental prototyping is an approach that supports system and component design. Naturally experimentation plays an important role in exploratory prototyping as well.

*Evolutionary Prototyping*

The goal of evolutionary prototyping is incremental system development, i.e., a successive development strategy with the following approach: A prototype is developed for those user requirements that are obvious from the start. The result serves as a base system for the later user and for the succeeding iterative process during which new user requirements are integrated. This approach no longer differentiates between prototype and product, yet the prototype designation is appropriate because the initial versions certainly cannot be viewed as the target system.

This approach requires that the extensibility of a software system not decline in the process of incremental implementation. That is, the redesign of software architectures must be possible in a simple way and with an economically feasible amount of effort. From the point of view of authors on the subject, this situation has not yet been achieved. Practice shows that complete redesign of an incrementally developed software system is often not carried out, even when necessary, because such redesign can often be too expensive. The result is a continuous decline in the quality of the system architecture. Evolutionary prototyping does not build a prototype on simulation. Prototypes are not viewed as throwaway; instead they are successively elaborated toward the final product.

In order to treat prototyping-oriented software development as a whole, it does not suffice to examine the various approaches; instead, the different types of associated products need to be discussed as well. Hence, we distinguish not only various approaches to prototyping but also the following categories of prototypes:

- complete prototypes
- incomplete prototypes
- throwaway prototypes
- reusable prototypes

A *complete prototype* is one in the classical sense, in which all the significant functions of the proposed system are present and complete. The experience gained in the production and use and the prototype itself form the basis for the final system development. Complete prototypes are hardly ever produced for software systems.

An *incomplete prototype* is a software system that permits the study of the usability and/or feasibility of individual aspects of the proposed system (e.g., user interface, system architecture, system components).

Prototypes are considered *throwaway* when the implementation of the prototype is not used in the implementation of the target system, when the prototype only serves as an executable model.

Prototypes are designated as *reusable* when significant parts thereof fulfills the quality principles of software engineering and can be integrated into the target system .

Experimental prototyping as defined above corresponds very much to exploratory programming, as described in the next section. In the rest of this book, prototyping therefore will be used as a generic term for exploratory and evolutionary prototyping, while experimental prototyping will be subsumed under the term exploratory programming. Using the terms this way permits the drawing of an exact line between prototyping as a paradigm that is applied mostly during the requirements definition process and eases communications problems between developers and clients, and exploratory programming as a paradigm that is applied during design and implementation with the purpose of evaluating various solutions for complex applications.

*Definition of the terms "prototype" and "prototyping"*

No definition of prototyping has won general recognition. The following definitions by Boar and Connell best describe the approaches identified above.

"A *prototype* is an easily modifiable and extensible working model of a proposed system, not necessarily representative of a complete system, which provides later users of the application with a physical representation of key parts of the system before implementation" [Boa83].

"A *software prototype* is a dynamic visual model providing a communication tool for customer and developer that is far more effective than either narrative prose or static visual models for portraying functionality. It has been described as

- functional after a minimal amount of effort
- a means of providing users of a proposed application with a physical representation of key parts of the system before system implementation
- flexible—modification requires minimal effort
- not necessarily representative of a complete system" [Con89]

*Prototyping* covers all activities necessary to make such prototypes available.

## 1.2.2 The Prototyping-Oriented Software Life Cycle

A prototyping-oriented software development strategy does not differ radically from the sequential life cycle-oriented one. The two are more complementary than alternative. The new aspect is that we explicitly state that the processes described by the sequential life cycle-oriented approach are performed iteratively rather then sequentially, and that we pinpoint where iterations should take place within the life cycle.

The prototyping-oriented software development strategy, as we see it (see Figure 1.3), differs from the sequential life-cycle paradigm in its approach and in the results produced in the individual phases of the life cycle. The phase distinction is maintained, but the requirements analysis and the requirements definition phases overlap considerably, and design, implementation and testing blend together a great deal. The phases become more stages of a continuous development process. For this reason we speak of activities rather than phases because we no longer have a strict delimitation of the activities into phases, as required by the sequential life-cycle paradigm.

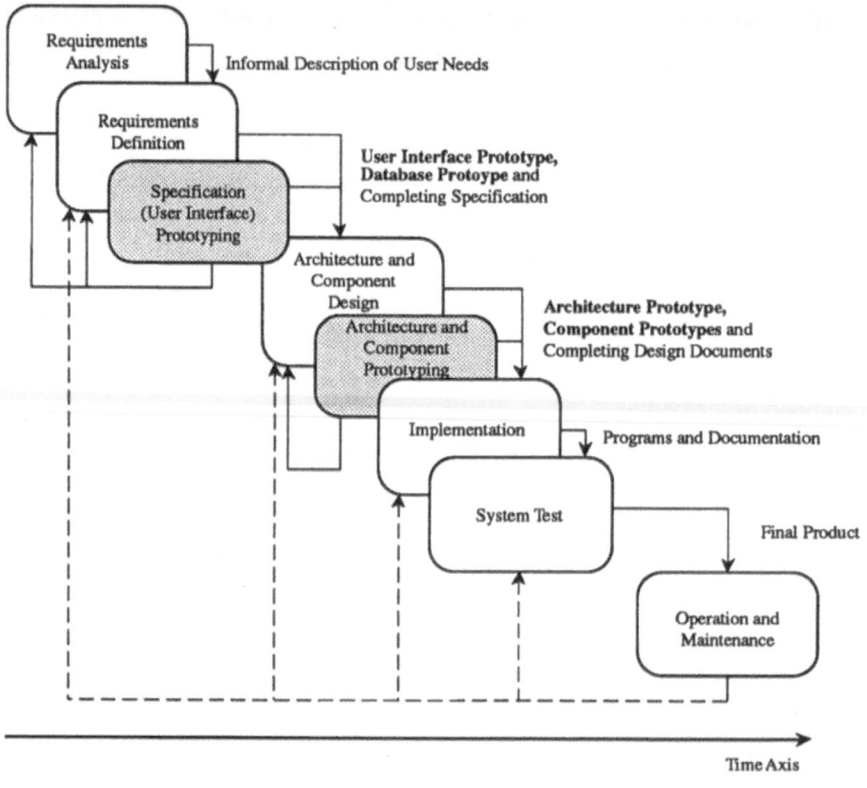

Figure 1.3. The prototyping-oriented software life cycle

Now we can discuss how the development process takes place according to this enhanced development model. After an informal description of user needs has been derived from a rough requirements analysis, a prototype of the external behavior is produced (with tool support). On the basis of this prototype, experiments are carried out that reflect real application conditions to evaluate whether the later user's requirements have been met. Under conditions close to reality, the software developer and the later user can test whether the system model has errors; they can check whether the later user's conceptions have been addressed or whether modifications are necessary. The production of a prototype is an iterative process (see Figure 1.4). Thus a life cycle is introduced within the life cycle through a "pseudo-implementation" as early as possible. This inner life cycle is terminated when the later user and the developer agree on the system model (prototype). This procedure corresponds to the exploratory approach.

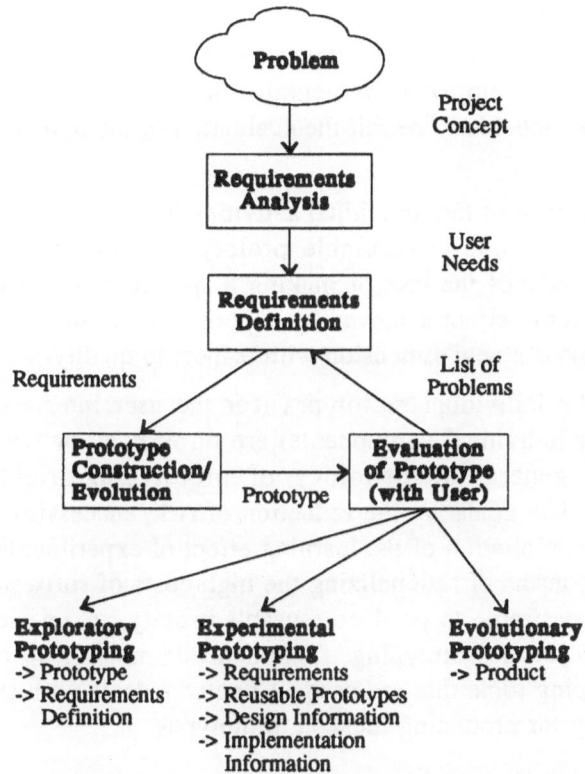

Figure 1.4. Software development using the prototyping paradigm

In reality it is impossible to design a suitable system architecture on the first try. For this reason a model of the system architecture (an architecture prototype) needs to be created as soon as possible in order to evaluate the quality of the system architecture. This again leads to a life cycle within the life cycle. The adequacy of the system decomposition, the conciseness and completeness of the component interfaces, and the extensibility of the system architecture can be experimentally tested under real conditions on the basis of such a prototype of the system architecture before the system components have been implemented. This procedure corresponds to the experimental prototyping approach. The risk of having to make extensive (hence expensive) architecture redesigns during the implementation phase is drastically reduced.

This leads to another significant difference between the two approaches. According to the sequential life-cycle paradigm, implementation occurs as late as possible and only after all the details of the requirements definition and design processes have been clarified. The application of the prototyping-oriented paradigm promotes the implementation of a prototype as early as possible. This is done because practice has shown that goals are more readily achieved if the requirements definition and the system architecture are developed incrementally on the basis of a model. The purpose of this model is to permit the evaluation of the dynamic behavior of the system.

The overlapping of the individual activities (see Figure 1.3) and the type of intermediate results—executable prototypes rather than mere static descriptions—reduces the risk of making a specification error or a design error. The learning effect achieved by experimenting with the phase results (prototypes) opens a new dimension with respect to quality assurance.

Whether the individual prototypes (for the user interface, the system architecture or individual components) are throwaway or reusable is irrelevant to the general methodology of prototyping-oriented software development. The goals are the reduction of risk, successful quality assurance, and the exploitation of the learning effect of experimenting under real conditions. In terms of rationalizing the high costs of software production, it is naturally desirable to produce reusable prototypes, i.e., to move to an evolutionary form of prototyping. This depends most of all on the quality of the prototyping tools that are used. Chapter 2 deals with such tools and their suitability for producing reusable prototypes.

## 1.2.3 Advantages and Disadvantages of the Prototyping Paradigm

The prototyping-oriented development paradigm has its strengths where the sequential life-cycle paradigm displays serious weaknesses. The strictly sequential development approach is replaced by an iterative approach. The overly ideal distinction between what and how, between goal and means, is softened. The validation process is simplified by the early availability of executable models, thus promoting quality assurance that accompanies the entire project. This is achieved without sacrificing the advantages of the sequential life-cycle paradigm.

*Advantages*

- Communication problems between developer and client diminish.

- The client learns early in the software development process what is feasible.

- Execution of results—which were represented as documents in a conventional development process—increases the probability of finding errors, inadequacies and incompleteness earlier in the development process. Thus redesign costs can be reduced.

- Iterations which took place during a conventional software development process are are incorporated into the paradigm. This results in a closer correspondence of the paradigm to reality.

- Prototyping-oriented software development brings about a significant increase in the following quality attributes: functional adequacy, user-friendliness, structuredness, modifiability, extensibility, correctness, and reliability.

- The approach reduces testing and maintenance costs; i.e., it generates increased productivity.

- Prototyping facilitates the scheduling of software projects because an improved requirements definition makes it possible to predict the implementation and testing investment more accurately.

- The risk of flops diminishes because experimentally validated models reduce the number of uncertain assumptions that are necessary.

*Disadvantages*

- Prototyping can lead to a nonconverging development process—the more the later user gets, the more he wants.

- If the later user sees a "working" software system at the end of the requirement analysis, it may be difficult to explain why it has to be designed and implemented again.

- There is the danger of delivering prototypes instead of products and thus forsaking software engineering principles. Sometimes the quality of the code of prototypes is not as good as required for a final version of a software product.

- It may be dangerous to develop exploratory prototypes of mainframe applications using prototyping tools on personal computers because the functionality and user friendliness of the prototype easily outgrows the functionality and user friendliness of the final application.

# 1.3  The Exploratory Programming Paradigm

The exploratory programming paradigm[1] was not developed by the
software engineering community. It evolved as a paradigm for the
development of artificial intelligence applications (i.e., novel, complex,
research-oriented software systems). While there exists no generally
accepted definition for exploratory programming, it was well described by
Sandberg [San87] in his paper about exploratory programming in Smalltalk.

> *"Exploratory programming involves producing a piece of software that
> attempts to meet the known, basic requirements of the system [to be
> developed]. This software is then tested in the product environment to
> find out how it fails. These failures lead to more requirements. The
> software is modified to meet these requirements, and tested again. This
> process is continued until the software performs adequately in the product
> environment. The requirements are not usually explicitly expressed by
> programmers, but are embodied in the code under development.*
>
> *Standard software engineering uses programming to implement a
> given specification. In contrast, exploratory programming is writing the
> specification."*

The following subsections describe the application of the exploratory programming paradigm and the resulting advantages and disadvantages.

## 1.3.1 Software Development Using the Exploratory
Programming Paradigm

*Exploratory programming* has evolved as a paradigm for the development
of applications where little or no experience exists that would permit a
developer to determine the whole set of requirements of a planned software
system, its feasibility, and the quality of particular technical solutions. The
only possibility to reduce the risks emerging from missing experience is to
implement and evaluate one or more solutions. If no suitable solution is
found, the requirements definition has to be adapted or the basic goals of the
project even have to be reconsidered. Because this happens frequently in a
research environment, the importance of exploratory programming is
stressed in many publications about development of knowledge-based
systems (artificial intelligence programming) ([Par86], [Mos85b], [She83]).

---

[1] There are many different names for the exploratory programming paradigm. We decided to use the
term "exploratory programming" because it is used most frequently and expresses the basic concept of
the paradigm satisfactorily. In the context of prototyping it is often called "experimental prototyping"
(e.g., [Flo84]), and in [Wal87] it is named "rapid productizing".

Software development using the exploratory programming paradigm starts (as every software development effort) with requirements analysis. The requirements analysis is followed by exploratory programming, a cyclical sequence of the classical software development activities (i.e., requirements definition, design, implementation) which are followed by evaluation (see Figure 1.5). During evaluation it is decided whether another cycle is necessary or whether the goals of the exploratory programming process have been reached.

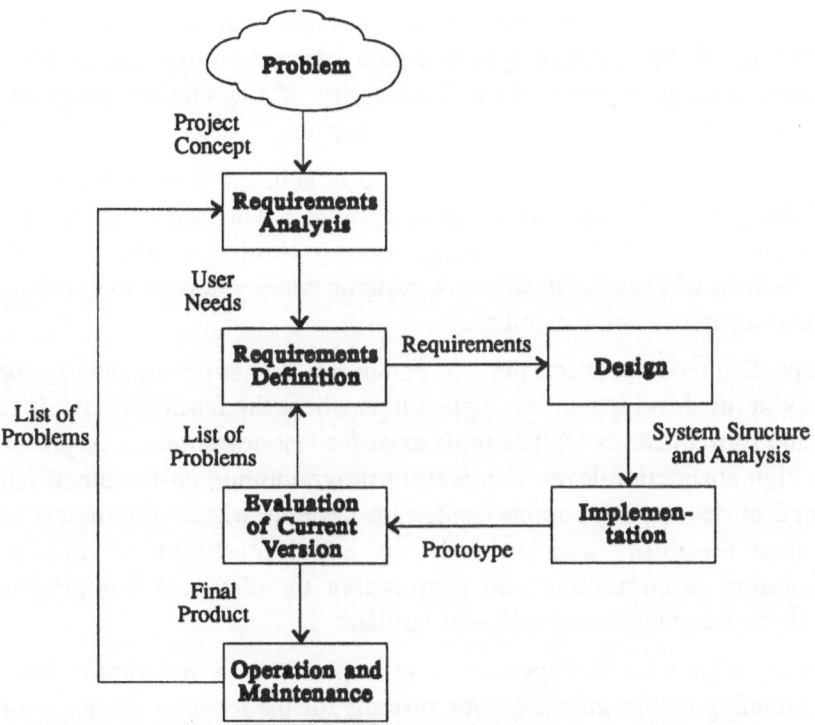

Figure 1.5. Software development using the exploratory programming paradigm

While the names and also the underlying ideas of the development activities are the same as in the sequential life-cycle paradigm, the proceeding and the goals differ profoundly. In a sequential approach, every phase is carried out only once, which implies that its results should be complete and correct. In an exploratory programming approach, on the other hand, every activity is carried out many times and each time only certain aspects are (re)implemented and evaluated.

Two approaches to exploratory programming can be distinguished: the *evolutionary* and the *experimental* approach. The goal of the evolutionary approach is to develop a final application by iteratively growing and refining the software system. The goal of the experimental approach, on the other hand, is to learn enough about requirements, design, and implementation strategies, to justify starting the last cycle, the "real" development process, during which the application is written from scratch.

An evolutionary approach has to be favored because of the reusability of its results. Nonetheless, it is expensive to achieve reusable results. A software system which should incrementally grow into the final application has to be designed and implemented with more care than a piece of code which serves only to examine certain aspects and can be discarded later. Which of the two approaches should be chosen depends mainly on the percentage of the software system which has to be implemented for mere experimenting purposes and on the quality of the chosen programming language and tools.

From the discussion above it can be concluded that exploratory programming is very similar to prototyping. The application of both prototyping and exploratory programming results in the evolutionary development of executable software systems which are used to continuously evaluate adequacy and feasibility.

The difference between the two paradigms is that prototyping is applied mostly in the development of applications where the feasibility risk is rather low and formalisms as well as tools exist for fast development of prototypes on a high abstraction level; exploratory programming, on the other hand, is applied in developing complex software systems where the highest risk is technical feasibility and little or no experience can be drawn on. Exploratory programming and prototyping therefore are complementary paradigms helping to ease different burdens.

Prerequisites for the application of exploratory programming are good programming environments and/or systems for the reuse of design information and source code that help to shorten the implementation/evaluation cycle as much as possible. The features of such programming environments and systems for reuse of design information and code are discussed in Chapter 3.

## 1.3.2 Advantages and Disadvantages of the Exploratory Programming Paradigm

*Advantages*

- The application of exploratory programming improves the requirements definition process by ensuring the adequacy and feasibility of a planned solution.

- Exploratory programming goes hand in hand with object-oriented programming—another technique for the improvement of the software development process. The development of large object-oriented software systems should always be an exploratory programming process. It is generally accepted today that it is impossible to get a good object-oriented system architecture without several redesigns.

- Exploratory programming usually leads to qualitatively better results than a sequential approach because it gives a developer the freedom to implement different solutions and to keep the best.

- Exploratory programming is complementary to prototyping.

*Disadvantages*

- The planning and control of a project where exploratory programming is heavily applied becomes difficult because exploratory programming is an adaptive process which does not support well-defined phases and phase results. The definition and control of milestones therefore becomes much more difficult and requires a better technical understanding on the part of a manager.

- Exploratory programming easily degenerates into a hacking approach to software development.

- Exploratory programming is not well-suited to developing software in large teams because a lot of flexibility is required in applying changes to the system under development.

- Exploratory programming can be quite expensive because it requires the implementation of certain application parts in an algorithmic programming language for experimentation purposes.

# 1.4 The Operational Paradigm

Zaves overview paper [Zav84] describes the application of the operational
paradigm as follows:

> *"During the specification phase, computer specialists formulate a system
> to solve the problem and specify this system in terms of implementation-
> independent structures that generate the behavior of the specified system.
> The operational specification is executable by a suitable interpreter. Thus
> external behavior is implicit in the specification (but can be brought out by
> the interpreter), while internal structure is explicit.*
>
> *This description may make an operational specification sound like a
> design, but it is not. First of all the structures provided by an operational
> specification language are independent of specific resource configurations
> or resource allocation strategies, while designs actually refer to specific
> run-time environments."*

The following subsections describe the application of the operational
paradigm and the resulting advantages and disadvantages.

## 1.4.1 Software Development Using the Operational Paradigm

Software development using the *operational paradigm* starts like a conventional software development process with a requirements analysis.
Afterwards an iterative requirements definition process is carried out which
consists of the formal description of requirements and their validation by
executing the formal description (see Figure 1.6).

Once the formal requirements definition is considered satisfactory, the
realization process starts. This realization process can either consist of conventional design and implementation processes, or it can be based on transformational implementation, i.e., the iterative application of transformations
on a formal specification, which leads to the final product.

The formalisms used to write formal descriptions are similar to programming languages. The main difference is that the abstraction level is
higher, so that decisions about resource allocation (which make up a considerable part of conventional software systems) can be ignored. Formal
specification languages can be distinguished by the abstraction concepts they
support (see [Fro89]). Typical abstraction concepts are functional decomposition, modular interface specifications together with preconditions and
postconditions, and finite-state machines. Typical data abstractions are abstract data types and objects as used in object-oriented programming.

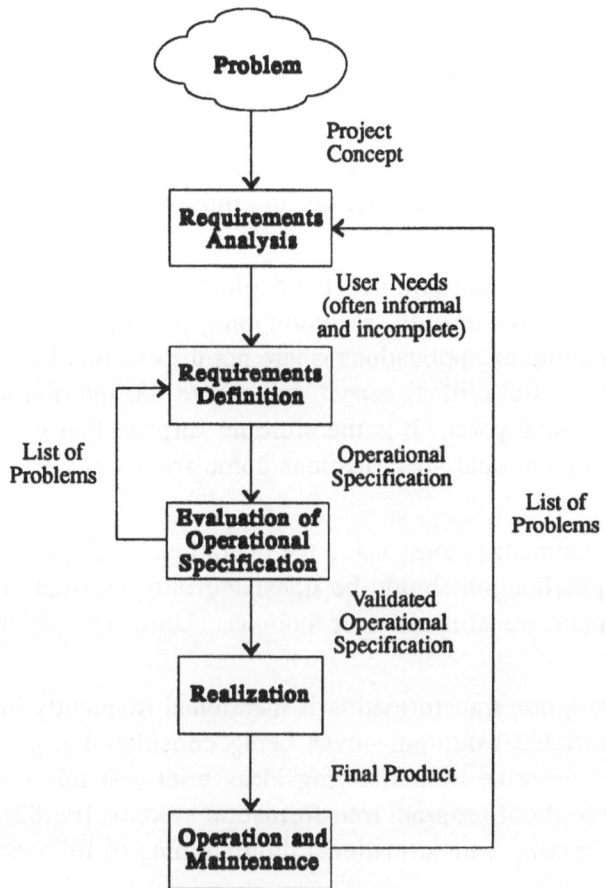

Figure 1.6. Software development using the operational paradigm

Zave (see [Zav84]) lists several differences between the conventional approach to software development and the operational approach. For instance, the conventional approach explicitly separates external behavior (the requirements) from internal structure. During a conventional design process functioning and performance of a mechanism have to be considered and high-level mechanisms as well as implementation constraints have to be incorporated at the same time. In contrast, the operational approach acknowledges the unavoidable interleaving of external behavior and internal structure. Since optimizations are done only during the realization process, problem-oriented considerations are separated from implementation-oriented ones.

The difference between the operational paradigm and specification prototyping is one of emphasis. In specification prototyping the external behavior is the important feature; it does not matter how this external behavior is achieved. In the application of the operational paradigm, by contrast, the internal structure of the software system is defined and evaluated. The external behavior can be observed during interpretation of a specification, but the formalisms for defining operational specifications usually do not permit the specification of the exact user interface. This is a consequence of the implementation independence of operational specifications.

The operational paradigm, like the exploratory programming paradigm, is therefore complementary to the prototyping paradigm. It is best applied in developing complex applications where not the external behavior (i.e., the user interface) is the critical aspect, but where the internal structure and logic are the critical parts. It is therefore no surprise that most application examples for operational specifications come from the area of distributed real-time systems.

In an development process using the operational paradigm, the validated operational specification should be translated into the final application by applying program transformation techniques. Unfortunately this has never been achieved.

Because program transformation is mentioned frequently in conjunction with the operational paradigm—even being considered a part of it (e.g., [Zav84])—we describe its underlying ideas briefly at this point. In their overview paper about program transformation systems [Par83], Partsch and Steinbrügge describe transformational programming as follows:

> *"Transformational programming is a methodology of program construction by successive applications of transformation rules. Usually this process starts with a (formal) specification, that is, a formal statement of a problem or its solution, and ends with an executable program. The individual transitions between the various versions of a program are made by applying correctness-preserving transformation rules. It is guaranteed that the final version of the program will still satisfy the initial specification."*

The goal of transformational programming is therefore to transform a formal specification automatically into an executable software system that is certain to satisfy the initial specification.

The result of the transformation phase is not only an implementation, but also a formal development record which contains all transformations and decisions made. Examples of transformations are change of representations, selection of algorithms, optimization, and compilation. Validation and maintenance are done on the specification level, and if modifications become necessary, the formal development record is used (in the ideal case automatically) to reimplement the system based on the new specifications. As a consequence the specification always describes the current system, even if it has been modified several times (see [Fro89]).

Today there are no products allowing for practical application of transformational programming, but there are many research projects whose goal is to develop such products. Descriptions of projects involved in developing semi-automatic tools to transform formal specifications into running software systems can be found in [Bal85] (overview), [Gre88], and [Fic85].

An overview of the operational paradigm, descriptions of various tools claiming to support the operational paradigm, as well as an extensive list of publications can be found in [Fro89].

## 1.4.2 Advantages and Disadvantages of the Operational Paradigm

The advantages of the operational approach are similar to the advantages of the prototyping paradigm described in Section 1.2. This is because the basic idea underlying the operational paradigm—i.e., the construction of executable software models during the requirements definition process—is very similar to the one underlying prototyping.

*Advantages*

- The operational paradigm takes an iterative approach to the specification and validation of software systems.

- The dynamic evaluation of operational specifications allows for much better validation than permitted by conventional review techniques.

- Operational specifications are not restricted to specific domains.

- There is a hope that automatic transformation of specifications into applications could eliminate conventional design and implementation activities and allow maintenance on the specification level.

- Formal specifications allow application of automatic consistency checks.

*Disadvantages*

- In order to execute a specification, all aspects relevant to execution but not implementation have to be described. This means that operational specifications are closely related to implementations in terms of addressed details.

- The hardest problem during the requirements definition process of software is communication with the prospective user. This problem cannot be solved with an operational approach.

- When executable specification languages are applied, implementation-dependent details have to be carefully avoided because otherwise the result is a design instead of a specification.

- In their report about a technology transfer project, Berliner and Zave [Ber87] observe that the biggest barrier to the use of their executable specification language was the difficulty and cost of teaching people. This corresponds with our experience that even toy application examples of executable specification languages are quite difficult to understand.

- Transformational programming is not yet ready for the development of large software systems.

# 2  Concepts and Tools for Prototyping

Many concepts and even more tools support exploratory and evolutionary prototyping. In order to give a representative overview the first two sections of this chapter discuss concepts and tools for

- user interface prototyping, supporting the requirements definition process, and

- prototyping of software architectures, supporting the design and implementation process,

which make it possible to translate the prototyping-oriented life cycle (see Section 1.2.2) into practice. These concepts and tools are application area-independent. In practice, prototyping has experienced its most widespread application in the development of information systems. Thus the third section is dedicated to the underlying concepts and tools supporting the

- prototyping of information systems.

Each section presents basic concepts underlying the respective kind of prototyping. Based on these concepts, criteria are derived for the selection of supporting tools. Finally, one exemplary tool is presented which is state of the art and lends itself to practical application.

## 2.1 User Interface Prototyping

Section 1.1 discussed the problems that occur in defining the requirements of a planned software system using conventional development strategies. Section 1.2 concluded that these problems can be mastered better if a requirements definition is developed stepwise on the basis of a model that permits the simulation of the system.

Nowadays *dialog-oriented systems*, in which human-computer interaction plays a central role, make up one of the largest application areas. The requirements definition of such dialog-oriented systems consists of at least the functional and nonfunctional requirements as well as the user interface specification. The functional requirements and part of the nonfunctional requirements (e.g., necessary response and processing times) are implicitly defined by the user interface since they are directly contained in or disguised behind the user interface. The *user interface specification* is therefore the most important part of the requirement definition and its quality is decisive.

The user interface specification and its underlying functional behavior can be represented much better and tested more effectively with an executable prototype than is the case with other means of representation.

The definition of nonfunctional requirements is not directly supported by prototyping. However, an executable model of the target system depicting the system's static and dynamic outward appearance does provide a good basis for the discussion of nonfunctional requirements.

An executable model at the user interface level also provides an ideal basis for communication among the client, the later users, and the developer. From this viewpoint, a user interface prototype does not merely serve a means for specifying the user interface of a target software system; instead it is an important basis for a complete and contradiction-free requirements definition.

In the following section we discuss the concepts necessary to develop such prototypes.

## 2.1.1 Concepts for User Interface Prototyping

The development of a user interface prototype usually consists of three parallel activities (see Figure 2.1). First, the user interface itself is developed using a convenient tool. Second, the functionality behind the user interface is enhanced. The form of the development and enhancement activities depends very much on the tool used. In order to permit the enhancement of prototypes, most prototyping tools provide interfaces to algorithmic languages. Third, a complementary specification is written containing information about functional and nonfunctional requirements that are not represented in the prototype. Experience shows that even if these further requirements are not inherent in the prototype, they usually emerge during the cyclical development and evaluation process.

The results of the user interface prototyping process are a *user interface prototype*, which is reusable in the case of an evolutionary approach, and a complementary *specification document*.

The influence of the user interface on the functional requirements makes such a process particularly interesting. Wassermann et al. call this an "outside-in" approach and speak of "external design" (see [Was86]). Contrary to a functionally-oriented, top-down approach, the requirements definition is created from the viewpoint of the later user rather than that of the system.

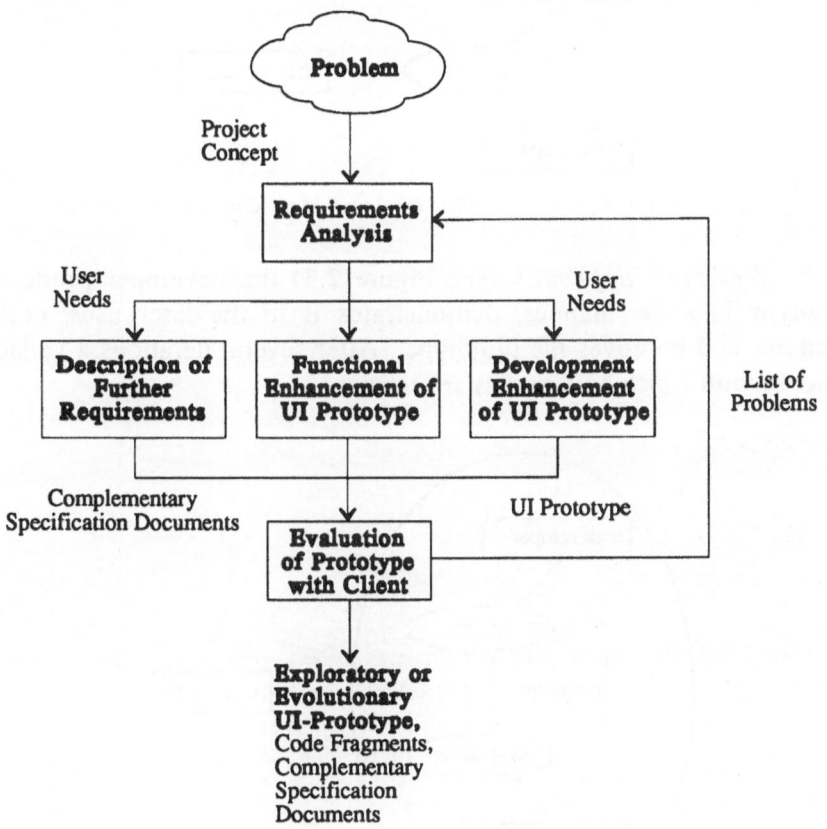

Figure 2.1. User interface (UI) prototyping

An examination of the production of a prototype poses the question of to what extent the later user is involved in the prototype design process.

Basically three approaches are possible for the development of user interfaces. These are distinguished by the degree and kind of participation on the part of the later users (see [Löw87]):

- participatory approach
- feedback approach
- exclusive approach

In the *participatory approach* (see Figure 2.2), the later user and the developer work together closely. If the team is small, the method can lead to high satisfaction and involvement on the part of the later user. Otherwise such a cooperative effort can be time-intensive and a source of conflict.

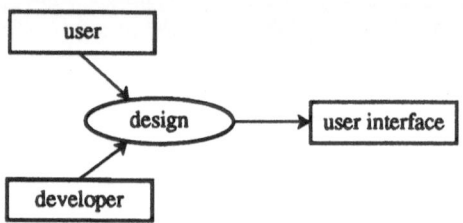

Figure 2.2. Participatory approach to user interface construction (see [Löw87])

In the *feedback approach* (see Figure 2.3) the developer produces a prototype in some manner, demonstrates it to the later user, collects reactions, and improves the prototype. After several iterations a version is achieved with which both parties are satisfied.

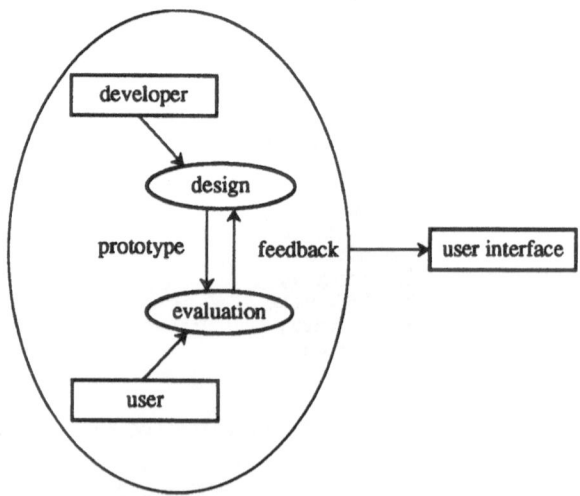

Figure 2.3. Feedback approach to user interface construction (see [Löw87])

These two approaches are quite widespread and have produced good results. They make it possible to validate the user interface already during the requirements definition phase.

The *exclusive approach* (see Figure 2.4) keeps the later user outside the development process. This approach is founded on the assumption that the later user has nothing to say to the developer in terms of the user interface, that in fact the later user's participation can be detrimental. Proponents defend this point of view with the argument that users tend to gravitate to older but familiar methods, that the other prototyping methods can lead to endless iteration, and that it is not even possible to satisfy all conceivable wishes.

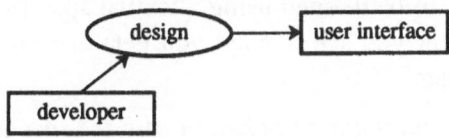

Figure 2.4. Exclusive approach to user interface construction (see [Löw87])

In order to achieve a user-friendly software system, the user interface design must consider human factors (see [Shn86]), e.g., ease of learning, performance, error rate per user, subjective satisfaction, ease of relearning after a period of non-use. The extent to which these factors can be incorporated is determined by the involvement of the later user in the requirements definition process, and on ergonomic and software engineering characteristics of the user interface.

We are convinced that the *feedback method* is best suited to incorporating the human factors; i.e., it best lends itself to a requirements definition process that makes optimal use of not only the later user's understanding of his needs and knowledge of his field, but also the experience and know-how of the software engineer. The feedback method also proves harmonious with the prototyping-oriented software life-cycle paradigm defined in Section 1.2.

User interface prototyping only makes sense if prototypes can be developed rapidly and incrementally, which is not possible without appropriate tools. Due to the importance of tool support in the user interface prototyping process, the next subsection provides a list of criteria to assist in the comparative evaluation of tools and the selection of the best-suited.

## 2.1.2 Selection Criteria for User Interface Prototyping Tools

User interface prototyping tools can be distinguished and evaluated according to the following criteria.

- *What kind of user interface is supported?*

  We distinguish two kinds of user interfaces: window-based, graphic-oriented user interfaces displayed on graphic (bitmap) screens on workstations or PCs, and character-oriented user interfaces on conventional monitors.

- *What kind of specification mechanism is provided?*

  User interfaces can be defined using a textual specification language or a WYSIWYG (what you see is what you get) drawing tool as the specification mechanism.

- *What abstraction level can be achieved with the specification formalism?*

  An important criterion for the usefulness of a user interface prototyping tool is the expressive power of its specification formalism. In defining a user interface, there are three aspects that a developer wants to specify on the highest possible abstraction level: layout, event handling, and consistency rules (e.g.,for input fields).

- *How are the user interfaces executed?*

  During the cyclical prototyping process, interpretive execution provides for short turnaround times. In the final product, however, generated code is executed more efficiently. Tools providing both kinds of execution mechanisms therefore best lend themselves to evolutionary prototyping.

- *What type of software architecture is supported?*

  There are two different software architectures which are currently supported by user interface prototyping tools. One architecture enforces a strict separation of the user interface and the functional parts of an application; the other architecture omits this separation.

  For many applications (e.g., simple bookkeeping systems), the user interface can be assembled from standardized components. This enables a complete separation of the user interface and the functional parts of the application. This strong separation allows a developer to build different user interfaces for the same application (e.g., a window-based or an character-based user interface). In other applications, such as ones with complex event handling (e.g., a CAD system), a complete separation of the user interface and functional parts is not possible. Nevertheless, with the help of application frameworks, such applications can be developed without significantly restricting their flexibility and modifiability.

- *How is it possible to extend the functionality of a prototype beyond what can be expressed in the specification formalism?*

   Some prototyping tools provide the possibility to extend the functionality with code written in an integrated algorithmic language. Others make it possible to add code written in a programming language of choice.

- *Does the generated code meet the general quality requirements of software engineering?*

   Does a clean interface exist in the generated code to allow the integration of handwritten code? For reasons of maintainability, reuse of code in the implementation of the target system is only practical if the generated code meets software quality requirements in terms of structuredness, readability, security and efficiency.

- *To what extent is the set of available user interface elements (gadgets/ widgets) extensible?*

   The type and number of required user interface elements (windows, buttons, menus, icons, scroll bars, etc.) varies depending on the area of application. New user interface elements are developed based on experience and ergonomic improvements. Whether such new elements can be integrated and how much effort is required to do so comprises another important evaluation criterion for prototyping tools.

### 2.1.3 DICE—a Tool Example

We chose DICE (Dynamic Interface Creation Environment) [Pre90] as our tool example for the following reasons:

- It is a typical example of a state-of-the-art development in the area of user interface prototyping tools.

- It supports the development of window-based, graphic-oriented user interfaces.

- It provides a WYSIWYG specification mechanism with high expressive power.

- Its interpretive execution mechanism ensures short turnaround times.

- It supports the development of applications with two different kinds of system architectures: applications where the user interface and the functional parts are strictly separated, and applications with a close integration of the user interface and the functional parts.

- It allows extensions of the functionality of a prototype in two ways: first, by connecting a separate process (which contains functional enhancements written in any language) over an interprocess communication interface; second, by generating object-oriented code for an application framework which can be extended by writing subclasses.

- It generates object-oriented code that meets the general quality requirements of software engineering.

- The set of user interface building blocks is easily extensible.

DICE is not commercially available. It was developed in a research project which was carried out in a cooperation between the University of Linz, and the University of Zurich. Because it forms part of the TOPOS tool set for prototyping-oriented software development, DICE is described in Chapter 7 of Part II, where TOPOS is presented.

## 2.2 Concepts for Software Architecture Prototyping

The designing of a software architecture—i.e., the decomposition of a software system into a set of cooperating components—is a creative process. During this process a developer has to make many subjective decisions that will have an effect on the quality of the resulting architecture. Because of the the large number and complexity of these subjective decisions, their adequacy cannot be verified very well.

Due to the difficulty of validating a system architecture, wrong or less than optimal decisions are frequently not recognized before the end of the development process. The possibility to dynamically validate a system architecture based on its abstract description—i.e., the *prototyping of a system architecture*—would therefore certainly lead to much better results.

A dynamic prototyping-oriented validation process would, for instance, make it possible to

- determine the adequacy of the decomposition of a software system into cooperating components

- check the completeness of the interfaces of the individual components

- validate the correctness of communication protocols for information exchange between the single components

- verify the extensibility and maintainability of a certain decomposition

We have selected two representative architecture prototyping techniques for discussion in this chapter. One, *prototyping of module-oriented software architectures*, supports the designing of applications consisting of one single process—where the emphasis of the design process is on the decomposition of a software system into sensible modules or objects. The other, *prototyping of concurrent systems* with Petri nets, supports the design of software systems consisting of a set of cooperating processes which eventually run concurrently and on different processors—where the emphasis is on the decomposition of the application into a set of processes and on the definition of the corresponding communication protocols.

## 2.2.1 Prototyping of Module-Oriented Software Architectures

A *module* is a collection of data structures and algorithms that communicate with the outside through a well-defined interface. Because of this interface the architecture of software systems consisting of various modules can be designed without bothering about the internal structure of a module. Furthermore, every module can be realized without knowledge about the system it will form a part of, as long as its functionality—as defined by its interface—is correctly implemented.

Module-oriented programming languages such as Ada [Ich79] and Modula-2 [Wir85] require the explicit separation of module interfaces and realizations. With such a language it is therefore possible to formally describe the structural aspects of a system architecture. A compiler tests only syntactic correctness of such descriptions, but not the semantic correctness of the architecture (i.e., the correct cooperation of the designed components).

In order to validate such an architecture, a developer has to make sure that it is possible to provide every service a module offers according to its interface definition. This means he has to check that all external services required to implement a specific exported service exist, i.e., that the required input data are available, and that all required output data can be generated and returned.

The security that all needed services exist can only be gained by simulating the implementation of the services exported by the modules. In this case a validation process consists of the simulation of data and control flows through the module interfaces for several realistic scenarios. For a module-oriented architecture, control flows are the procedure calls carried out between modules. Data flows consist of the parameters passed with these procedure calls.

The approach of running through realistic scenarios mentally or on paper is widely used in practice and described in software engineering textbooks as review and walkthrough (e.g., [Fai85], [Som85]). The problem with this approach is that it becomes extremely difficult to track the whole data and control flow during the simulation of large applications. The approach becomes completely unrealistic as soon as all the scenarios have to be played through again after changes were applied to a system architecture.

A prerequisite for the simulation of large, complex software systems based on their architecture definition is therefore the availability of a tool which represents the current state of execution and makes it possible to trigger control and data flows. Furthermore, it must be possible to record and replay data and control flows in order to validate an architecture after changes were applied.

### 2.2.1.1 How to Prototype Module-Oriented Software Architectures

Figure 2.5 illustrates a prototyping-oriented architecture design process carried out with the kind of tool support prescribed above. After the requirements analysis process an iterative prototyping-oriented system architecture design process is started. It consists of two activities which are carried out alternately.

First, the system architecture or parts of it are designed and described in the formalism understood by the supporting tool (e.g., as Ada package descriptions or as Modula-2 module descriptions). In parallel with the proper design activity, a complementary specification is written that contains information about all design details which cannot be expressed formally.

Second, experiments with the architecture description are carried out in order to validate it. These experiments are simulations of data and control flows which would occur in the implemented application during real scenarios. Every simulation that is carried out is recorded and can be replayed during later validation activities.

The architecture prototyping process ends after the successful simulation of several realistic scenarios when the developers are sure that the components of the designed system architecture cooperate correctly and that the design fulfills the requirements described in the requirements definition.

At this point no guarantee for the completeness and correctness of the system architecture can be given; however, the probability that errors or incompletnesses will be found during the following implementation process is drastically reduced compared to a conventional design process where completeness and correctness are only checked by carrying out review cycles.

The results of a prototyping-oriented architecture design process are validated module interfaces, recorded simulations, and complementary specifications which capture further details. The recorded simulations define the inner working of the designed modules and can therefore be reused as specifications for the implementation of the modules or as dynamic documentation during maintenance.

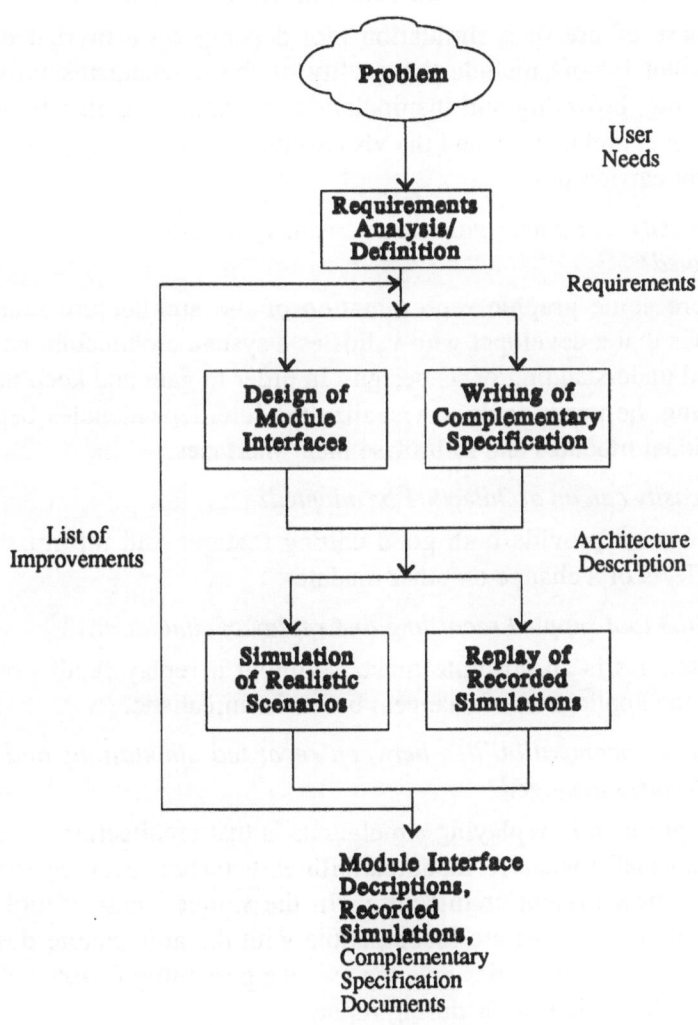

Figure 2.5. Prototyping of module-oriented software architectures

Simulating a software system in order to validate its architecture requires adequate tool support. Due to the importance of tool support the next subsection provides a list of criteria to assist in the comparative evaluation of tools and in the selection of the best-suited.

### 2.2.1.2 Selection Criteria for Architecture Prototyping Tools

Architecture prototyping tools can be distinguished and evaluated according to the following criteria.

- *How is the management of the simulation process supported?*

  The ease of use of a simulation tool depends on a myriad of details. Important factors include the quality of the mechanisms provided for observing, browsing and manipulating the data items that flow through the system architecture and the visualization of simulation steps that were already carried out.

- *How easily can a user gain an overview of the system architecture being simulated?*

  Is there some graphic representation of the architecture model? It is obvious that a developer who validates a system architecture has to have a good understanding of its design. In order to gain and keep this understanding, he needs tools to visualize the interdependencies between the individual modules and to browse their interfaces.

- *How easily can an architecture be adapted?*

  A tool must provide both good editing features and information about the effects of a change on other modules.

- *Does the tool support recording and replay of simulations?*

  This feature is an absolute must. Without a replay facility validation (after the application of changes) becomes unrealistic.

- *How are incompatibilities between recorded simulations and changed architectures managed?*

  A big problem in replaying simulations is that architectures can change. This normally leads to incompatibilities between recorded simulations and the new system architecture. In the simplest case a tool discards simulation steps that are incompatible with the architecture description. More advanced strategies give the user the possibility to apply changes to the simulation before or during replay.

- *Is it possible to execute existing application parts while only the newly designed modules are simulated?*

Everybody who has developed large software systems can imagine the effort needed to entirely simulate applications in a realistic way. It is therefore important that reusable application parts as well as evolutionary prototypes can be executed, while only the newly designed modules have to be simulated.

- *Does the tool provide the possibility to reuse recorded simulations for other purposes?*

  The usefulness of recorded simulations is not limited to their replay during validation of changed system architectures. With adequate tool support they can also be used to generate stubs of implementation parts of the simulated modules, and to complement the component specification for the implementors.

### 2.2.1.3  SCT—a Tool Example

We chose SCT (System Construction Tool) [Bis89] as our tool example for the following reasons:

- It provides a comfortable user interface for guiding and visualizing architecture simulations and forms an exploratory programming environment.

- Its comfortable programming environment supports the browsing and adapting of a system architecture.

- It provides a record-and-replay mechanism for architecture simulations.

- It supports the direct execution of existing application parts, the interpretation of parts currently under development, and the simulation of newly designed parts.

- It permits the use of recorded simulations as dynamic specifications of simulated parts, to generate stubs of implementation parts, and as a testbed for newly implemented parts.

SCT is not commercially available. It was developed in a research project which was carried out in a cooperation between the University of Linz, and the University of Zurich. Because it forms part of the TOPOS tool set for prototyping-oriented software development, SCT is described in Chapter 8 of Part II, where TOPOS is presented; SCT's architecture simulator is discussed in Section 8.6.

## 2.2.2  Prototyping of Concurrent Systems with Petri Nets

The problems in specifying and designing *concurrent systems* are neither the user interfaces nor the internal structure of processes or applied algorithms, but the decomposition into processes and the definition and validation of the protocols used for communication between these processes. Furthermore, concurrent systems frequently consist of a number of time critical parts.

In order to define and validate these protocols, formalisms are needed to represent processes and communication between them, and tools are required to check specifications written in these formalisms for syntactic and semantic correctness. If appropriate tools are available prototyping can be applied for validation of the dynamic aspects by simulating and executing the resulting specifications.

Today several such formalisms enjoy practical application. The most widespread among them are data flow diagrams, Petri nets, and SDL.

- *Data flow diagrams* are the most informal approach to modelling processes and communication (data flows) between them. Processes usually are described informally and the data flows are defined by referencing the data model. Because of their informality and the resulting ease of use, they are mostly applied for analysis and specification of complex business administration systems. While the informality brings good results for high level representations, it does not allow extensive checking of syntactic and semantic correctness, and prototyping-oriented validation becomes almost impossible. Data flow diagrams are therefore not discussed further. For additional readings about data flow diagrams, see [Mar89], [Pet88], [Ros85], and [DeM78].

- *Petri nets*, in contrast to data flow diagrams, base on a mathematical foundation [Bes86]. This makes it possible to verify resulting nets for various aspects such as connectivity and avoidance of deadlocks. Furthermore, execution of Petri nets is formally defined. For an overview of Petri net analyzers and simulators, see [Fel87] and [Ige86].

- *SDL* (Specification and Description Language) is the specification language for parallel systems, standardized by CCITT [CCI85] and largely used by telephone constructors. SDL consists of two graphic formalisms: one for the description of processes, and one for the representation of the structure of a system of processes, which provides blocks for the grouping of processes and channels for the grouping of signals that are exchanged between processes (see [Cav88]). There are many tools supporting graphic editing, checking and simulation of SDL diagrams (e.g., [Alg88], [Cav88]). SDL was developed for the specification of telephone systems. Nowadays it is applied more and more for specification of general real time systems.

Both Petri nets and SDL have proven to be useful for the specification and design of large practically applicable concurrent systems. The main difference between Petri nets and SDL in the field of architecture validation is that the tools for the design and execution (simulation) of Petri nets are better suited for a prototyping approach than similar tools for SDL. For this reason the rest of this chapter first describes *PrT-nets*, a kind of enhanced Petri nets, and how they can be used to specify a concurrent architecture. Afterwards *SPECS*, a tool for the design and prototyping-oriented validation of enhanced PrT-nets, is presented.

### 2.2.2.1 PrT-Nets[1]

*General Petri Nets*

A general Petri net consists of S-elements (places) and T-elements (transitions) which are connected with directed arcs. Arcs connect a T-element with an S-element or vice versa. S-elements represent preconditions for transitions and are therefore passive components. T-elements trigger changes in the states of their associated S-elements. When a T-element is triggered, it deactivates its preconditions and enables its postconditions. Graphically, T-elements are represented as boxes, S-elements as circles, and arcs as arrows.

In Petri nets black tokens are used to indicate the state of a system. A precondition—represented by an S-element—holds if the corresponding place is marked with a token. When all preconditions of a transition hold, it is fired and its postconditions begin to hold (see Figure 2.6).

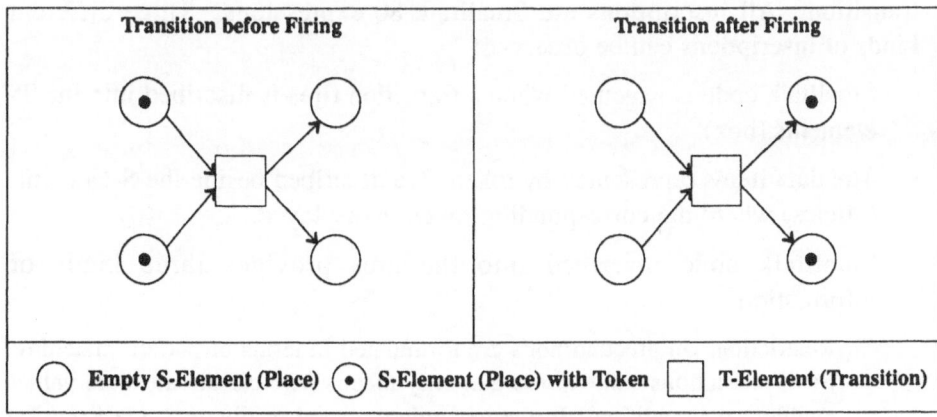

Figure 2.6. Petri net with fireable transition (left) and after firing this transition (right)

---

[1] The following description of Petri nets and their enhancement to PrT-nets is adapted from [Däh87].

Concurrency is a natural concept in Petri nets because no explicit sequence of execution is defined. Rather, the execution of a transition is triggered when its preconditions become true. During the execution of Petri nets it is even frequently the case that the prerequisites of many transitions become fulfilled at the same time, which results in their concurrent triggering.

*Predicate/Transition-nets*

Predicate/Transition-nets (PrT-nets) are a step toward a higher abstraction level. This increase in the abstraction level results from the introduction of individual tokens. While a token in a Petri net represents a boolean value, a set of attributes can be associated with a token in a PrT-net. The S-elements of a PrT-net, therefore, represent not only simple conditions but also complex predicates. The value of such an S-element is determined by the set of tokens it holds and by the attribute values of these tokens.

The increased modelling power of PrT-nets makes it possible to drastically reduce the size of basic Petri net models. For this reason they are a widely used class of high level nets (see [Gen81]).

PrT-nets can be further improved. One improvement is the possibility to describe the data types and values associated with tokens as well as actions to be taken when a transition fires in a programming language. For ease of execution, interpretive programming languages such as Smalltalk-80 or Prolog have usually been chosen for this kind of extension (e.g., [Sch89], [Däh87]).

Figure 2.7 shows an enhanced PrT-net before and after the firing of a transition. All inscriptions are Smalltalk-80 expressions. Three different kinds of inscriptions can be observed:

- Smalltalk code is executed when a transition fires is inscribed into the T-elements (box).

- The data items represented by tokens are described beside the S-elements (circles) where the corresponding token is displayed.

- Smalltalk code inscribed into the arcs provides three kinds of information:

  - Restrictions on preconditions are formulated in terms of pattern matching. Such restrictions can express that only tokens with certain attribute values enable a precondition. In the example depicted in Figure 2.7, *<#red,X>* defines that the S-element *predicate 1* has to contain at least one token with *#red* as its first attribute before it becomes a valid precondition.

  - Attributes of tokens can be bound to variables. These bindings hold during the evaluation of preconditions, during the execution of the code inscribed into the transitions, and during generation of the output token. *<Color,Y>*

defines, for example, that the first attribute of a token stored in S-element *predicate 2* is bound to the variable *Color* and the second attribute to the variable *Y*.

- Third, the form of the output tokens is described in the code inscribed into the output arcs. For example, *<Color,Z>* on the output arc defines that the output token consists of the value of the variable *Color* (i.e., of the first attribute of a token coming from the S-element *predicate 2* ) and of the value of variable *Z* which is calculated.

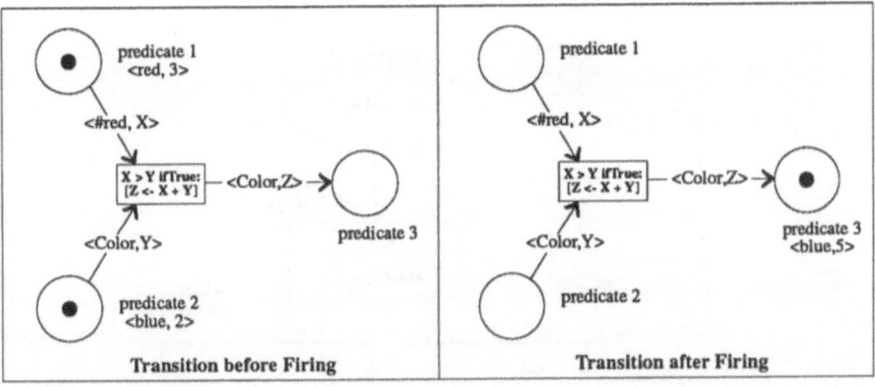

Figure 2.7. Enhanced Petri Net with firable transition (left) and after firing this transition (right) [Däh87]

Another enhancement is the introduction of a mechanism allowing for refinement of transitions in hierarchically lower diagram levels (e.g., Figure 2.8). Such enhanced PrT-nets have the same modelling power as data flow diagrams, but still base on a mathematical foundation. For this reason enhanced PrT-nets are gradually being applied for specifying administrative business software [Sch89], [Rei87].

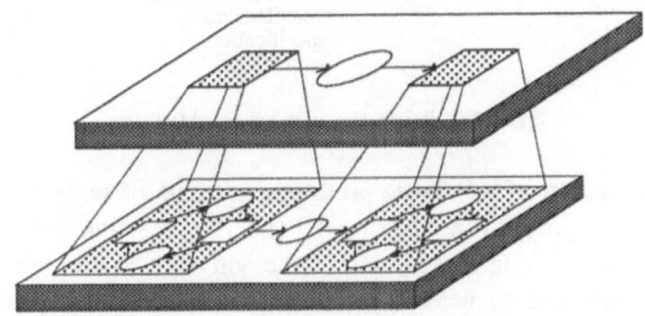

Figure 2.8. Hierarchical refinement of a PrT-net [Däh87]

Finally, PrT-nets can be augmented to represent the time required to carry out transactions. This explicit representation is very important for specification and prototyping of real-time systems that are highly coupled with the external world and have to meet strict time limits.

### 2.2.2.2 How to Prototype Distributed Systems with PrT-Nets

Prototyping with enhanced PrT-nets (see Figure 2.9), like all other prototyping processes, consists of two activities: (re)implementation and (re)evaluation of the current prototype version. These two activities are carried out iteratively until a satisfying solution is found.

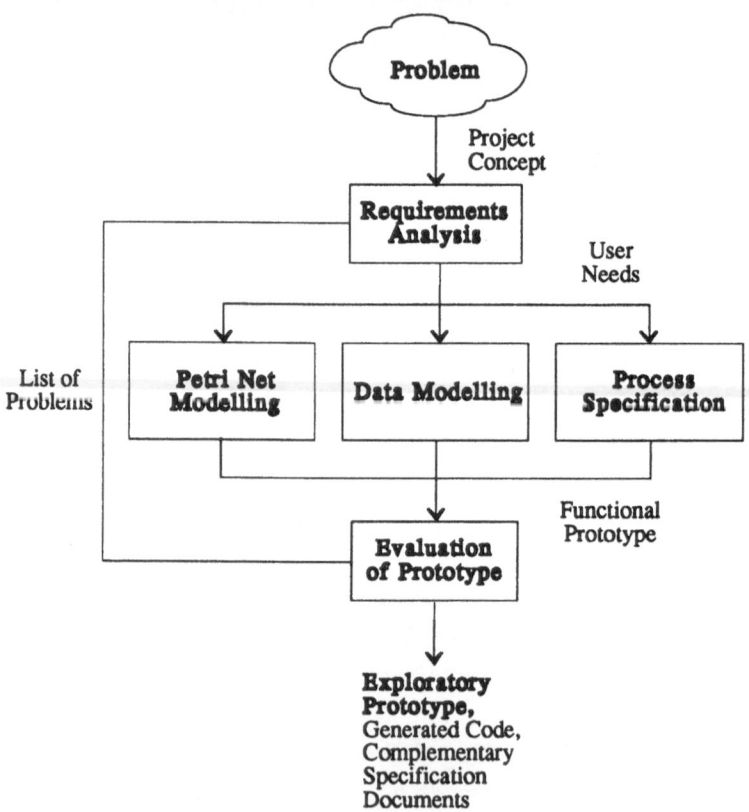

Figure 2.9. Prototyping with enhanced PrT-nets

The implementation of a PrT-net prototype consists of three activities: net modelling, description of the data model (i.e., the possible data types of tokens), and programming of as much of the activities carried out during the firing of a transition as needed for a realistic simulation (process specification).

Evaluation is usually carried out using a graphic net simulator. Such a tool allows for specification of an initial set of tokens. Based on this initial setting, the simulation is then carried out. During simulation the tool captures information such as the number of firings and data transmission rates. How the simulation can be influenced by the developer, and what kind of information is gathered depend on the applied tool.

The difference between prototyping with enhanced PrT-nets and the prototyping approaches described in Sections 2.1 and 2.3 is that PrT-net prototypes are not built and evaluated to ensure the quality of the external behavior on the user interface level. They serve instead to check the external behavior on the level of communication protocols, i.e., the correctness, feasibility, and efficiency of these protocols as well as of the structure of the communicating processes.

The results of such a prototyping process are an exploratory prototype and complementary specifications. Depending on the supporting tools, code implementing the communication protocols and parts of the code implementing the functionality of the processes can be generated.

Due to the importance of tool support for designing and validating PrT-net prototypes, the next subsection provides a list of criteria to assist in the comparative evaluation of tools and the selection of the best-suited.

### 2.2.2.3 Selection Criteria for Tools Supporting Prototyping with PrT-Nets

Tools supporting prototyping with PrT-nets can be distinguished and evaluated according the following criteria.

- *What kind of PrT-nets are supported?*

  There are different kinds of PrT-nets. They distinguish themselves by the programming language they provide for the definition of token types, triggering restrictions, and process behavior. The programming language determines the expressive power and the time that is required to switch from design mode to simulation mode. Furthermore, for certain nonalgorithmic programming languages such as Prolog, some amount of training is required before developers familiar with algorithmic languages can use them.

- *How well are browsing and editing of PrT-nets supported?*

  In order to keep an overview of large PrT-nets representing complex software systems, a developer needs a lot of support. The minimum support required is a tool providing a browser for the nested diagram structure. The manipulation of nets should also be supported by a graphic WYSIWYG editor.

- *Can the simulation be carried out interactively?*

  Interactive simulation tools that allow direct monitoring of simulations and for easy browsing and changing of the current state of simulation are a must.

- *Can simulations be recorded and replayed?*

  During a prototyping-oriented validation of large complex PrT-nets—as during the validation of large module-based architectures—a lot of time has to be invested in defining input data and checking output data. For this reason it is important that a tool make it possible to record entire simulations and to replay them during the validation of a PrT-net after changes were applied, as well as for documentation purposes.

- *Is there a possibility to generate code, and how portable is this code?*

  While it is usually difficult to reuse the source code of the inscriptions, it would frequently be attractive to reuse the formally specified communication protocols by generating code from a PrT-net and integrating this code with the newly implemented behavior of the individual processes. Because the processes of a concurrent system frequently run on different hardware platforms, the portability issue is of special importance in this context.

### 2.2.2.4 SPECS—a Tool Example

We chose SPECS [Däh87] as our tool example for the following reasons:

- Its combination of hierarchical Petri nets with Smalltalk-80 inscriptions makes it possible to specify prototypes on a high abstraction level.

- The features and user interface of the tools it provides for editing and interactively simulating enhanced PrT-nets are state of the art.

- It permits the generation of C code which implements the behavior of a specific PrT-net.

SPECS was developed at the ETH Zurich and is commercially available. It runs on a wide variety of hardware platforms. The following description is adapted from [Däh87].

SPECS consists of two tools: a graphic *net editor* which is used for editing and browsing a prototype as well as for visualization of simulations, and a *control panel* which makes it possible to control a simulation.

## The Net Editor

The net editor was designed according to the Smalltalk-80 user interface conventions [Gol84]. Its user interface was therefore implemented on the basis of windows, pop-up menus, and the mouse as a pointing device. Graphic elements can be directly selected and manipulated by clicking and dragging. Like most applications based on direct manipulation of graphic objects, it is therefore highly self-explanatory. Figure 2.10 shows the screen during editing of a model representing two stations communicating with the alternating bit protocol—a simple protocol which works by attaching a sequence bit to each message to detect losses of data in the channel. Three different levels of the model are displayed in editor windows. The sheet directory in the upper right corner displays the current hierarchical structure of the model.

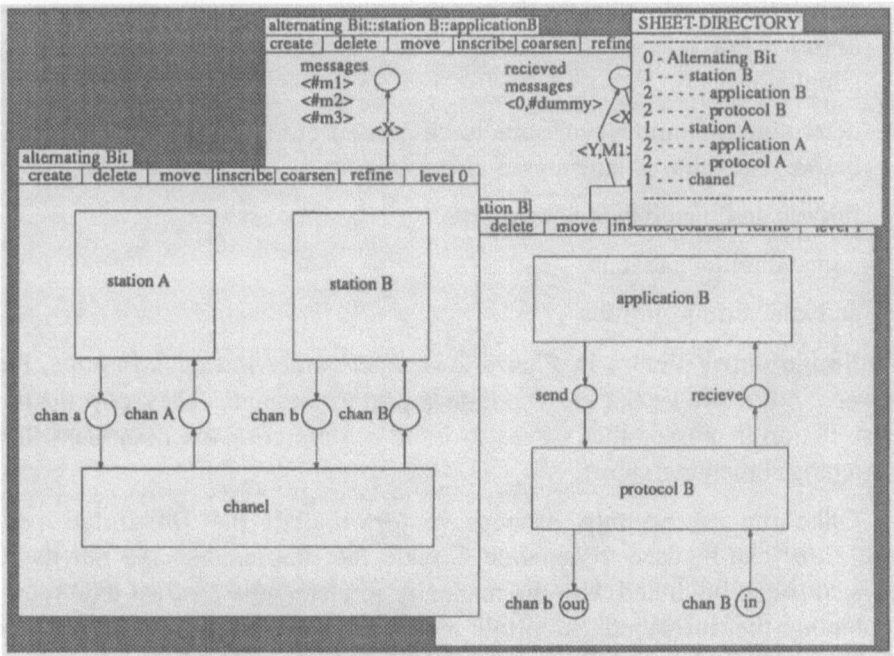

Figure 2.10. SPECS net editor [Däh87]

After a model consisting of several nets has been checked for completeness and consistency, it can be simulated any time during the design process. During a simulation tokens are represented as black points (or a custom designed bitmap) and displayed at the places where they are currently located. Their values are described below the description of the corresponding place. In the active editor window the token flow is animated during a transition by visibly moving the tokens from place to place. For every element of the simulated model (places, transitions, nets and arcs) a statistics window displaying a bar graph can be opened. The values to be depicted in the bar graph are computed from the automatically gathered data by a user-selectable function.

*The Control Panel*

The control panel of the simulator shown in Figure 2.11 serves to control the simulation. It consists of a subwindow containing push buttons and a message subwindow which serves to display information about the executed simulation steps as well as other messages. The push buttons serve to:

- switch step mode on and off (i.e., going from a mode where the simulation is interrupted after one transition was fired, to a mode of continuous execution or vice versa)

- switch time mode on and off (i.e., switching into a mode, where the time a transition takes, as defined in the model, is considered during simulation)

- determine the number of steps to be carried out (transitions to be fired) before execution is interrupted in step mode

- browse and manipulate breakpoints

- add and remove tokens

- activate various utilities

While the upper picture in Figure 2.11 shows only the push buttons, the lower picture shows the corresponding pop-up menus. They pop up if a push button is pressed that serves to issue a more complex command than switching something on/off.

Once the prototyping process is terminated, the integrated *code generator* can be used to generate C code that implements the net itself. This code can be linked with the manually implemented abstract data types, replacing the inscribed Smalltalk code in order to get an executable application. If changes or extensions to these protocols become necessary later in the development process, they can be implemented with SPECS on the level of PrT-nets and are available in the application after the corresponding C code has been generated anew.

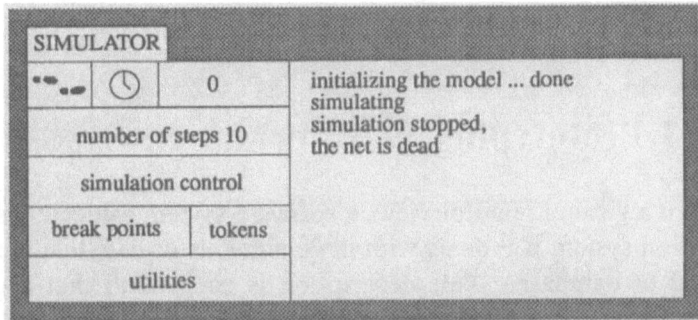

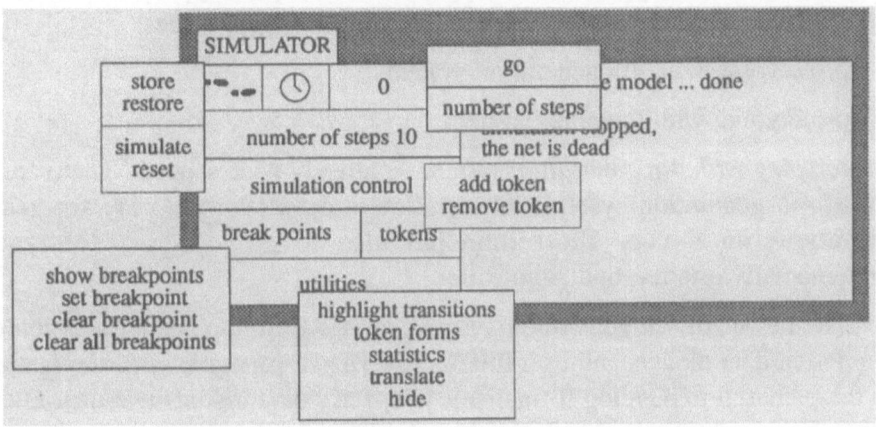

Figure 2.11. SPECS simulations control window [Däh87]

*Suitability for Prototyping*

SPECS is excellently suited for exploratory and evolutionary prototyping of concurrent systems for the following reasons:

- It provides a formalism consisting of a mix of Petri nets and Smalltalk-80. This formalism makes it possible to specify communicating processes on a high abstraction level as with Petri nets and to implement as much of the functionality of these processes in Smalltalk-80 as needed for the planned experiments.

- It supports the prototyping-oriented validation of a PrT-net in an excellent way with its flexible simulation mechanism, with the way it visualizes the events occurring during simulation, and with the short turnaround times, which make it possible to switch immediately from design to simulation and vice versa .

- It provides a code generator which makes it possible to evolve a prototype into the final application.

# 2.3 Prototyping of Information Systems

From a general point of view, a software system can be considered an information system if it deals with large amounts of data that are stored in some kind of database. This description is so general that a great variety of software systems can be called information systems. This variety necessitates a lot of different approaches for prototyping information systems. Today there are two especially promising approaches:

- prototyping with 4th generation systems
- prototyping with hypertext systems

*Prototyping with 4th generation systems* is already widely used. There are a lot of 4th generation systems which allow a developer not only to create prototypes in a very short time but also to grow these prototypes incrementally into the final application.

The power of 4th generation systems comes from the standardization of supported data models and user interfaces. The advantage of standardization is the potential to develop formalisms to specify data models and user interfaces on a very high abstraction level. That is, it becomes possible to specify the "what" instead of the "how". The disadvantage of standardization is its limitation of the application area of 4th generation systems to the development of software systems with standardizeable data models and user interfaces.

*Hypertext systems* make it possible to manage data and arbitrary links between data items. Reading a hypertext means navigating through a network of linked data items by studying data items and following promising links. With a hypertext system that supports both text and graphics as data elements, it is possible to simulate a wide range software systems.

A new class of hypertext systems provides, besides standard hypertext functionality, the possibility to manage stacks of arbitrary linkable data structures. The combination of the simulation of user interfaces with the management of data structures makes hypertext systems a very interesting approach for the prototyping of information systems.

Prototyping with 4th generation systems and prototyping with hypertext systems are complementary approaches. 4th generation systems excel in prototyping and evolutionary development of standardizable information systems. Hypertext systems make it possible to prototype information systems that exceed limits imposed by 4th generation system standardization. The increased flexibility offered by hypertext systems also has its costs: increased prototype development effort and nonreusable mock-up prototypes.

## 2.3.1 Prototyping with 4th Generation Systems

4th generation systems are in use for developing and maintaining a significant part of data processing applications. They had an impact on the data processing business like nothing else since the development of COBOL. Every concept with such success becomes difficult to define because everybody producing a tool claims that the tool supports the new concept perfectly, which results in a blurring of the initial concept. Because there exists no exact definition of what a 4th generation system is, most authors offer lists of features which a typical 4th generation system provides (e.g., [Hol86], [Mar85]).

We use the term 4th generation systems as tools allowing for implementation of entire information systems on a high abstraction level. They are built around (relational) database management systems and enable the developer to specify/implement the following parts of information systems on a high abstraction level:

- data model
- user interface
- printed reports
- consistency rules

Furthermore, they provide standard search, retrieval and sort facilities and interfaces to algorithmic languages for the realization of other features.

### 2.3.1.1 How to Prototype with 4th Generation Systems

Like user interface prototyping, prototyping with 4th generation systems consists of a cyclical process where (re)development and (re)evaluation of the prototype alternate. In contrast to user interface prototyping, 4th generation systems allow not only the specification of static and dynamic aspects of the user interface, but also of the underlying data model and the connection between the database (as defined by the data model) and the user interface. 4th generation systems, therefore, allow the fast evolutionary development of prototypes of entire information systems. A client does not have to be confronted with a mock-up, but always sees the incrementally growing application.

Prototyping of information systems (see Figure 2.12) starts with the designing of the data model, the integrating foundation of every information system. Based on this data model, input masks are specified which make it possible to enter information into the database. Output masks are designed to browse this information. Menus and other means for dialog management are defined. Report forms for the retrieval and display/printing of information are specified. Consistency rules are formulated.

The administration of the database, the human/machine dialog, the transfer of the information from the user interface to the database and vice versa, the searching and sorting of data, as well as the enforcement of consistency rules are automatically managed by the 4th generation system.

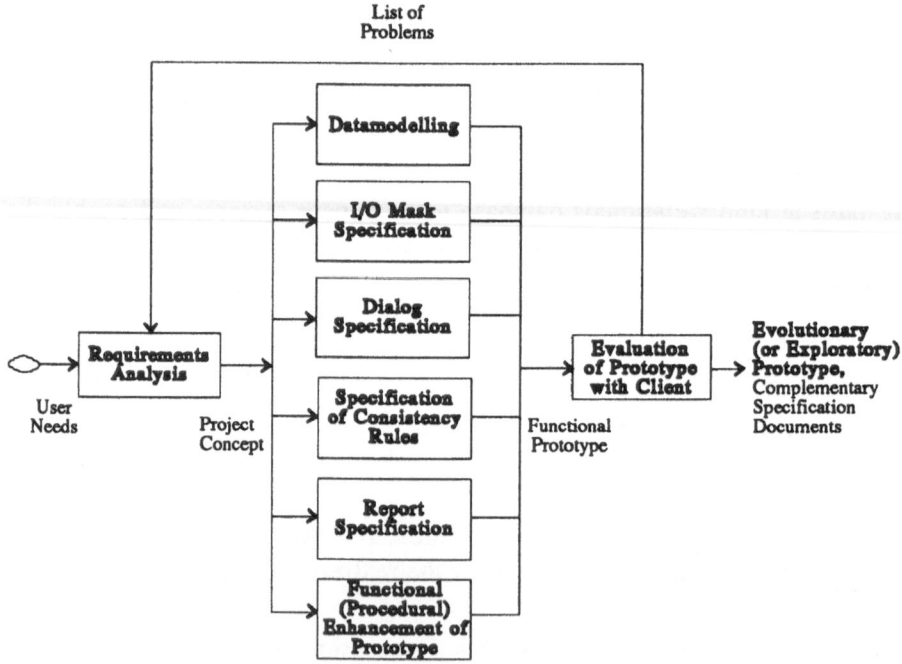

Figure 2.12. Prototyping with 4th generation languages (adapted from [Mar85])

The result of this proceeding is an executable prototype which was realized without algorithmic programming and which, therefore, is based mainly on standard functionality provided by the 4th generation system. This initial prototype is then successively evolved by improving the standard functionality, and by adding further application-specific functionality, which has to be implemented in an algorithmic programming language.

Prototyping of information systems is usually an evolutionary process which ends with the final application as its result, but in certain cases it can be economical to consider the prototype a mere vehicle for requirements definition. This is, for example, the case if the final application needs to be implemented in an algorithmic language for efficiency reasons. In such cases it is possible to prototype applications in a few weeks using 4th generation systems, while the conventional implementation takes several person-years.

### 2.3.1.2 Selection Criteria for 4th-Generation Systems

4th generation systems can be distinguished and evaluated according to the following criteria:

- *Does it provide means to specify data models, user interface layouts, dynamic aspects of the user interface, consistency rules, and report forms?*

- *On which abstraction level are the various aspects specified?*

  Data model, reports, masks, menus, buttons and other dialog elements are best specified with WYSIWYG drawing tools.

- *Are the different specification, generation, and execution tools well-integrated?*

  The developer sees a good 4th generation system as a single tool with a consistent user interface. Integration of the various results (e.g., data model, reports) into a working application should be transparent.

- *Does it provide a suitable algorithmic language and programming environment to support the functional enhancement of a prototype?*

  The most important aspects that determine the quality of an algorithmic programming language imbedded into a 4th generation system are the concepts for abstraction and modularization it provides and the degree to which the language and its programming environment are integrated into the 4th generation system.

  Algorithmic code which is used to enhance the functionality of an information system usually consists of a large number of small functional parts that have to communicate. This communication usually consists of procedure calls and global data that is accessed by different procedures. In order to prevent the cluttering of the global name space, it is important that the language provide some kind of data hiding mechanism. Furthermore, a sound scheme for procedure calls and parameter passing is required to reduce the number of global variables and to make it possible to share algorithms which are used more than once.

- *Is the turnaround time short enough to make the tool suitable for use in a prototyping process?*

  Most 4th generation systems with such a short turnaround time rely heavily on interpretive execution.

- *Is it possible to develop applications with satisfying run-time efficiency?*

  4th generation systems providing only interpretive execution cannot be used to realize medium-sized or large applications. For the development of such applications, 4th generation systems generating code are better suited.

- *Does the 4th generation system provide for easy understandability and modifiability of information systems built with it?*

  During every development process and especially during a prototyping process, it is important that an information system can be understood and changed quickly. A 4th generation system can strongly improve understandability and modifiability by enforcing a system architecture standard. Furthermore, it is important that an application can be changed even after data has been entered and that the system guarantees consistency among the various parts of the program as well as between data and application.

### 2.3.1.3  4th Dimension—a Tool Example

In a study carried out on the basis of the selection criteria described above, four 4th generation systems were compared [Sei90]. 4th Dimension (4D) [Aci90a] proved to be best-suited for prototyping-oriented software development.

In order to give an overview of 4D, this section first describes the structure of a 4D application. Afterwards, the various editors allowing a developer to specify/implement an information system are briefly outlined. Finally, a short overview of the execution mechanism is given and 4D's suitability for prototyping-oriented development of information systems is discussed. Further technical information can be obtained from the documentation of 4D [Aci90a].

4D applications consist of:

- relations (the data model)

- layouts used to visualize, manipulate, and print relations and views (the user interface)

- layout procedures coupled with layouts used mainly for initialization of layouts and for checking consistency after data manipulations by the user

- menu bars for the invocation of commands

- global procedures used to factor out standard behavior and to control the execution of commands invoked from menus

Figure 2.13 gives an overview of the structure of a typical 4D application. After starting up a 4D application, the user issues commands by selecting items from the pull-down menus. Every possible menu selection is logically connected to a global procedure, which is called on selection of the menu item.

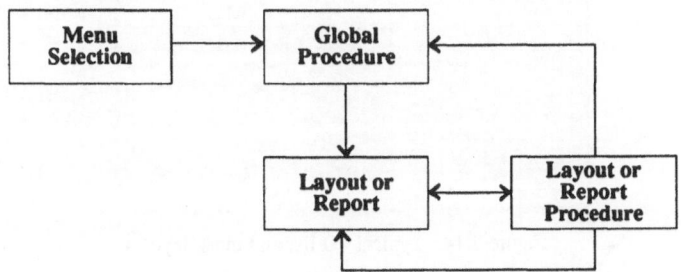

Figure 2.13. Typical 4D application structure

In the global procedure any kind of computation (programmed in the integrated algorithmic language) can be carried out. In order to display, manipulate, or print relations and views a layout is invoked from the global procedure.

A layout is coupled with a relation or a view and serves to display or print the corresponding records in the form of lists (see Figure 2.14 above) or to display, print, and manipulate single records in the form of masks with powerful interaction elements (see Figure 2.14 below).

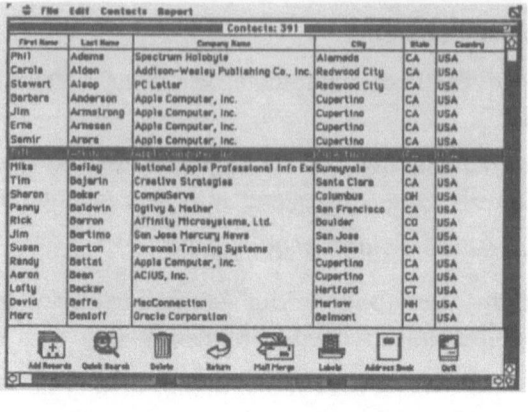

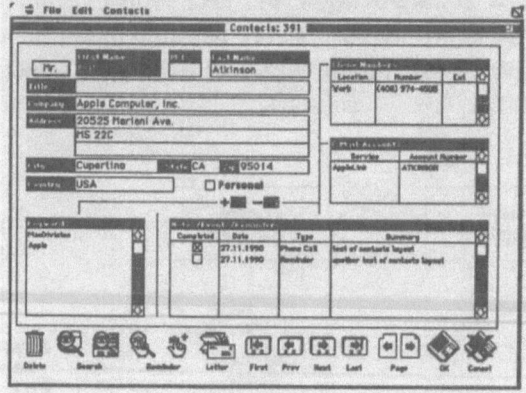

Figure 2.14.  Typical 4D list and mask layouts

Every layout is connected with its layout procedure. This procedure is called automatically once before a record is displayed, after every change to the record, after a push button is pressed, and after the layout is left. It serves for initializations, consistency checks, computations, and clearing work. A layout procedure can also call global procedures and invoke other layouts/reports.

The *data model* is manipulated with a graphic editor. Besides the (expected) operations to manipulate the data model that can be invoked from the menu displayed in Figure 2.15, the data editor makes it possible to arbitrarily change the layout of the relations (files). Furthermore, zooming support is provided, which helps a developer to keep an overview of large data models. The supported data types are displayed in Figure 2.16 which shows the dialog invoked by the selection of the "Change Field" or "New Field" command.

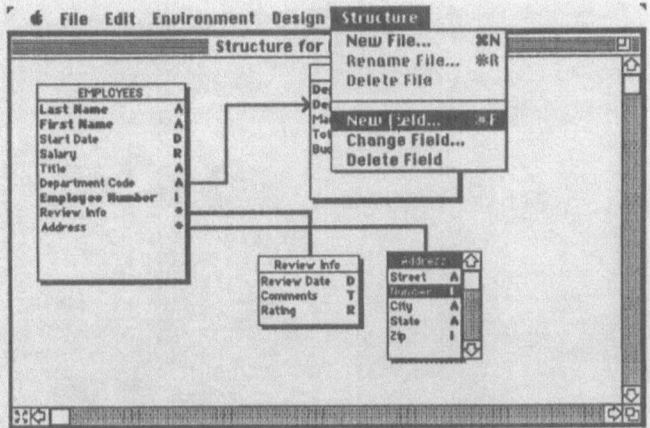

Figure 2.15. 4D data model editor

Various kinds of *input/output-layouts* and *reports* can be generated automatically. In order to generate a layout, a developer selects the fields to be
displayed/printed in the *Select fields* list. In addition, the developer chooses
one of the standard masks (see Figure 2.17); or the field labelled *custom* can
be selected in order to design a layout from scratch. The selected fields can
either be all or a selection of the fields of a relation, or they can define a
view.

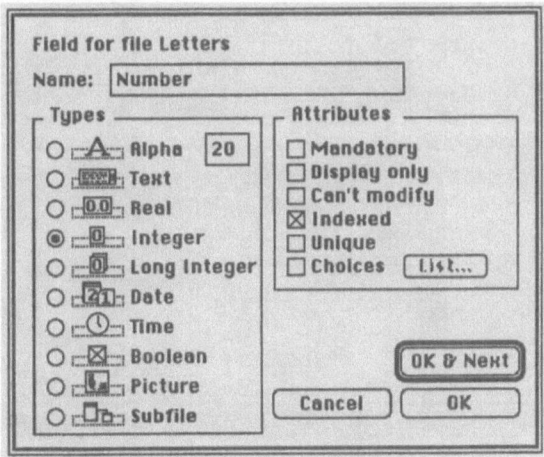

Figure 2.16. 4D data type specification dialog

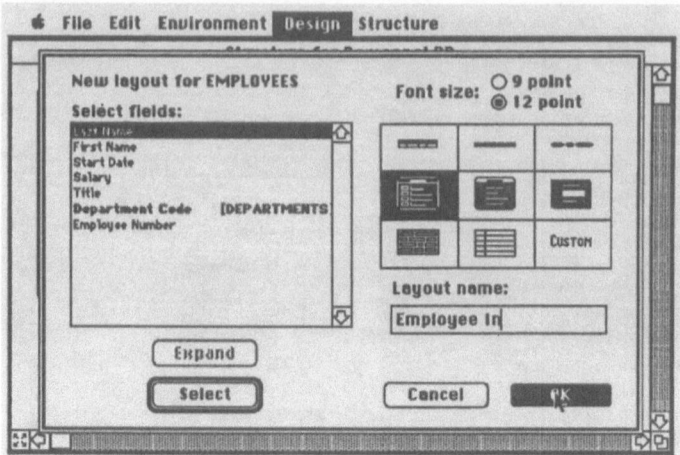

Figure 2.17. Interface to the 4D layout generator

Starting with a generated layout or from scratch, *input/output-layouts* and *reports* containing variable fields, record fields, push buttons, radio buttons, arbitrary graphics and much more can be drawn with a graphic editor (see Figure 2.18). In order to give an impression of the available interaction mechanisms, Figure 2.19 shows the list of the gadgets provided by 4D.

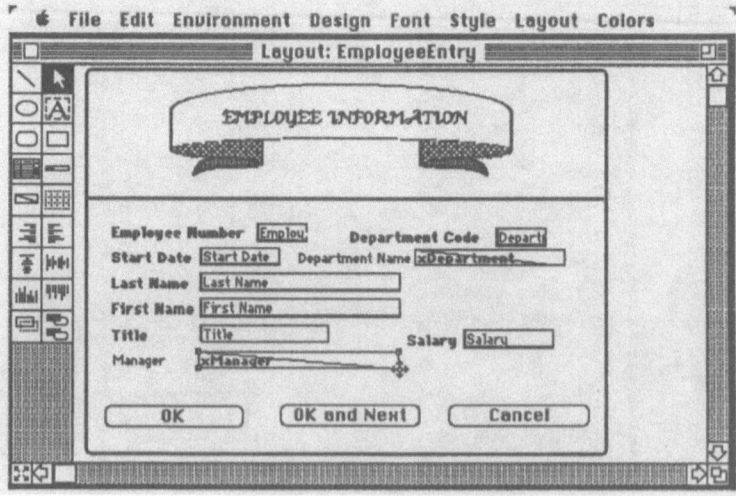

Figure 2.18. 4D layout editor

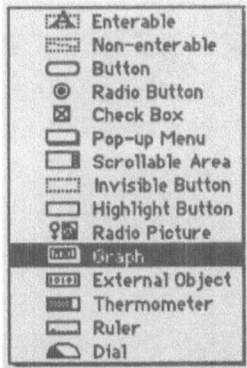

Figure 2.19. User interface gadgets provided by 4D

Pull-down *menus*, shortcuts and global procedures to be called on selection of the corresponding menu item can be specified with the menu browser/editor depicted in Figure 2.20.

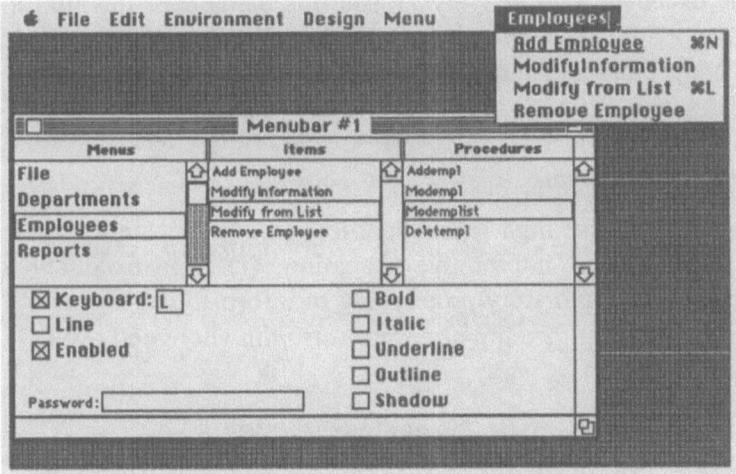

Figure 2.20. 4D menu browser/editor and simulator

*Global procedures and layout procedures* can be edited in the comfortable syntax-sensitive editor depicted in Figure 2.21. Editing is eased by three scrollable lists located at the bottom of the editor. They allow fast insertion of programming language key words and for browsing and insertion of the names of relations and fields as well as of the names of the available procedures.

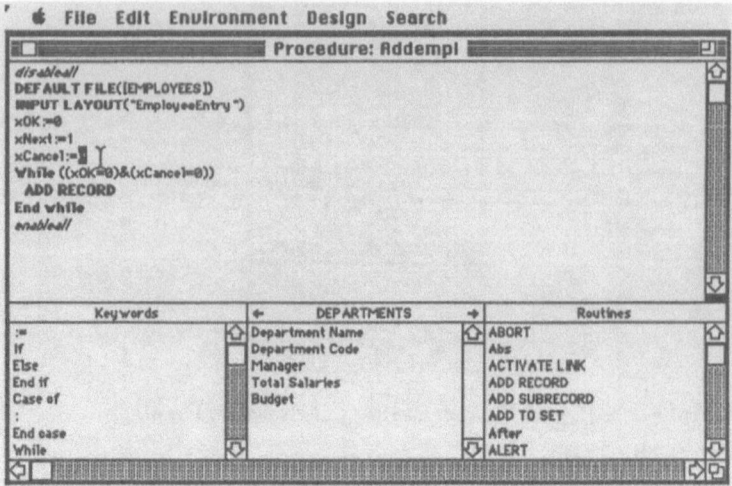

Figure 2.21. 4D Code editor

All application parts specified and implemented with the editors depicted above are executed interpretively. Restarting the application after a change has been applied takes only seconds. During execution a dynamic debugger helps to understand and debug the procedures written in the integrated algorithmic language.

*Suitability for Prototyping*

Providing easy to use high level specification/implementation facilities as well as instantaneous interpretive execution, 4D is an excellent tool for evolutionary and exploratory prototyping of information systems. We have applied it in different medium-sized projects with very good results.

## 2.3.2 Prototyping with Hypertext Systems

In [Par89b] hypertext is defined as follows:

> *"Hypertext can be simply defined as the creation and representation of links between discrete pieces of data. When this data can be graphics or sound, as well as text or numbers, the resulting structure is referred to as hypermedia. ... Hypertext is simultaneously a method for storing and retrieving data. It incorporates the notion of linking pieces of information, allowing users to navigate through a network of chunks of information. Information is provided both by what is stored in each node and in the way the information nodes are linked to each other."*

General hypertext systems which provide linking services for text and graphic objects lend themselves readily for the simulation (prototyping) of software systems with modern graphic user interfaces. The resulting prototypes are finite state automata in which screens represent states and transitions are triggered by following a link. General hypertext systems therefore provide a functionality similar to general user interface prototyping tools described in the previous section. The difference is that prototypes created with user interface prototyping tools frequently can be used as part of the final application while hypertext prototypes are mere mock-ups. The advantage of the hypertext approach is that a great variety of user interfaces can be prototyped (simulated), while user interface prototyping tools provide only a restricted number of interaction mechanisms. A widely known example of a general hypertext system is Intermedia [Gar86].

General hypertext systems lack two features which are needed to build more than mere mockup prototypes for information systems. They are missing a formalism to express functionality which is not connected with links, and they do not allow the organization of sets of similarly structured data items, as relational databases do.

These two shortcomings were overcome by hypertext systems that support the so called note card concept. This concept bases on the notion that data are stored in information fields on note cards, and these notecards are organized in stacks. A single card can therefore be considered a record, and a stack consisting of note cards containing the same information fields is analogous to a relation of a relational database.

Compared to a relational organization, which can be emulated, the note card concept is much more general because of the linking capabilities of hypertext systems. Links make it possible to connect single cards in arbitrary ways and to build any kind of data structure.

All hypertext systems which support the note card concept also provide an algorithmic language that makes it possible to express functionality that is not connected with links. These languages are used to write scripts that are associated with user interface objects such as push buttons, data fields, or entire cards. The execution of a script is triggered when a user manipulates the corresponding field. This scripting mechanism is very similar to the way 4th Dimension (see Section 2.3.1.3) supports the algorithmic enhancement of the functionality of information systems.

More information about general hypertext systems can be found in [Par89b], [Shn89], and [Fli88].

## 2.3.2.1 How to Prototype with Hypertext Systems

The main difference between prototyping with 4th generation systems
(Figure 2.12) and prototyping with hypertext systems (Figure 2.22) is that
in the latter many well-defined steps such as data modelling and report
design are carried out with tool support. In prototyping with hypertext
systems, a developer primarily gets support to simulate any kind of
prototype behavior. All other aspects such as the data model and
consistency rules have to be documented in complementary specifications.
The two approaches are clearly complementary. 4th generation systems
excel in fast evolutionary prototyping of standardizable information
systems. Hypertext systems are the method of choice for exploratory
prototyping of information systems with features going beyond the limit of
what can be implemented with 4th generation systems.

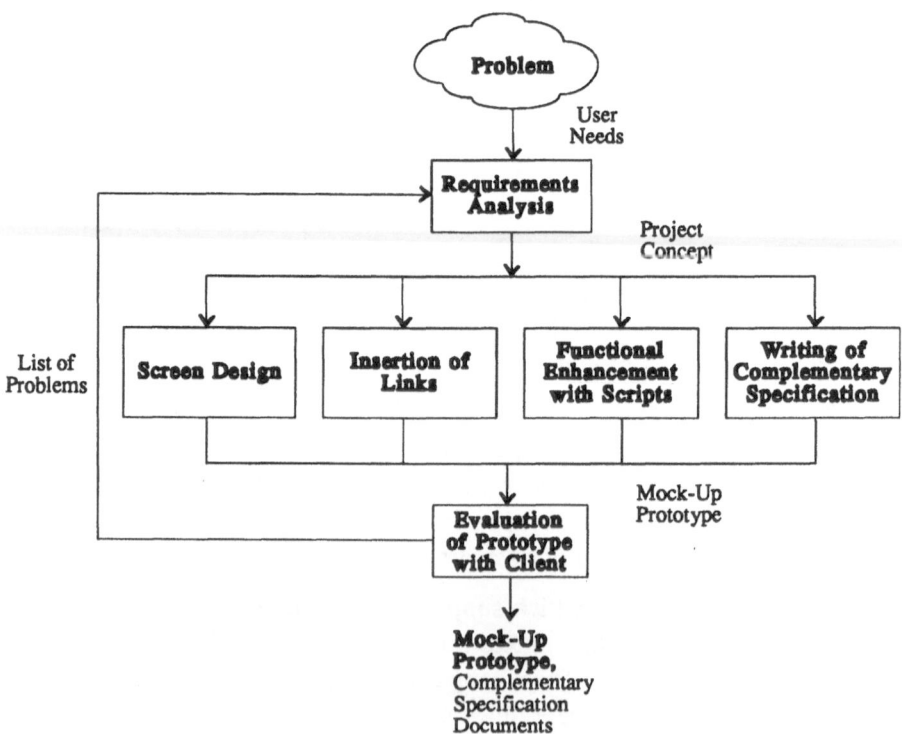

Figure 2.22. Prototyping with hypertext systems

Prototyping of information systems with hypertext systems starts with an
informal designing of the data model. Based on this data model and on the
functional requirements collected during requirements analysis, the screens
are designed to represent the various possible states of the user interface and

the transitions between these states are modeled by inserting links. Afterwards, scripts are implemented which realize further functionality for
certain parts of the user interface where a more realistic behavior is
required.

Parallel to the realization of the prototype, complementary specifications
are written that cover all functional and nonfunctional requirements that
were not incorporated into the prototype.

The result of this proceeding is a mock-up prototype which is evaluated
with the client and then refined during an iterative prototyping process. At
the end of this prototyping process the results are a validated requirements
definition, consisting of an exploratory—and therefore not reusable—prototype and a set of complementary specifications.

### 2.3.2.2 Selection Criteria for Hypertext Systems

Hypertext systems can be distinguished and evaluated according the criteria
below. Further general criteria can be found in [Nie88].

* *What kinds of media are supported?*

  Does it allow the management of text only, or are graphics and sound
  supported also? For prototyping, the combination of text and graphics is
  a must.

* *Does it provide the possibility to enhance the functionality beyond the
  manipulation of links?*

  In order to build prototypes which are not mere concatenations of screen
  drawings, it is important to have some kind of a programming language
  to customize the behavior.

* *Is some kind of data model supported?*

  In order to store more than plain text and graphics, it is important to
  have the possibility to define data fields and their organization. The
  most common data model today is that of note cards organized in stacks
  of similar cards.

* *Does it provide a design tool which allows the drawing and manipulation
  of objects instead of bit maps?*

  A major shortcoming of many hypertext systems is that the user
  interface consists of bitmaps that have to be painted. This encumbers the
  drawing and evolution of user interfaces because user interface elements
  cannot be easily moved, grouped, or aligned once they are painted.

- *Is the turnaround time short enough that the tool is suited for use in a
  prototyping process?*

Most hypertext systems available today rely on interpretive execution
allowing for instantaneous reexecution after modifications.

### 2.3.2.3 HyperCard—a Tool Example

General hypertext systems lack two features that are needed to build more
than mere mock-up prototypes for information systems, as mentioned
above. They are missing a formalism to express functionality that is not
connected with links, and they do not allow organization of sets of similarly
structured data items, as provided by relational databases.

*HyperCard* [Goo88] provides features which make it possible to
overcome exactly these shortcomings. Its data management is based on the
notion of stacks of similarly structured note cards. These cards can contain
different kinds of data fields and interaction objects. In order to add
functionality, scripts can be added to objects and executed upon user
manipulation of these objects.

We chose HyperCard as our tool example because of this combination of
features which makes it an excellent prototyping tool, because it was the
original tool supporting the note card paradigm, and because it is still the
most widespread.

This subsection gives a short overview of the structure of a HyperCard
application and some glimpses of its development environment. It discusses
the application of HyperCard in a prototyping process. Further information
about HyperCard can be found in [Goo88] or in one of the flood of other
books that have been published.

A HyperCard application consists of note cards organized in stacks.
Every note card consists of a background, which can be shared among
several cards of the same stack, and a foreground which is card-specific.

Every foreground and background consists of pictures, buttons, and data
fields. Pictures are drawn with a graphic editor. This editor is also used to
design the overall layout of cards (i.e., foreground and background) and to
manage buttons and data fields. Figure 2.23 shows a card of a time management stack and the palette of the drawing tools.

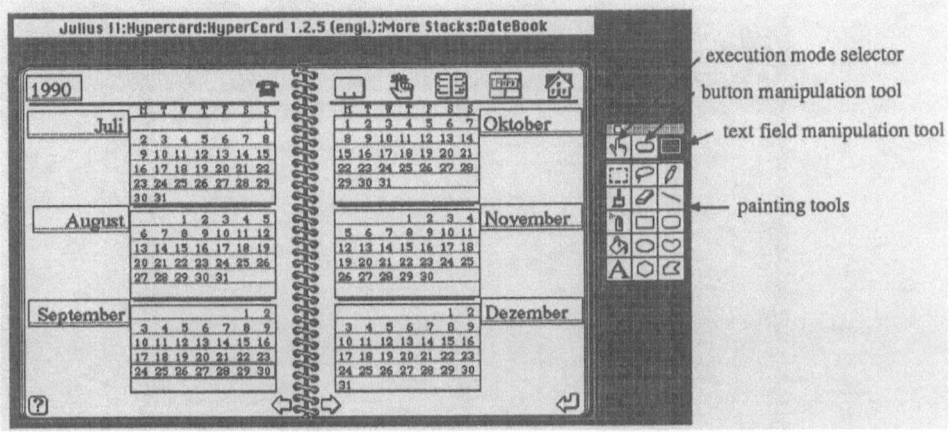

Figure 2.23. Card of a time management system with tool palette

HyperCard links start from buttons or data fields and lead to cards. They can be inserted either manually—by indicating a button and a card with the mouse—or from code. A mouse click on a linked item causes the display of the linked card. Figures 2.24 and 2.25 show how a new button—which was inserted with the *New Button* command—is linked to a card. After the new button is doubble-clicked, its property sheet is displayed (Figure 2.24), which serves to define the button's look and behavior. Clicking the *Link To* button (Figure 2.24) enables link mode. In this mode the user can browse through the stacks until the card to be linked is found. The button and the selected card are then linked with the *This Card* command (Figure 2.25).

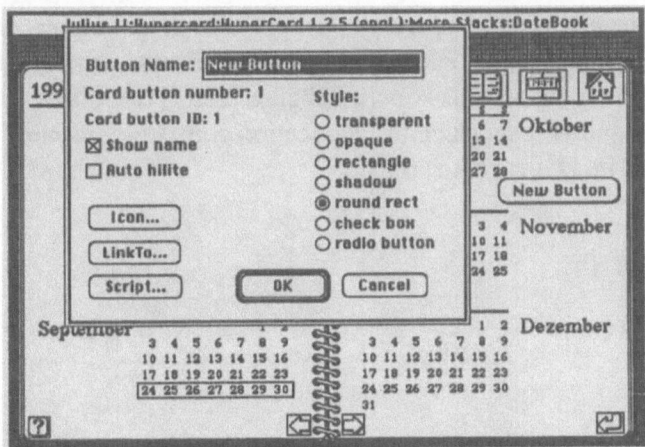

Figure 2.24. New button with its property sheet

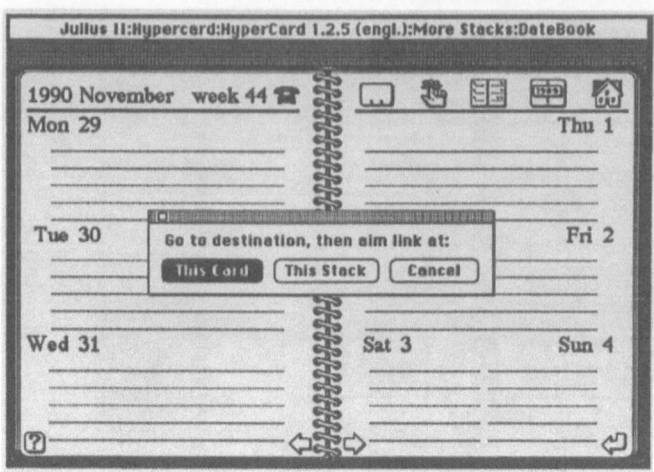

Figure 2.25.  Linking the new button with a card

HyperCard provides a very simple but nonetheless powerful means of managing data. In HyperCard every card can be considered a record. The data fields on the card can then be interpreted as the fields of the record. By putting only homogenous cards into one stack, it is possible to create a data structure which corresponds closely to a relation, and linking different kinds of cards makes it possible to build arbitrary data structures. An example of a stack of homogenous cards is the *DateBook* stack, which consists of a set of cards representing one week each. One card of this stack is displayed in Figure 2.25. Other cards could, for example, be accessed by leafing through the stack with the ⇨ buttons.

HyperCard also provides HyperTalk, a programming language for customizing the behavior of a hypertext. HyperTalk scripts can be connected to stacks, backgrounds, data fields, and buttons. Scripts are called on user-triggered events (e.g., a mouse click). Figure 2.26 gives a little sampling of HyperTalk by showing a calculator application consisting of one single card, with (most of) its HyperTalk scripts.

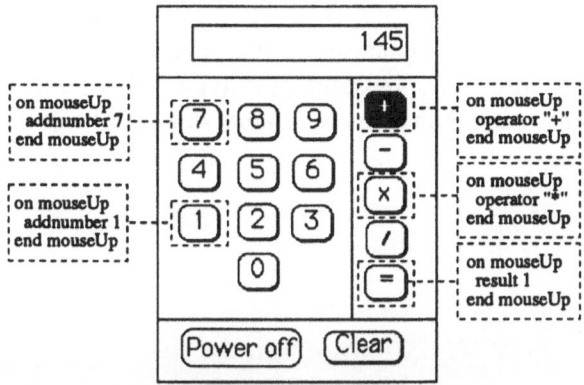

**Calculator Card Script**

```
on openCard                                  on operator vChar
  global power                                 global vOperand, vResult, vOperator, power
  put "off" into power                         if power="on"
end openCard                                   then
-- ********************************               result 2
on closeCard                                     put vChar into vOperator
  put "" into card field "Display"               if vOperand<>0
end closeCard                                    then
-- ********************************                 put vOperand into vResult
on addnumber vDigit                                 put 0 into vOperand
  global vOperand, vResult, vOperator, power      end if
  if power="on"                                end if
  then                                       end operator
    if vOperand <> 0                         -- ********************************
    then                                     on result vArt
      multiply vOperand by 10                  ...
    end if                                   end result
    add vDigit to vOperand
    put vOperand into card field "Display"
  end if
end addnumber
```

Figure 2.26. HyperCard application example

## Suitability for Prototyping

HyperCard is an excellent prototyping tool because its flexibility makes it possible to prototype almost any kind of user interface and database. Nonetheless, HyperCard is no replacement for a 4th generation system because it usually takes more effort to implement an experimental prototype with HyperCard than to build an evolutionary prototype with a good 4th generation system. However, HyperCard and 4th generation systems are complementary tools because HyperCard makes it possible to apply prototyping in developing applications with features going beyond the standardized databases and user interfaces that can be achieved with a 4th generation system.

While HyperCard prototypes can be built in a relatively short time., they are almost always mock-ups and cannot be reused as part of the final application. Nonetheless, experience shows that it is better to invest some weeks in the development of a nonreusable prototype before several person years are wasted in the realization of a system that does not meet the requirements of the later user.

# 3 Concepts and Tools for Exploratory Programming

*Exploratory programming* has evolved as a paradigm for development of novel complex applications where the main risk is feasibility and where little or no experience can be drawn on to help a developer in determining the quality of a particular solution. In such a situation the only sensible approach is to implement different solutions and to compare the results. If no suitable solution is found, then the requirements have to be reconsidered.

In order for exploratory programming to be reasonable, the cost of experimentation has to be low. The cost of experimentation depends on two factors: the costs of implementing an initial version of a software system and the costs of evolving it. Thus the time to write the code for an experiment must be short enough that the code can be discarded if the idea fails to produce the desired result.

The costs of experimentation depend on the suitability of the applied programming language and programming environment for fast implementation, modification, and reuse of code. Furthermore, they depend on the availability of a base of reusable software and on the processing power provided by the hardware.

Programming languages and their underlying concepts influence the way developers think and therefore also the overall design and the design of particular components of software systems. This influence becomes even stronger in exploratory programming, where the separation between design and implementation becomes blurred.

This means that programming languages have to fulfill certain requirements to be suitable for exploratory programming. Their semantic density should be high to express much functionality in little code without violating structural quality requirements. Furthermore, they should provide concepts supporting programming in the large, programming in the small, modifiability, and extensibility.

During exploratory programming it is important that experimentation not be impeded by long turnaround times and that programmers not have to worry about trivialities such as allocating and freeing memory.

Programming environments support two kinds of activities: programming (i.e., editing, execution, and debugging) and management of software systems under development. Exploratory programming requires special support from programming environments. The length of turnaround times depends, for example, on the execution mechanisms provided by the programming environment. Modifiability and extensibility of a software system are strongly influenced by the support a programming environment gives a developer toward gaining an overview of static and dynamic aspects of a software system. Furthermore, it is important that a programming environment support the management of an application under development and that it provide mechanisms for easing teamwork on dynamically evolving software systems.

While hardware will not be discussed further, it is important to recognize that powerful workstations are a prerequisite for the successful application of exploratory programming. Modern programming environments offer a vast amount of functionality, but they also need much processing power. Window-based, graphic-oriented user interfaces using a mouse as input device come hand in hand with modern powerful workstations, and they are a must for the realization of high information interchange between developer and computer. This information interchange can be further improved with large screens that make it possible to display more information in a better structured way.

Section 3.1 discusses requirements of programming languages for exploratory programming without giving an overview of general programming language features. Section 3.2 discusses factors which determine the quality of an exploratory programming environment and presents an exemplary environment. The higher the degree of reuse of design information and code, the faster new experimental systems can be built. Section 3.3 starts by describing prerequisites and concepts for reuse of design information and code. Then it presents an application framework (an object-oriented standard application) allowing for a high degree of reuse in developing dialog-oriented applications that support direct manipulation of graphic objects.

# 3.1 Programming Languages

The strong influence of the *programming language* on the success of an exploratory programming process is evident. Nonetheless, it is extremely difficult to select the "best" programming language at the beginning of a project for the following reasons:

- A programming language for exploratory programming has to fulfill a lot of partially contradictory requirements.

- The serious evaluation of a programming language requires its application in the realization of at least a medium-sized software system.

- Many pragmatic arguments, such as the availability of a programming environment for a certain hardware platform, the education and experience of developers, the sometimes almost religious worship of evaluators for a certain language have to be considered.

An in-depth analysis of the factors which influence the suitability of a programming language for exploratory programming together with the necessary discussion of the various concepts underlying the programming languages available today would fill a book on its own. For this reason we decided to present in this section only the following short list of the most important criteria.

- *What kind of high-level structuring mechanisms does the language provide?*

  The larger a planned software system is, the more important become high-level structuring mechanisms which support programming in the large and therefore the structuring of a software system on architecture level. This is because the modifiability and extensibility of a large software system depend mostly on the quality of its system architecture.

  Good structuring mechanisms include modules, as provided by Ada and Modula-2, and classes, as provided by object-oriented programming languages.

- *Which concepts are provided to ease reuse of design information and code?*

  This aspect is of paramount importance in exploratory programming and for this reason is discussed in depth in Section 3.3.

- *Which concepts are provided to promote understandability and readability of code ?*

  Understandability and readability depend on the provided structuring concepts and the documentation value of the language used.

The claim for simplicity in the context of readability should not be underestimated. Typical examples of languages that make it possible to write sensible code which becomes almost unreadable because of the many different ways something can be achieved are C and C++. Good examples of languages favoring the writing of readable code are Pascal, Modula-2, and Smalltalk, which were designed with simplicity and readability in mind.

- *Does the language permit the concise formulation of algorithms?*

During exploratory programming much code is written which has to be discarded later. For this reason it is important that the code written in a programming language have a high semantic density, which means that little code has to be written to implement an algorithm. Unfortunately, it also has to be considered that a too high semantic density can lead to poor readability of source code.

An example of a programming language with high semantic density is APL. APL makes it possible to formulate complex algorithms in a few lines—which are hardly comprehensible for anybody but the implementor. Because of its semantic density APL is excellently suited for prototyping of short algorithms, but absolutely unsuitable for exploratory programming of large software systems.

- *How simple and concise is the syntax of the language?*

The simplicity of the syntax not only has an effect on the readability of software systems, but also on the quality of the available programming environments.

It is therefore no surprise that the programming environments for the Molochs among the currently used programming languages such as Ada and C++ are of a much lower quality than programming environments for simple and concise programming languages such as Pascal, Modula-2, and Smalltalk.

- *Does the structure of the language favor short turnaround times?*

For exploratory programming, short edit-compile-go cycles are very important. An important prerequisite for short turnaround times is separate compilation of class and module interfaces and their corresponding implementation parts. This is very important because otherwise the interfaces have to be recompiled together with every compilation unit in which they are used.

- *Does the language implementation permit efficient execution?*

  The efficiency of execution is of secondary importance during exploratory programming, but it has to be considered if an evolutionary approach is taken. Fortunately, it today is only seldom a factor that really restricts the language selection because of the extreme advances that have been made in processor and compiler technology.

Further information can be found in [Mey90], [Set89], and [Ghe87], which deal with programming languages and their underlying concepts in general.

# 3.2 Programming Environments

In the context of an exploratory programming process, the purpose of a *programming environment* is to support the developer in carrying out the development/evaluation cycle as fast as possible. A Developer needs support to manage, browse, and edit the software system under development, to execute it, and to obtain as much information about its static and dynamic aspects as possible.

Section 3.2.1 describes various concepts for supporting all these activities. Section 3.2.2 presents an exemplary programming environment to illustrate these concepts.

## 3.2.1 Concepts Underlying Programming Environments

*Execution Mechanisms*

The following three aspects prove relevant in comparing various execution mechanisms in the context of exploratory programming:

- the time needed for the preparation of execution
- the time efficiency of execution
- the influence of the execution mechanism on the effort required to implement features supporting exploratory programming

The execution of compiled code is certainly faster than the interpretation of source code, but the compilation and succeeding linking process can take a lot of time. Interpretation, on the other hand, can be started immediately after a software system has been modified.

Interpretive execution has a positive effect on the quality of the programming environment because an internal representation that is interpreted usually contains much more information about the executed software system than the object code. In order to build a programming environment supporting compilation followed by direct execution, all information needed later for browsing and debugging purposes has to be extracted and stored during compilation. During debugging, the information about the current dynamic state of the system has to be tediously reconstructed from the current location in the object code and from the information which was extracted during compilation.

Almost all programming environments propagated for exploratory programming rely on interpretive execution. The only argument against interpretation is its slower execution speed, which normally is not crucial for exploratory programming. Execution speed is, however, crucial for the practical application of most software systems. For this reason, there are two different kinds of programming environments.

The first kind of environment is suitable for exploratory programming and relies on interpretive execution. Such environments provide short turnaround times and much information about static and dynamic aspects of a software system—which makes them suitable for analyzing, browsing, and debugging software systems. They are mostly applied in research-oriented environments. Good examples for such environments are Smalltalk-80 [Gol84], Interlisp [Tei84], [She83] and Genera [Wal87].The second kind of environment is applied in developing products and relies on compilation, providing less support to the developer.

In recent years various approaches have been taken to develop environments providing much information, short preparation times before execution, and direct, fast execution, i.e., environments incorporating the advantages of both approaches presented above.

One of them is to shorten the compilation process with one pass compilers and dynamic linking and loading. The environments based on this approach provide preparation times almost as short as interpretive environments. The programming environments did not improve that much, however, because the problem of information extraction, storage, and recalculation is not addressed. Successful examples of environments based on this approach are the Lightspeed programming environments (e.g., [Sym89]), MacMETH [Mac86], and the Oberon system [Wir88], [Rei91].

Another approach is to improve the execution speed of the established environments for exploratory programming. Methods for partial compilation of languages like Lisp, Smalltalk-80, and even Prolog have been developed. The resulting semidirect execution is only slightly less efficient than direct execution of conventional programming languages.

A further approach is to shorten the preparation time before direct execution and keep the extracted information in an internal representation, making it possible to develop more comfortable programming environments. There are two ways in which reduced preparation time can be achieved. First, changed code parts are recompiled incrementally (i.e., *only* changed code is recompiled), and the resulting object code is dynamically linked and loaded. Second, the software system is executed hybridly. This means direct execution of code that is stable and interpretation of code that is under development.

Successful examples for environments with incremental compilation are Objectworks for C++ [Par90] and Cedar [Swi86], [Tei85]. Commercially available environments relying on hybrid execution are Saber-C and Saber-C++ ([Sab90], [Kau88], [Sab88]).

In summary, it can be said that a programming environment for exploratory programming has to provide short turnaround times and as much information as possible about static and dynamic aspects of a system. The programming environments that best fulfill these requirements usually base on interpretation or incremental compilation.

### Gathering Information About Static Aspects of a System

Information about *static aspects* of a system includes all kinds of information which can be extracted from a software system without executing it. The quality of a programming environment depends on which information is provided, how it is presented, how long it takes to get the information, and whether the information is also available for incomplete software systems.

Every useful programming environment has to provide some kind of project management system to keep track of the various artifacts a software system consists of, as well as of the overall structure of the system itself. Typical information about the overall structure of a software system includes its constituent modules and their interdependencies, the class hierarchy in an object-oriented software system, the location of the source code of modules or classes, the location of other project-related files, and libraries needed to execute the software system. This information can be used for a lot of purposes, such as for in keeping track of the overall structure of the system, for automatic recompilation after changes, for easing browsing and editing.

A developer needs a lot of information in order to understand the working of a software system and the effects of a change. Typical information is where types, variables, procedures and constants are defined and used. In order to be useful, this information has to be presented to the developer instantly upon request. Furthermore, it should also be available for incomplete software systems that contain errors. This is especially important in exploratory programming, where the overall structure of a software system has to be changed frequently. During restructuring, information about definitions and references of system components is important although the software system is probably in an inconsistent state.

Every software developer knows that it is almost impossible to keep an evolving software system consistent with the corresponding documentation. For this reason documentation is frequently written at the end of the implementation activity and many ideas and much information are lost. Most of the time it is not worth writing extensive documentation in the course of an exploratory programming venture. Nonetheless, there are certain ideas about possible improvements and concepts needed to understand the current implementation which have to be managed by the developer. This information is mostly managed on paper or with a text processing system. The results are piles of paper containing ideas and concepts which rapidly become obsolete because the system changes faster than the information can be found and updated. Hypertext is a new approach that promises at least partial solutions to these problems by providing the possibility to directly connect various documents with one another. Using hypertext, ideas and concepts described in different documents are linked to the code. After a change in the code, the programming environment can remind the developer to update certain documents or to discard them.

According to this description, hypertext systems not only improve consistency but also greatly improve the possibilities to organize and find information about programming systems which are not directly deducible from the code. Hypertext features are therefore important building blocks of an exploratory programming environment. While there are many general documentation systems supporting hypertext, Objectworks for C++ [Par90], ET++ [Gam89], and DOgMA [Sam91] are programming environments including hypertext facilities. A general introduction to hypertext can be found in [Shn89] and [Con87].

*Gathering Information About Dynamic Aspects of a System*

Information about *dynamic aspects* of a software system is collected during execution. It can be classified according to debugging information, information about dynamic aspects of the application structure, performance monitoring, and test coverage information.

The most important information needed during exploratory programming is collected with debuggers, run-time data inspectors, and editors during the execution of an application. These tools allow for stepwise monitoring of the execution, for setting breakpoints at specific location, for setting breakpoints which are triggered on indicated conditions, for inspection of the current state of execution, and for browsing and editing the run-time data.

While debuggers are indispensable for finding errors, they are at least as useful for understanding complex software systems by monitoring their execution. This understanding of how a software systems works is crucial during exploratory programming because the developer is frequently confronted with the problem of making major changes to scarcely documented software systems and therefore needs support to understand their consequences.

There are many programming environments providing good debuggers. For this reason it is difficult to recommend further readings, but an example is described in Section 3.2.2.

Information about the dynamic aspects of an application structure is important in working with modern application frameworks, which standardize the control flow and the layouting of graphic objects to a sizable degree by providing standard event handler chains and hierarchies of nested objects, which are configured at run-time (see Section 3.3). In order to understand the inner working of an application written with an application framework, it is important to know the current state of these event handler chains and object hierarchies. An example of a tool supporting the monitoring of this kind of information is presented in Section 3.3.2.

Performance monitoring information consists of reports about which procedures were called, how many times they were called, and how much time they took for execution. Such information is needed to monitor and optimize software systems. During exploratory programming this is important if several solutions are evaluated which have to meet strict time limits. Examples of performance monitoring tools are the UNIX Gprof and Prof tools (see [Tar87]).

Test coverage information indicates which procedures or even possible program paths were executed during experimentation. This kind of information is certainly not needed during an experimental proceeding, but becomes important during the final testing and should therefore also be part of a programming environment for exploratory programming.

*Editing Support*

A developer spends a remarkable percentage of time editing. A comfortable *program editor*, therefore, is an indispensable part of any programming environment.

State-of-the-art editors allow direct manipulation by selecting code with the mouse and issuing commands from pull-down or pop-up menus. They usually provide commands such as cut, copy, and paste for moving and duplicating text, dialog boxes for specifying complex find/change operations, and much more.

An important point is that all commands can be issued by selection from a menu or by using a shortcut, making the editor both easy to learn and fast to use. Even the best program editors cannot provide all the functionality a developer sometimes needs. It is therefore important that the editor provide a macro language allowing the developer to implement custom high-level commands (e.g., [Gam86b], [Sta81]).

Furthermore, an editor can support automatic customizable pretty printing with various kinds of indentation and different fonts for key words and other code, freeing the developer from another tedious task and enhancing the readability of the resulting code. An example of customizable pretty printing is described in [Bla89].

In order to back out of experiments which have proven to be dead ends and to undo other erroneous manipulations, the program editor of an exploratory programming environment should provide a history mechanism which allows for *undoing* and *redoing* any number of basic editing manipulations. If the changes are saved on a disk, such a mechanism can also be used to redo all manipulations since the last save after a system crash occurred. The Smalltalk-80 environment, for example, provides such a mechanism.

At the end of the Seventies syntax-directed editing was a widely used buzzword. Different systems for automatically generating syntax directed editors [GAN85], [Rep84] as well as a wide range of programming environments with syntax-directed editors were developed (e.g., [Pro84]). The advantage of syntax-directed editors is that they enforce syntactical correctness during editing. The disadvantage is that most known systems are much too rigid, making the editing process slow and tedious. While syntax-directed editors are seldom applied in practice because of their rigidity, partially syntax sensitive editors providing incremental syntax checking and pretty printing are integrated into practical programming environments.

Good examples are 4th Dimension [Aci90a] and the Lightspeed programming environment family (e.g., [Sym89]).

## Configuration Management and Version Control

The management of all but very small software systems requires discipline on the part of the developer and tool support for keeping track of the current configuration, for managing different versions of an evolving system, and for undoing changes. While all these aspects are receiving more and more attention in conventional development projects, they are decisive for exploratory programming, where the software system under development changes much faster.

In exploratory programming various solutions for a problem are implemented and compared. Managing different versions manually is tiresome, but it becomes really awesome if code shared by different versions is duplicated and a single change has to be inserted into all these versions manually. A programming environment should therefore provide a tool for version control which permits a developer to comfortably manage a set of versions. Examples of a version-control systems are SCCS [Roc75], RCS [Tic85] (running on UNIX platforms) and the Projector [App91] (running on the Apple Macintosh).

A problem that is seldom addressed by exploratory programming environments is teamwork. Nonetheless, experience shows that small teams working on a dynamically evolving software system lose much time in communicating about applied changes if they work on a common version, or they lose a lot of effort in manually integrating their different versions into a common version from time to time. An interesting approach to support such teamwork is employed by SUN's NSE (the network software environment) [NSE89]. Working with NSE, every developer has the impression of working on a proper version, while NSE transparently ensures that every file which was not changed is shared and only changed files are duplicated. Because of its knowledge about who has changed what, NSE can then ease the integration process by visualizing which code parts were changed and by merging the versions as indicated by the developer.

Depending on the implementation language and the execution mechanism, various information is needed to update the system after changes were applied. This is no trivial task, especially if hybrid software systems are developed that consist of code in different languages and various kinds of libraries. A programming environment should thus take care of the current configuration of a software system and provide for automatic preparation of execution after changes were applied. Widely used tools, such as MAKE [Fel79], which is distributed with all UNIX operating systems, are not acceptable. They require that the developer manually describe all update dependencies between the various system components (which leads to all kinds of time-consuming errors).

In summary, configuration management and version control tools are indispensable parts of a programming environment supporting an exploratory approach. Unfortunately, they are available today in neither the required quantity nor quality.

Further information about configuration management and version control systems can be obtained from [Rei89], [Tic88], [Win88], and [Leb84].

### 3.2.2 Smalltalk-80—a Tool Example

Smalltalk-80 is one of the best and most widespread systems for exploratory programming. For this reason we chose Smalltalk-80 to exemplify some of the concepts discussed above. Because of its quality, much has been written about Smalltalk. Best known are the three books written by the developers of Smalltalk-80 ([Gol85], [Gol84], [Kra84]), which are recommended as further readings. More detailed information about Smalltalk-80 can be found in [LaL90].

Smalltalk-80 is a tool supporting object-oriented software development. For this reason a complete understanding of this subsection requires a basic knowledge of object-oriented programming. A short overview of the concepts underlying object-oriented programming are give in Section 3.3.1. For further reading we recommend any of the following books: [Bud91], [Boc90], [Mey88].

First, the basic organization of Smalltalk-80 is described. Then its browsers are presented as an example of tools for editing and information gathering[1]. The description closes with a very simple but typical scenario of exploratory programming in which the Smalltalk-80 tools are heavily used.

*Basic Organization*

In the Smalltalk environment several tools are available at any time. Each of these tools runs in one window and many instances of a tool can exist at the same time. A window is (de)activated when the mouse (pointer) is moved across its border. This makes it possible to carry out different or related tasks almost in parallel.

---

[1] The first part of this subsection is adapted from [Die87], a good overview of Smalltalk-80.

Using Smalltalk-80, the developer is never caught in time-consuming edit-compile-and-go cycles. It is instead possible to edit a piece of code in the debugger after an error was found and immediately continue the current execution.

*Obtaining Information About Static Aspects of a System*

Because the application's source code and the source code of the whole programming environment are contained in one class tree, beginners often wonder where the program is. Programming in Smalltalk-80 is mainly adding new subclasses and testing them immediately in the context of interpretive execution. Being able to understand and enhance the class tree, therefore, is critical to productive Smalltalk-80 programming.

Smalltalk-80 provides different kinds of browsers to examine and edit the class tree. The system browser shown in Figure 3.1 contains several subwindows. The subwindow at the bottom is a text editor which displays the code selected in the four subwindows along the top.

Subwindow 1 contains a list of class categories which serve to manage several groups of classes. The category *Collections-Sequenceable* for example, groups several classes that manage sequenceable collections. The selection of a class category results in the displaying of the corresponding classes in subwindow 2. The same grouping mechanism is also provided for methods. Subwindow 3 contains the method categories, and subwindow 4 the corresponding methods.

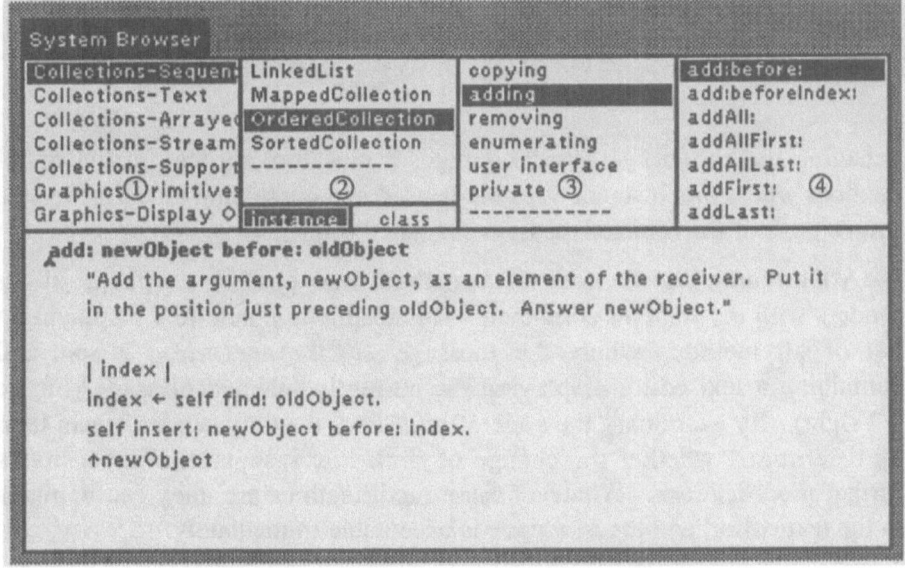

Figure 3.1. Smalltalk-80 system browser [Die87]

The *instance/class* pair below subwindow 2 serves to switch between the object and the class view. In the object view (*instance*), subwindows 3 and 4 present information about messages understood by instances of the selected class. In the class view (*class*) they display information about messages sent to the selected class, which is itself a Smalltalk object.

Let's suppose the developer has applied a change to the class *OrderedCollection*, resulting in a change in the semantics of the instance variable *firstIndex*. This requires examining all methods where *firstIndex* is used and which could be affected. The developer therefore wants to automatically retrieve all these methods.

There are several ways to achieve this. One way is to select the class *OrderedCollection* in the browser. Using the pop-up menu shown at the left of Figure 3.2, the command *inst var refs* is selected. As a result another pop-up menu appears, listing all instance variables of the selected class as depicted at the right of Figure 3.2.

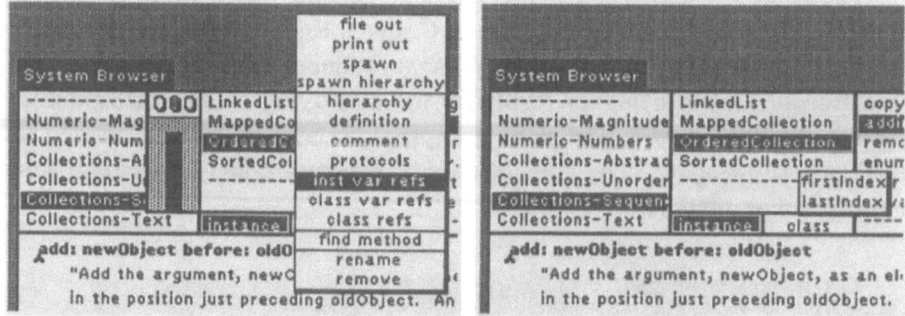

Figure 3.2. Smalltalk-80 class browser menu (left) and menu containing all instance variables
of the selected class (right)

Selecting the variable *firstIndex* creates a new tool showing a list of all methods where this instance variable is used and containing an editor for the source code of the selected message (Figure 3.3 left).

After examining the code of a method, it is possible to obtain all its senders with the *senders* command. This results in a new tool displaying a list of all methods where the message *add:beforeIndex:* is sent and containing a text editor displaying the currently selected message (Figure 3.3 right). By examining the code of *addField*, the only sender, it can then be determined whether the change of *firstIndex*'s semantics necessitates further modifications. Whatever these modifications are, they can be made in the text editor, and the new code is executable immediately.

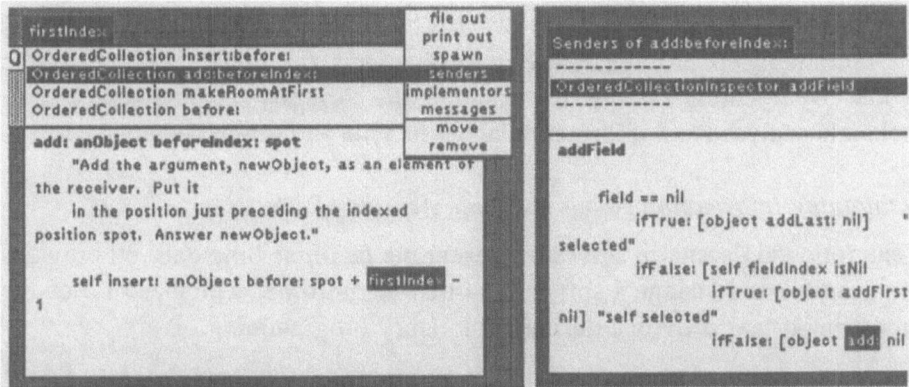

Figure 3.3. Method browser (left) and result of the *senders* command (right)

The *senders*, *implementors* and *messages* commands are effective message tracers. They serve to determine all senders and implementors of a selected message, or they provide a pop-up menu of all messages occurring in the source code of a selected message.

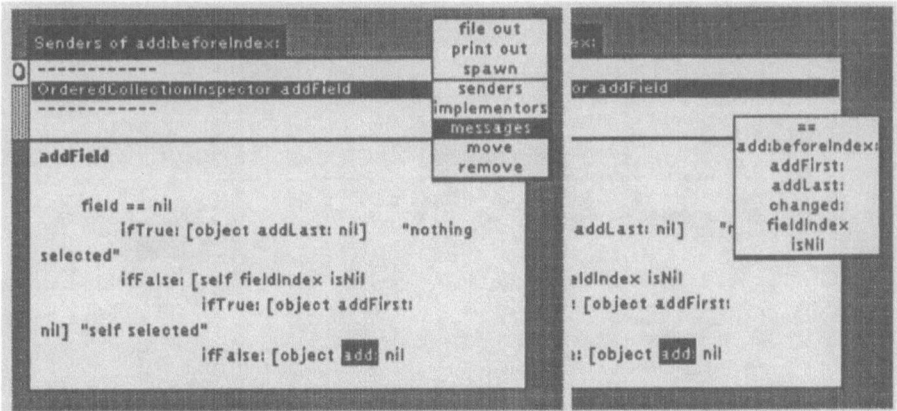

Figure 3.4. Method browser menu (left) and result of the *messages* command (right)

In the pop-up menu resulting from the *messages* command, a method can be selected for further examination (Figure 3.4 right). These commands help the user to browse through the system during implementation and debugging.

Smalltalk-80 source code is analyzed incrementally as new classes as well as messages and their associated methods are defined. The code is manipulated in the text editor, where the developer triggers the analysis of a method by selecting the *accept* command. If the code contains a syntax error, an appropriate message is inserted directly into the source code.

Smalltalk-80 provides further mechanisms for understanding source code. By selecting *explain*, for example, the currently selected source code token is analyzed and information about its type and origin is displayed.

### Obtaining Information About Dynamic Aspects of a System

The following scenario serves to present the facilities Smalltalk-80 provides to examine and change a software system at run-time, which is one of the most important activities during exploratory programming.

At the begin of the scenario the developer has discovered the class *Pen*, a class for drawing lines on the screen. In order to learn more about *Pen*, the developer starts the execution of the sample application *penSampler*, which is provided as a class method of *Pen*. Figure 3.5 shows how the execution is triggered by selecting the command *do it*, which could be done in any subwindow containing an editor.

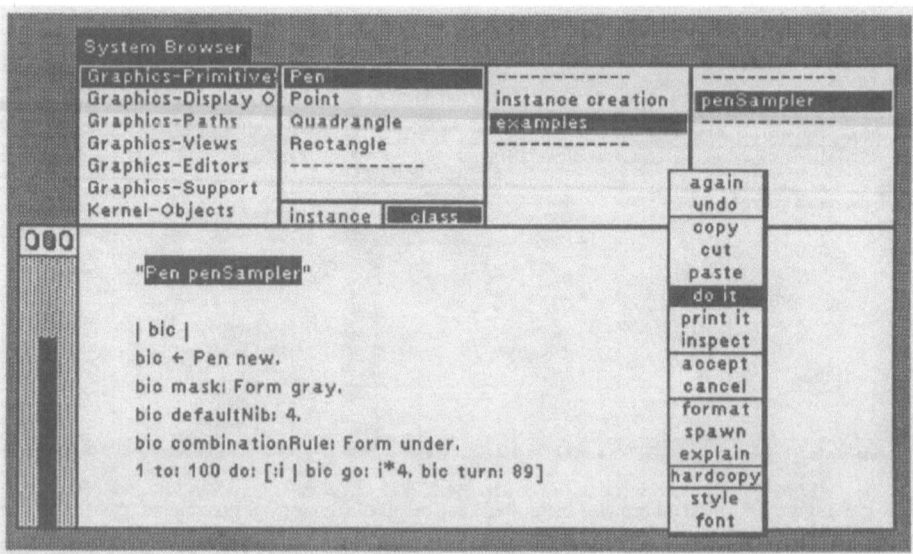

Figure 3.5. Starting of the sample application *penSampler* from a Smalltalk-80 system browser

After seeing that the application draws a geometric figure, the developer decides to interrupt the program in order to learn more about the application and so presses the interrupt key. Upon being prompted by the system for how to react on this interrupt, the developer selects *debug*

(Figure 3.6 left). At the right of Figure 3.6 the resulting debugging tool is depicted.

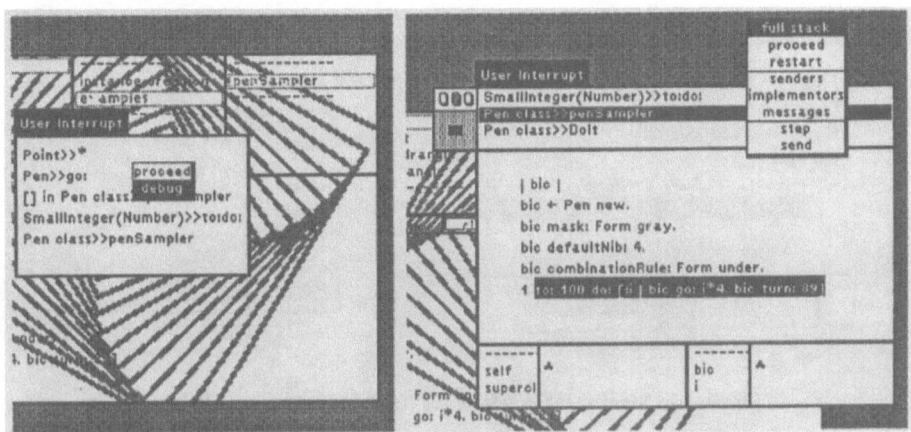

Figure 3.6. Smalltalk-80 interrupt handler (left) and debugger (right)

The debugger consists of several subwindows. The subwindow at the top displays a list of the currently active methods; this corresponds to the procedure call stack in a conventional programming environment. Selecting a method causes its code to be displayed in the editor below it, where the code at point of interrupt is highlighted. The two subwindows at the bottom left serve to select and display the instance variables, and the two subwindows at the bottom right serve to select and display the temporary local objects (local variables).

The displayed pop-up menu contains commands for controlling execution. The next statement could be executed (*step*), the next message could be sent (*send*), or execution could be continued by quitting the debugger (*proceed*).

After having studied the code, the developer turns to the internal representation of *bic*, an object of class *Pen*. Selecting *bic* and choosing the *inspect* command from the pop-up menu (Figure 3.7 left) produces an inspector displaying all of *bic*'s instance variables in a list. When one of them is selected, its value is displayed in the editor on the right side (Figure 3.7 right).

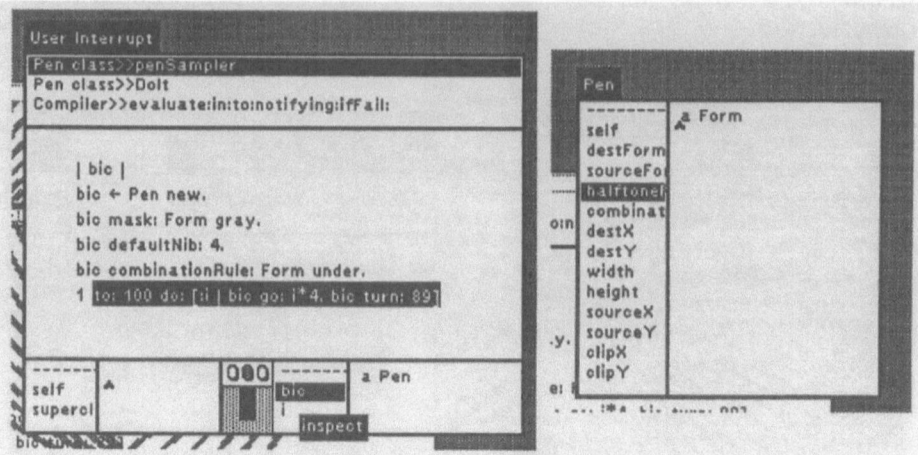

Figure 3.7.  Starting inspection of *bic* (left); inspector for *bic* (right)

Knowing that colors are represented as forms, the developer wonders about the meaning of the three forms *destForm*, *sourceForm*, and *halftoneForm*, and decides to learn about them by carrying out an experiment.  After selecting *halftoneForm*, the developer writes the code to create a new instance of *Form* in black.  This instance is created and assigned to *halftoneForm* by selecting *accept* (Figure 3.8 left).

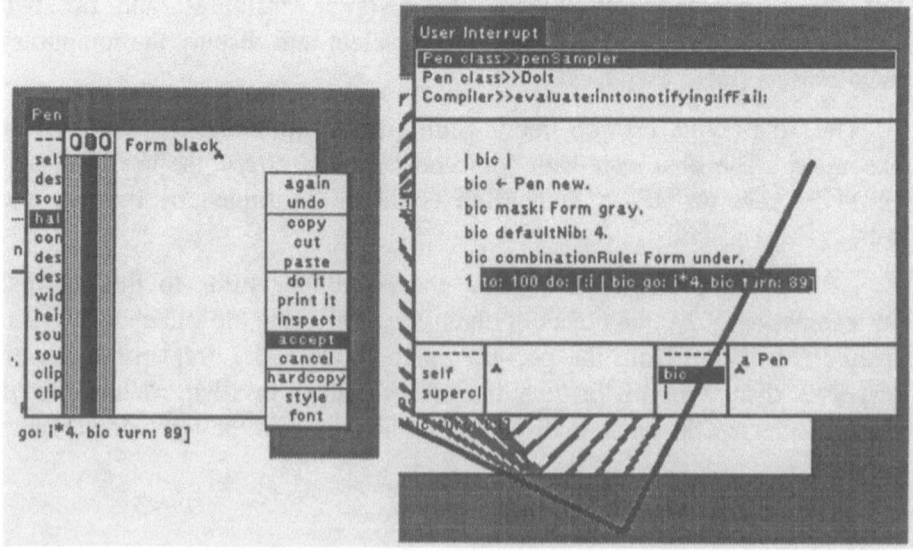

Figure 3.8.  Inspector for *bic* (left); debugger beneath continued drawing (right)

The developer then initiates the next execution step by selecting *step* in the debugger and draws conclusions from the fact that the color of the lines changes from gray to black (Figure 3.8 right).

The way in which screen dumps for this description were made is another example of exploratory programming. In order to make a screen dump of a tool together with a pop-up menu, the class *pop-up menu* had to be changed. The understanding of where pop-up menus are managed and how it is possible to delay the purging of the menu from the screen took the author about ten minutes. Without the debugging and inspecting tools described above, this would have been much more difficult.

*Conclusions*

This short presentation of a subset of the tools provided by the Smalltalk-80 programming environment makes clear how comfortably exploratory programming is supported by Smalltalk-80. In applying this programming environment, a developer has the possibility to quickly realize an idea and dynamically determine its quality—which is the basic idea underlying a prototyping-oriented approach.

Furthermore, the discussion above shows unquestionably that the economical application of exploratory programming relies heavily on the support provided by programming environments. This is also the reason why programming environments suitable for exploratory programming have to fulfill much higher quality requirements than programming environments that are used during the implementation process of a conventional software development project.

# 3.3 Reuse of Design Information and Code

Extensive reuse of design information and code is an old dream of software developers and an important prerequisite for prototyping-oriented software development. Every developer knows the feeling of *déjà vu* when coding the same algorithm again and again. Jones estimates [Jon84], for example, that less than 15 percent of the code written in 1983 was unique, novel, and specific to individual applications. However, while reusability is a strategy of great promise, it is one whose promise has been largely unfulfilled.

In order to reuse code, it has to be located, understood, and usually adapted as well. At least two approaches could be taken to attain a better degree of reusability:

The *management approach*, tries to oblige developers to write good documentation about the interfaces and inner workings of their software components, to design them for reuse, and to store them in databases. This approach was chosen with a certain degree of success in the so-called "software factories" [Mat81], but it is of very limited use for exploratory programming. As soon as an application area is so well-understood that there are enough documented software building blocks, exploratory programming looses its reason for being.

The *technological approach*, tries to find software development techniques better suited for reuse[2]. In the novel, complex areas where exploratory programming is applied, few reusable building blocks exist. For this reason, concepts are required that allow easier adaptation of building blocks that do something similar to what is needed and frameworks that free the developer from reinventing what is common to most applications.

This section describes concepts on programming language and application levels and provides examples of their effects on the achievable degree of reuse. The first subsection starts by discussing why and how the degree of reuse of code depends on the structuring concepts provided by programming languages. Then system architecture structuring concepts are described which permit the reuse of significant application parts including parts of the concepts embedded in the architecture design. The second subsection is dedicated to ET++, a representative example of software systems which are based on modern structuring concepts on language and application levels, and which allow a high degree of reuse in developing dialog-oriented applications.

## 3.3.1 Concepts for Reuse of Design Information and Code

*Structuring Concepts on the Language Level*

The technological advances which have improved the reusability of code stem from a continuous improvement in the structuring of software systems.

Monolithic assembly programs, for example, are scarcely reusable. The possibility to isolate functionality in procedures with explicitly defined interfaces considerably improves reusability compared to assembly code. An area of successful reuse of procedures is scientific computation, where excellent libraries for numeric applications exist.

---

[2] "Give your poor, huddled projects a decent technical environment in the first place. Then worry about whether you are managing them properly" [Mey87].

*Procedures* support the reuse of algorithms by making it possible to group a set of instructions, but they do not improve the reusability of complex data structures. This kind of reuse is achieved with higher structuring concepts such as those provided by Ada *packages* [Ich79] and Modula-2 *modules* [Wir85]. They allow the grouping of procedures together with declarations of types, constants and variables. A module (package) may thus be devoted to a single data structure and its associated operations.

In terms of reusability, these techniques are useful but limited [Mey87]. They are useful because encapsulating groups of related features provides compact, easily documentable interfaces for collections of procedures and implementations of abstract data types. But they are limited because they do only what they do, and every modification requires the duplication of the whole module and the modification of the copied code.

*Genericity*, a further concept provided, for example, by Ada and Clu [Lis86], makes it possible to define a module with generic parameters that represent types. Instances of the module are then produced by supplying different types as actual parameters. This improves reusability because just one generic module is written instead of a group of modules that differ only in the types of objects they manipulate.

*Object-oriented programming* is a concept which is intended to increase the reusability of code by orders of magnitudes. Object-oriented programs consist of cooperating *objects* which are similar to abstract data types—i.e., they encapsulate both data and operations. Each object is described by a *class* which defines its corresponding data and operations.

We address two concepts that distinguish object-oriented programming from module-oriented programming, polymorphism and inheritance. These two concepts are particularly relevant to reusability, which is of great importance for exploratory programming and prototyping. For further reading about object-oriented programming, we recommend one of the three books [Bud91], [Boc90], [Mey88].

*Polymorphism* means that something which is named by an identifier in a program can take on several shapes. This holds for variables as well as for operations. Variables are able to refer to objects of different (but related) data types. Depending on the type of an object (not necessarily the type of the referring variable), a certain operation may result in the execution of different action sequences. The binding of abstract operations to concrete actions is performed at run-time (see [Str91]). Polymorphism therefore improves reusability by making it possible to formulate abstract operations independently of the concrete types of the objects they are working on.

The basic idea underlying *inheritance* is that each class has a superclass from which it inherits data definitions and operations. The class itself can then introduce new operations, replace inherited operations and add new data definitions. Inheritance therefore promotes reuse by making it possible that several classes share code which is implemented in a common superclass. Furthermore, it facilitates the adaptation of existing classes by the writing of subclasses which change the behavior of the superclass by overriding some operations, and which extend its functionality by introducing new operations and data definitions.

Figure 3.9 shows a part of the class tree of *quadworld*, a Smalltalk-80 application for drawing various kinds of quadrilaterals. (The complete *quadworld* application is described in [Sch86].) The class *Quadrilateral* and its subclasses provide a good example of the effects of inheritance. While three methods had to be written to create general quadrilaterals, only one or two of them had to be rewritten in order to implement special kinds of quadrilaterals, whereas the other methods were reused.

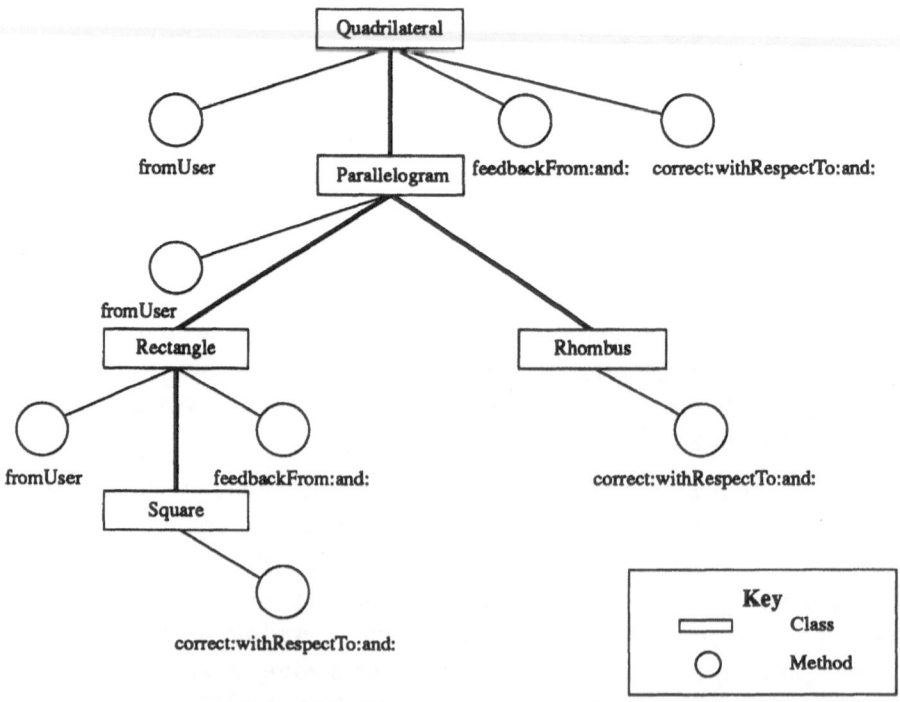

Figure 3.9. *Quadrilateral* and subclasses with methods for creation of quadrilaterals [Sch86]

The *quadworld* example shows that inheritance results not only in easier adaptability but also in significant reuse. (In order to adapt a class, its code does not have to be copied.) This results in software systems written with significantly less source code—up to a factor of ten. For examples, see [Cox84] and the experiences with ET++ described in the next subsection.

The advantages of applying object-oriented programming—greater flexibility, easier adaptability, and a smaller amount of code that has to be written—make it suited to support a prototyping-oriented approach and exploratory programming.

### *Structuring Concepts on the System Architecture Level*

While structuring concepts on the programming language level make it possible to increase reuse to a certain degree, reuse can be further improved if not only code but also parts of the design of a system architecture can be reused. Such reuse is possible for various application areas, but its greatest benefits can currently be obtained in developing dialog-oriented applications with modern user interfaces. For this reason the rest of this subsection discusses the concepts for reuse of design information and code in developing dialog-oriented applications.

Modern interactive applications provide comfortable user interfaces consisting of menus, dialog boxes, scrollable lists and many other elements (which can be manipulated with a mouse). Implementing such interfaces requires complex code. The reimplementation of this code for every application would be too expensive, especially if we want to build prototypes for exploration purposes. Concepts therefore had to be found to implement it once and reuse it afterwards.

One step in this direction was the introduction of toolboxes. They provide modules (abstract data types) to handle such aspects as managing and drawing graphic objects, windows, menus, dialog boxes and much more. Typical examples of toolboxes are the Apple Macintosh Toolbox [App85] and ET [Gam86a]. They not only provide abstract data types for user interface handling but also for operating system tasks such as file management and network communication.

Using such a toolbox means writing a main routine, receiving user and operating system events, and distributing these events to managers provided by the toolbox or to hand-coded managers as depicted in Figure 3.10.

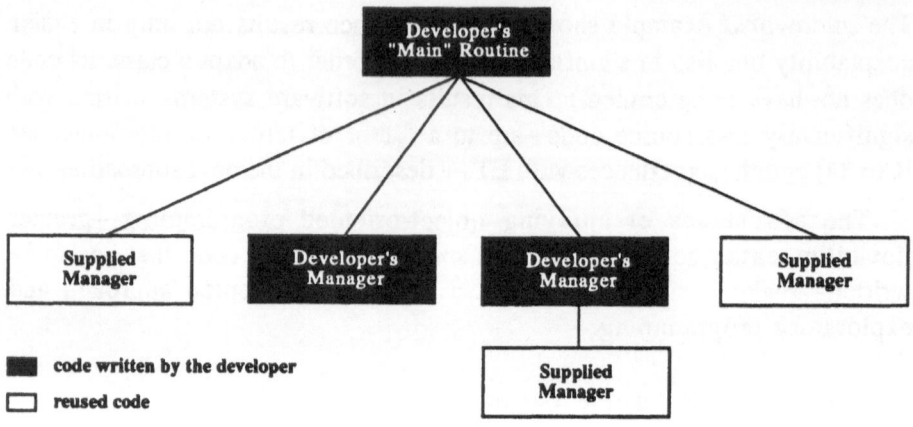

Figure 3.10. Structure of an application developed with a toolbox (adapted from [Sch86])

While a toolbox helps the developer to manage various resources on a high-level, it was recognized that applications with modern graphic interfaces had much more in common. The main routine, dialogs for opening, closing and saving of documents, as well as undo/redo mechanisms repeatedly provide nearly identical functionality. For this reason, *standard applications* were developed. These standard applications have certain hooks where a programmer can place custom code to implement the functionality of the application. Such standard applications are distributed with most toolboxes.

A problem of standard applications implemented with toolboxes is that they cannot be extended where such an extension was not explicitly foreseen. A menu manager, for example, provides exactly predefined menus. Extending the functionality of these menus would result in changing the menu manager or in writing a new one. Changing a manager is usually impossible because the source code of commercial toolboxes is not available, and writing a new one is too expensive.

The problem of adapting existing modules is diminished by the application of object-oriented programming. The resulting object-oriented standard applications are called *application frameworks*. An application framework consists of a set of classes defining the standard components of an application such as windows, documents, menus, undoable commands, as well as their cooperation.

The development of a software system based on an application framework consists of the insertion of application-specific functionality into the framework. This is achieved by writing subclasses of framework classes which define new and/or override existing methods. The difference compared to the development of an application with a toolbox is that the standardized code is not used only as a library, but that it is extended and adapted using polymorphism and inheritance as depicted in Figure 3.11.

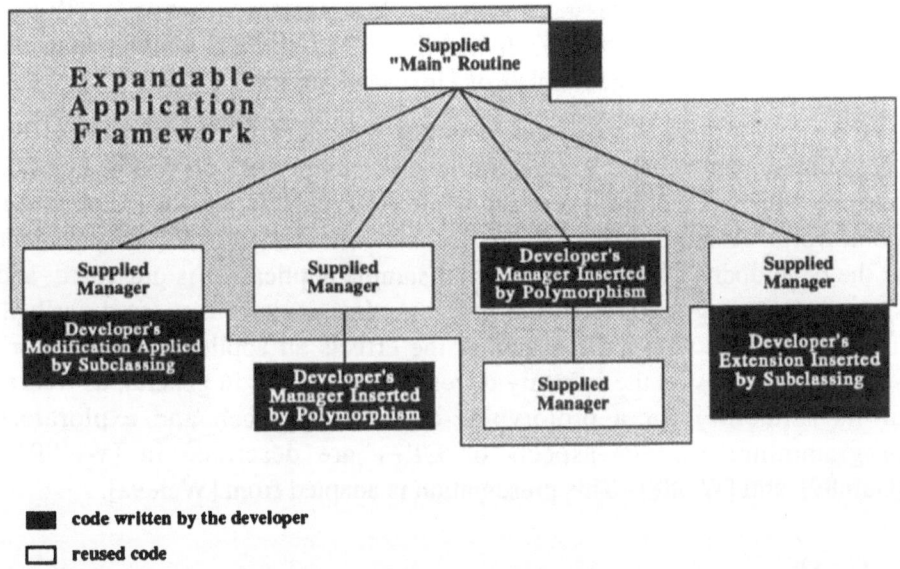

Figure 3.11. Structure of an application developed with an application framework (adapted from [Sch86])

Practical use of application frameworks is just starting. Nonetheless, a certain number of application frameworks are already available. The best known examples are MacApp [Bia88], ET++ [Wei89a], and NextStep [Tho89]. The Smalltalk-80 class tree contains also a sort of an application framework.

In order to give an impression of the potential for reuse of design information and code availed by application frameworks, and to show their impact on exploratory programming and prototyping, the next subsection presents an example.

### 3.3.2 ET++—a Tool Example

We have selected ET++ as our tool example because both its functionality and the quality of its implementation represents the current state-of-the-art, and because it has proven its quality in numerous development projects at universities and in industry.

ET++ is a homogenous object-oriented class library that includes a programming environment. With high-level application framework components, it integrates user interface building blocks, basic data structures, and support for object input/output . The main goals in designing ET++ were to substantially ease the building of highly interactive applications with consistent user interfaces that adhere to the well-known desktop metaphor, and to combine all ET++ classes into a seamless system structure. ET++ is available in the public domain. It was developed on SUN workstations and has been ported to a large number of Unix workstations.

For the purpose of this book it is not necessary to describe the ET++ class library and its application framework components in depth. For this reason, this subsection presents a short overview of the application framework classes, how they cooperate, and what functionality they provide to the developer. Furthermore, a small sample application is presented, and some outstanding features of the programming environment are described. The section ends with a discussion of the effects an application framework such as ET++ has on the software development process in general, as well as of its suitability for a prototyping-oriented approach and exploratory programming. Various aspects of ET++ are described in [Wei89a], [Gam89], and [Wei88]. This presentation is adapted from [Wei89a].

*Overview*

Because ET++ was designed for the highly interactive applications as known from the Apple Macintosh, the components of typical ET++ applications are similar to those of a Macintosh application. The classes *Application, Document, View,* and *Command* are basically derived from MacApp [Bia88] and therefore display similar behavior. Figure 3.12 depicts a part of the ET++ class tree, providing a first impression of ET++'s structure (boxes represent collapsed subtrees, and nodes marked with a bullet represent classes of the sample application to be presented later).

An ET++ application consists of a single instance of the class *Application,* which controls the application as a whole and manages any number of Documents. A *Document* is an abstract class that encapsules the data structure or the model of an application and "knows" how to open and close documents and how to save them on disk. The functionality provided by *Document* makes it very easy to write applications such as multidocument editors.

The main task of a standard ET++ application is displaying a document's data structures. Instances of the class *VObject* or subclasses thereof are the basic components for implementing the entities of the model (the data stored in the document) as graphic elements.

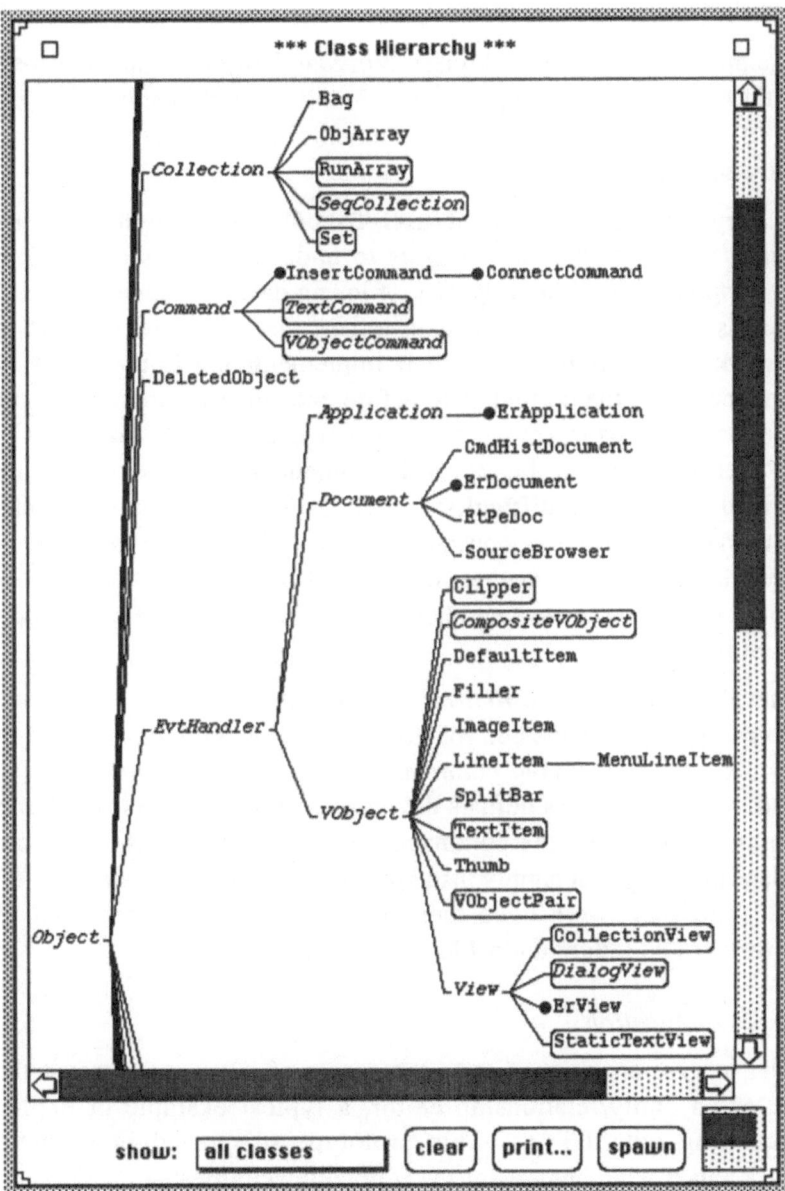

Figure 3.12. Overview of a part of the ET++ class tree

The class *View*, another subclass of *VObject*, represents an abstract and arbitrarily large drawing surface. Its main purpose is to factor out all control flow necessary to manage displaying, scrolling, zooming, and printing as well as maintaining a current selection of *VObjects*. A

*Document* can be associated with any number of Views, all showing the same model in various representations.

The application framework class *Window* defines the standard behavior of an ET++ window and implements window-related methods like *moving*, *resizing*, and *closing*. It also implements the mechanism to ease and optimize screen updating.

A very important aspect of user friendly applications is *undoable commands* because they allow users to undo the effects of errors and to explore applications without the risk of losing data. Implementing undoable commands, unfortunately, is a pain unless there is some support from a framework. One approach for their implementation is to collect enough information about the current state before executing a command in order to be able to reverse its effect when the user selects "undo". For a single-level "undo", this state can be discarded whenever the next command is performed. It is very difficult to build a totally automatic yet efficient framework for undoable commands. But it is possible to design a framework that factors out the flow of control, leaving only the decisions regarding what state to save and how to "do " and "undo" a command to the programmer.

The abstract class *Command* defines the protocol, while the class *Document* implements the control flow for dealing with a *Command* object. To implement an undoable command, a subclass of *Command* has to be derived. Such a subclass defines the necessary state variables and methods for doing and undoing the command. ET++ applications never perform commands directly, but simply instantiate command objects and pass them to ET++. The framework calls their methods and frees command objects when they are no longer undoable.

## A Sample Application

In order to give an impression of the power of ET++, we present the prototype of an entity/relationship editor, a typical example of exploratory programming with ET++. This prototype (displayed in Figure 3.13) provides a user with support for the following activities:

1) loading, storing, and printing entity/relationship diagrams

2) managing multiple diagrams in windows supporting horizontal and vertical scrolling and tiling

3) inserting and deleting symbols for entities and relationships

4) cutting, copying, and pasting groups of entities and relationships

5) connecting entities and relationships

6) inscribing text into the graphic representations of entities, relationships, and connections, which results in the immediate adaptation of the size of entities and relationships according to the size of the text

7) moving graphically represented objects

8) manipulating multiple selections

9) undoing any manipulation

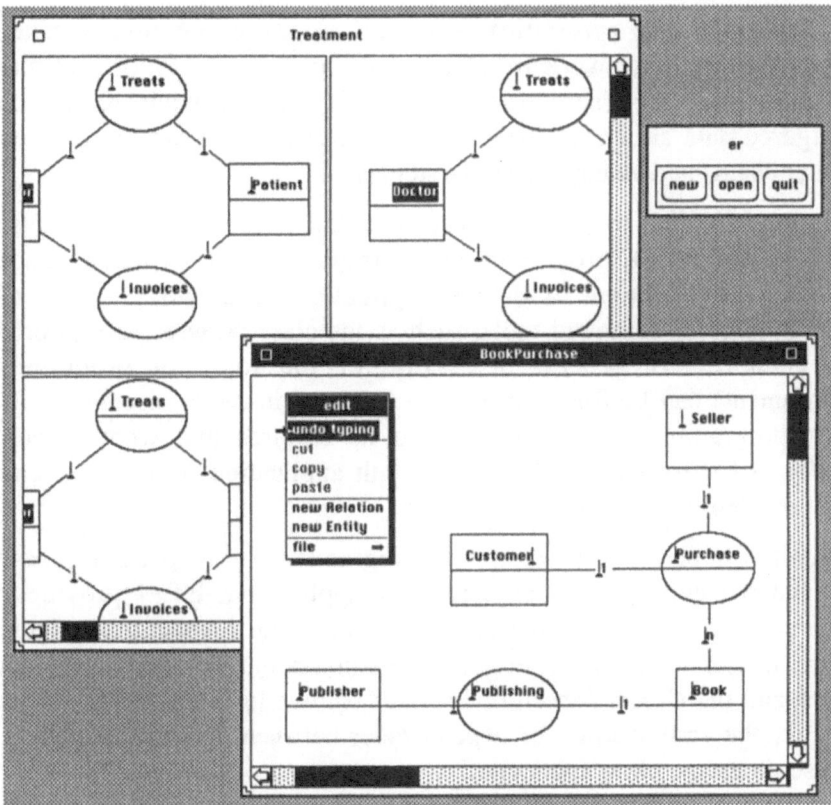

Figure 3.13. Entity/relationship editor

In implementing the prototype, its developer did not have to bother about the realization of the functionality described by points 1, 2, and 7 because it was already implemented in the ET++ framework. The concepts for the realization of the functionality addressed by the other six points are built into the framework. It was therefore possible to customize and enhance the functionality for this practical application with minimal effort.

The implementation of the prototype took two days during which eight classes and 613 lines of C++ code (including empty lines, comments, and lines containing only a bracket) were written. Five of the eight newly implemented classes and their location in the ET++ class hierarchy can be found in the class tree displayed in Figure 3.12. The missing three classes consist of the classes implementing the graphic representations of entities and relationships, and an abstract superclass which would be located in the contracted class tree that has *CompositeVObject* as its root.

## The ET++ Programming Environment

The development of application frameworks leads to new requirements for programming environments because a developer needs a lot of information to understand the (sometimes complex) standardized, dynamically configured data structures inherent to application frameworks (e.g., event handler chains and visual object hierarchies).

In the following we give an overview of the most important concepts and tools of the ET++ programming environment that explicitly support software development with an application framework. All other programming environment tools, such as the class browser, are ignored in this context. A general discussion of the topic of programming environments can be found in Section 3.2. An in-depth discussion of the ET++ programming environment and its features that were especially developed for software development with application frameworks can be found in [Gam91].

As it is important for exploratory programming to help a developer understand the current state of a running application, ET++ provides the *Inspector* and the *Object Structure Browser*. The *Inspector* (depicted in Figure 3.14) can be applied to get information about the state of any active object, and the *Object Structure Browser* (shown in Figure 3.15) serves to visualize the various kinds of dependencies between the objects making up the user interface of an application.

The *Inspector* provides a list of all classes, together with the number of active objects of each class, in the upper left subwindow. The selection of one of these classes (*Expander* in our example) results in the displaying of the addresses of the active objects in the top center subwindow. If one of these object addresses is selected, its instance variables are displayed in the large subwindow at the bottom. These instance variables are organized according to the inheritance hierarchy of the classes in which they are defined (the names of abstract classes being displayed in italics and the name of the actual class being displayed in boldface). The instance variable *modified*, for example, is inherited from the abstract superclass *CompositeVObject* and its value is *true*.

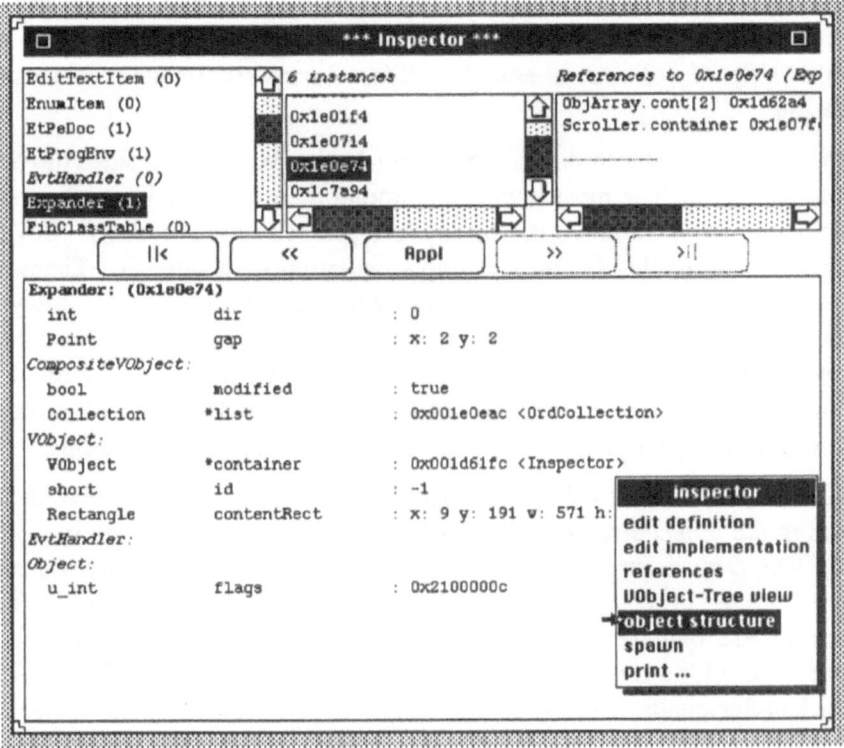

Figure 3.14. ET++ inspector providing information about active objects

Besides the explicit selection of an object, the *Inspector* provides three further browsing features:

- It makes it possible to browse through a graph of interconnected objects by simply clicking on a pointer to an object of interest, which is then displayed in the *Inspector*. In our example it would make sense to click on the instance variable *container* to inspect the enclosing visual object of the displayed *Expander* object. Once a path through a graph of objects is traversed, it is possible to traverse it again in both directions with the ||<, <<, >>, >|| buttons.

- It permits a developer to get a list of all the objects which have references to the current object by selecting the *references* command in the menu. This list is then displayed in the top right subwindow. The current object in our example is referenced by two objects, an

*ObjectArray* and a *Scroller*. These objects can be inspected by simply clicking on them.

• Depending on the type of the currently selected object, special tools can be invoked to visualize its relations to other objects. Such special browsing tools are, for example, list browsers that facilitate the browsing of collections and the *Object Structure Browser* discussed below.

There are other ways to display an object in the *Inspector* besides the ones discussed above. The most interesting among them is to click on any object of a running application while two keys are pressed simultaneously. Beyond the availability of this feature, its implementation is of interest. Thanks to the uniform handling of visual objects—which results from the framework approach—it sufficed to implement the feature for the abstract base class *VObject* because all other visual object classes inherit it. After the required 20 lines of code were written, the feature was also available for all standard and custom designed visual objects of the already existing applications.

The *Object Structure Browser* displayed in Figure 3.15 was invoked by selecting the *object structure* command in the *Inspector* as shown in Figure 3.14. The *Object Structure Browser* can be used to graphically visualize various kinds of framework-specific and general dependencies. Two examples are depicted in Figure 3.15. One is the event handler chain emphasized with a black line starting from the object of class *Thumb*. This event handler chain determines the way events are passed from object to object until an object is found that knows how to react on this specific event. The other is the container hierarchy highlighted with a thick dotted line, which is the list of objects which hierarchically contain the selected object of class *ImageButton*.

Further information that can be visualized is the objects which depend on the currently selected object via the change propagation mechanism, the objects which reference the current object, and the objects which are referenced from the current object.

Other commands of interest that are available in the *Object Structure Browser* are *inspect*, which displays the selected object in the *Inspector*, and *promote*, which makes the selected object the root object of the displayed object graph.

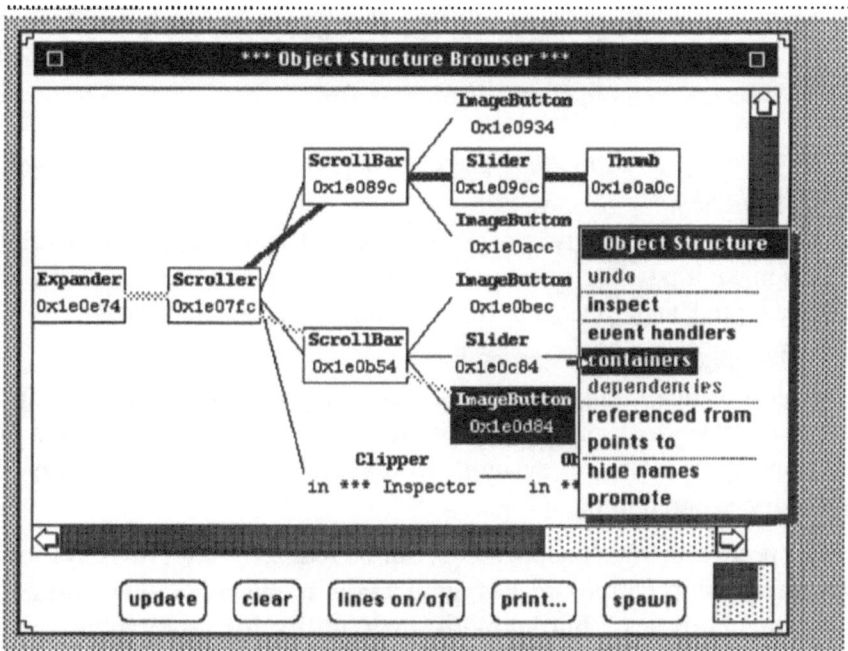

Figure 3.15. ET++ object structure browser depicting a visual object hierarchy

*Experience with ET++*

Weinand et al. write in [Wei89a] that, according to their experience, writing a complex application based on ET++ can result in 80% less new source code than without an application framework. As an example they mention a drawing tool similar to MacDraw which they developed based on ET++. The source code of this drawing tool consists of about 4000 lines of code, whereas the implementation of MacDraw based on the Macintosh Toolbox required almost 8 times as much.

The effort needed to learn an application framework is sizable, as general experience in the development of strongly interactive tools with application frameworks shows. The adaptation of the framework to a concrete, complex task requires a good understanding of the cooperation among the framework components. Fortunately, the effort invested in learning an application framework is usually more than recompensed in shorter development times and in better results.

The initial distribution of ET++ was accompanied by the hope that others who developed software with ET++ at various sites would contribute a number of reusable class trees for integration into the framework. Until now this has not been the case, which confirms our feeling that the realization of widely reusable classes requires a lot of farsightedness, excellent developers, and a strong dedication to the development of reusable components.

*The Significance of Application Frameworks for Exploratory Programming and Prototyping*

The outstanding characteristic of object-oriented application frameworks is that they make it possible to *reuse* not only code but also *entire designs* that can be adapted and extended for a concrete application, thanks to the underlying object-oriented concepts.

Because of these outstanding characteristics, the application of object-oriented frameworks significantly speeds up the initial implementation and evolution of a software system, which makes them ideal tools for exploratory programming.

The speed with which applications can be realized—e.g., two days for an entity/relationship editor—makes application frameworks interesting for prototyping purposes. Furthermore, their utility for prototyping can be improved by high-level tools such as DICE (see Chapter 7), which provide a further abstraction level. Tools like DICE make it possible to specify the layout and parts of the handling of user events with a graphic editor, while the rest of the application can be evolutionarily implemented with the underlying application framework.

# 4 Additional Aspects of Prototyping

This chapter rounds out Part I by emphasizing the organizational aspects of prototyping rather than the technical ones. During many discussions with practitioners we were asked the same few questions over and over again. For this reason we decided to formulate this chapter as a sequence of questions and answers. Similar questions with answers from a different prospective can be found in [Con89].

*Are there classes of applications which are especially suited to prototyping?*

A widespread point of view is that prototyping is a useful approach for specifying and implementing business applications—i.e., information systems—but that prototyping can hardly be applied in developing technical and scientific applications—i.e., process automation and real-time software.

Our point of view is that the development of every application for which the requirements or the feasibility cannot be determined without any doubt should be carried out in a prototyping-oriented way in order to eliminate the most risky uncertainties, as we have already discussed in depth. Such risks of ill-formulated requirements or technical infeasibility exist in almost all software projects carried out today (especially in technical and scientific applications), so that the application of prototyping certainly will result in benefits.

The reason why many people still think that prototyping is an approach for developing information systems stems from the fact that the (measurable) benefits obtained from prototyping depend on the available tool support, and this tool support is better for prototyping of information systems than for prototyping of technical and scientific applications. As we have shown with the example presented in Section 2.2.2, this support has improved considerably recent years.

*Who participates in a prototyping effort and to what degree?*

Recommendations range from 50% later users, 50% developers to 100% later users, which corresponds to "end user computing" during which the developers participate only as consultants. Our experience shows that prototyping brings best results if a team is built consisting of developers and later users who share the effort equally.

*Do you recommend end user computing in conjunction with prototyping?*

The development of applications by the later user usually is a prototyping-oriented explorative process. This is mainly because the later users usually lack the technical background to get even small systems right the first time, which forces them to take an exploratory approach.

The advantage of end user computing are:

- elimination of communication overhead between developers and later users

- minimization of acceptance problems because the later users have done the designing themselves and therefore have fewer possibilities to offload the responsibility

- reduction of the education effort at the beginning of the practical application of the software system because the users should already know it well

The disadvantages of end user computing are:

- forfeiting of the detection of organizational weak points resulting from the collaboration of external developers

- increased risk of inconsistency and incompleteness

- increased risk of redundant development efforts

- neglected integration of various software solutions

- the fact that the best applications developed today were not written by the later users because good design requires a lot of experience

From our point of view, end user computing should be discouraged except for very small simple applications which can be developed using spreadsheet software or small PC-based database systems.

*Who has the responsibility for the results of a prototyping process?*

During specification prototyping the developers and later users have to collaborate closely and therefore also to share the responsibility for the results. This is also illustrated by the fact that the resulting requirements definition is understood as a contract between developers and later users.

During architecture prototyping and exploratory programming the developers have the complete responsibility and the later users help only in formulating realistic scenarios and in collecting test data.

*Is it possible to apply prototyping as an evolutionary strategy which results in a software system which can be considered a product?*

This is possible, but it depends on the suitability of the available tools. Today there are few tools which fulfill the requirements in terms of performance, abstraction level, generality, security, and readability of the resulting product.

Good examples of tools which are suited to an evolutionary approach are 4th Dimension, the 4th generation system described in Section 2.3.1, and TOPOS, the prototyping-oriented software development environment presented in the second part of this book.

*What is the difference between a prototyping-oriented and a top-down development approach?*

Software development according to the sequential software life cycle can be understood as a top-down process because the software system under development is refined successively from the requirements definition, to a system architecture design, to the implementation of the individual components.

Prototyping employs the same approach, except that the intermediate results such as the requirements definition or the system architecture description are validated by experimenting with running software systems. A prototyping-oriented software development approach is therefore usually also carried out top-down.

Exploratory programming, on the other hand, can result in a bottom-up or inside-out approach when it is applied in developing software systems of application areas which are novel or scarcely understood. This is because it is usually not possible to formulate complete requirements definitions for such software systems. In this case the requirements are discovered during the iterative evolution of the application, which leads to a bottom-up or inside-out approach.

*Are time-tested methods such as structured analysis and structured design compatible with a prototyping approach?*

From our point of view, prototyping and traditional techniques such as structured analysis and structured design are complementary approaches.

Structured analysis and design makes it possible to semiformally describe requirements and to methodically transform them into a system architecture design. User interface prototyping, the simulative execution of the functional parts of a requirements definition, and architecture prototyping could certainly improve a development process based on structured analysis and design. For this reason modern CASE tools offer more and more components which support prototyping of various aspects of the later application.

*What is the effect of prototyping on costs, risks and quality aspects?*

Prototyping does not significantly reduce development costs. In certain cases the application of prototyping can even increase them. The advantages of prototyping are significant improvements of quality factors such as functional adequacy, user friendliness, modifyability, extensibility, and reliability.

Prototyping as a quality assurance measure leads to reduced costs of the overall software life cycle because maintenance and operating expenses can be diminished thanks to the increased overall quality.

Furthermore, prototyping reduces the overall risks inherent in a development process by providing means to dynamically validate parts of the requirements definitions, to ensure feasibility, and to test the system architecture before the entire application is implemented.

*Does prototyping lead to new risks in software development?*

The application of prototyping leads to a significant reduction of risk factors throughout the software life cycle, but it also introduces new risks. The most important of them are:

- the risk that the requirements definition process does not converge because the more the later users get, the more they want

- the risk that applications are built that provide more functionality and cost, therefore more than what is economically reasonable

- the risk that prototypes are delivered as products because of pressure from the clients

*Are special software and hardware required to successfully apply prototyping?*

From our point of view, special software and hardware are required to obtain the full benefits of prototyping. The fast development and evolution of software systems certainly requires supporting tools which make it possible to specify certain aspects of prototypes on a high abstraction level instead of implementing them in an algorithmic programming language. Modern hardware is of importance because modern software development tools provide comfortable user interfaces which cannot be implemented on mainframes and which need the processing power provided only by today's workstations.

*What is the perspective of the commercial application of prototyping?*

Experience with prototyping clearly shows that the application of prototyping can lead to qualitatively better software systems and to reduced overall costs. Because of this experience and the impression we have won from the marketplace, we see the following trends for the application and support of prototyping:

- The prototyping paradigm will replace the sequential software life cycle in the next 3-5 years as the process model in many newly started development projects.

- Significant improvements of prototyping tools which were made in research projects will be integrated into commercially available tools.

- New software development methods contain prototyping activities.

- The number of companies applying prototyping is quickly growing.

# Part II

## TOPOS — A Toolset for Prototyping-Oriented Software Development

An awareness of the processes that underlie problem solving becomes most valuable when you are having difficulty. If you are observant, you can often catch yourself failing to
1)    *identify* potential problems,
2)    *define* them appropriately,
3)    *explore* a variety of possible approaches,
4)    *act* on your ideas, or
5)    *look* at the effects of your actions.

By becoming aware of the possible sources of difficulties, you have a much better chance of approaching problems in optimal ways.[1]

---

[1] from "The Ideal Problem Solver", J.D. Bransford and B.S. Stein [Bra84]

# 5 Overview of TOPOS

In the first part of this book, we presented various concepts and approaches supporting a prototyping-oriented exploratory software development process. We discussed the possibilities, advantages and disadvantages, as well as the limits of their application. We have furthermore shown that it is unrealistic to apply prototyping and exploratory programming without adequate tool support. An important part of the discussion of the presented concepts therefore centered on the topic of what kind of tool support is required to efficiently support their application. Because of these discussions, a considerable portion of Part I dealt with tool technology and with selected examples for various kinds of tools.

Part I presented isolated tools as examples that support individual concepts or approaches. Such isolation does not suffice, however, to adequately support the prototyping-oriented life-cycle model. This model can best be supported by an integrated software development environment in which prototyping, exploratory programming, and all other activities of the software development process are supported. The goal of Part II is therefore to outline the structure and application of such a software development environment. This goal can be best achieved by presenting one single coherent example.

We have selected TOPOS, a working prototype of such a software development environment, as our example. Products that adequately support both prototyping and exploratory programming are not commercially available today; however, we are convinced that the concepts embodied in TOPOS will find application in development environments to be marketed in the near future.

TOPOS was realized and practically applied during a research cooperation of the University of Zürich, the Johannes Kepler University Linz, and Siemens Munich.

# 5.1 Basic Requirements on TOPOS

From the discussion in Part I and conclusions drawn therefrom, the following basic requirements can be formulated for a state-of-the-art prototyping-oriented software development environment. Each requirement is followed by an explanation of how it is fulfilled by TOPOS and by a discussion of the approaches that were taken in the design and realization of this software development environment.

*All prototyping activities described in the prototyping-oriented life-cycle model have to be supported.*

A prototyping-oriented software development environment therefore has to provide tools which make it possible to apply prototyping during the specification, design, and implementation processes.

The goal in developing TOPOS was to support at least all prototyping-oriented activities described in the prototyping-oriented software life cycle. In order to achieve this kind of overall support, a distinction between prototyping during the requirements definition process, and prototyping during the design and implementation process was made.

For the former kind of prototyping, a user interface prototyping tool was implemented which supports the requirements definition process as well as the design of the human-machine interface. For the latter kind of prototyping, a tool was realized which supports prototyping-oriented system architecture validation as well as exploratory programming.

*The various prototyping tools which support different stages of the development process have to cooperate.*

In the course of a prototyping process, various aspects of an application are best prototyped with different tools, e.g., the user interface, the data management, and the system architecture. It is therefore important that the prototypes which are realized with different tools can be integrated in such a way that they can be presented as one single prototype in order to give a realistic impression of the application under development.

In order to combine diverse prototyping tools, TOPOS provides an interprocess communication interface as well as a dynamic binding mechanism. With this kind of support it becomes easy to integrate the execution mechanisms of different, independently developed prototyping tools. Furthermore, TOPOS provides support for the management of documents and prototypes which were developed with the diverse tools.

*It has to be possible to easily modify and extend a prototype.*

During a prototyping-oriented software development process, exploratory and evolutionary prototypes are developed and have to be improved successively during various implementation-evaluation cycles. These iterative implementation activities frequently lead to an increasing deterioration of the overall structure of a prototype. This degenerative tendency makes it decisive for the quality of a prototyping-oriented software development environment that it provide specification and implementation formalisms that are sound from a software engineering viewpoint. Such formalisms provide good abstraction and structuring concepts which permit a developer to greatly reduce the degree of degeneration as well as the effort needed for restructuring.

TOPOS achieves easy modifiability and extensibility of prototypes by providing prototyping formalisms which were designed with these goals in mind. The user interface prototyping tool improves modifiability and extensibility of prototypes by increasing the abstraction level on which a prototype is described. On this high abstraction level an initial user interface prototype as well as modifications and extensions to it are simply drawn. The effect of this approach is that the structures of the implementation and the run-time behavior of a prototype correspond so closely that almost no deterioration of the overall structure is possible. The exploratory design and programming environment supports modifiability and extensibility by supporting an algorithmic programming language that is sound in terms of software engineering criteria.

*Turnaround times have to be short (while a prototype is being iteratively improved).*

During a prototyping-oriented iterative development process, the waiting time before reexecution after modification or extension is critical, because this turnaround time is an important factor in determining the number of economically feasible development/evaluation cycles. The constraints imposed by excessive turnaround times become especially restrictive if a prototype is dynamically improved during a meeting with the later user. Such collaboration moves from tiresome to unrealistic if it takes several minutes before the effects of minor changes can be evaluated.

All tools comprising TOPOS provide interpretive execution mechanisms to guarantee short turnaround times. This approach enables almost instantaneous evaluation of a prototype after modifications.

*Prototypes and prototype components should be reusable.*

In the ideal case, the various prototypes that were developed for a software systems should be incrementally evolved into the final application. A prerequisite for this kind of reuse is that the code to be reused conform to the general software quality criteria. The percentage of code which is written during the prototyping process and which can be reused during the succeeding implementation process is therefore a measure of the quality of a development environment as well as of the quality of the formalisms it supports for prototyping and exploratory programming.

Reusability of the user interface prototypes is achieved by providing a code generator which produces code in an algorithmic language that implements exactly the same behavior as the interpretively executed (graphically specified) prototype. Both the prototype and this generated code communicate via the same procedural interface with the functional application parts. This means that the step from the flexibly evolvable prototype to the final application consists of nothing more than an automatic generation and compilation process.

*Conventional development activities have to be supported.*

A lot of activities are carried out during a prototyping-oriented software life cycle which are not directly related to prototyping, such as component management, version control, and documentation. In order for an integrated set of tools to be considered a software development environment, these activities also have to be supported.

TOPOS provides a set of tools that support important housekeeping tasks such as component management, version control, and documentation.

# 5.2 Basic Concepts Underlying TOPOS

As shown in discussions in Part I, two kinds of activities have to be carried out during a prototyping-oriented software development process: prototyping as exploration of the requirements the software system under development should fulfill (i.e., specification prototyping), and prototyping as exploration of different possible realization approaches for the specified requirements (i.e, exploratory programming).

It is obvious that these two kinds of prototyping are different activities. The internal structure and the external representation of the results (the prototypes) as well as the abstraction level on which the prototypes are developed differ drastically, so that two different kinds of tool support are required.

While the two kinds of prototyping processes differ profoundly, they nonetheless have to be integrated in order to achieve a homogeneous development process. It therefore seems appropriate to structure a prototyping-oriented software life cycle as depicted in Figure 5.1.

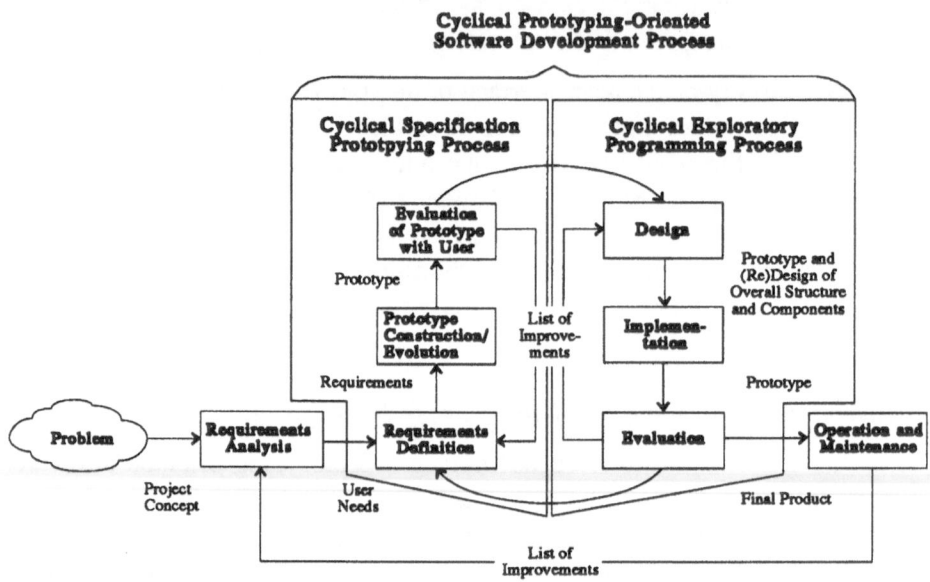

Figure 5.1. The prototyping-oriented software development process

A prototyping-oriented software development process (as described in Figure 5.1) consists of three iterative cyclical subprocesses: *specification prototyping*, *exploratory programming*, and *prototyping-oriented software development* itself. Specification prototyping and exploratory programming were already discussed in Part I. The novelty in this life cycle is that the two known processes are grouped into one comprehensive iterative process, while they were previously considered as separate processes.

The unified process was introduced because specification prototyping and exploratory programming are complementary approaches, from which can be concluded that it makes sense for the two processes to coexist in one single software development process. Such a unification is especially appropriate when an evolutionary approach to software development is taken.

During an evolutionary software development process it can, for example, make sense to enhance the behavior of a user interface prototype with application parts developed with exploratory programming. Another example is the prototyping-oriented evolution of a user interface prototype during an exploratory programming process. The cyclical nature of the unified process can be deduced from these two examples, where specification prototyping and exploratory programming are carried out in an interwoven way.

From the integration of specification prototyping and exploratory programming follows that the software system under development will consist of parts implemented in different formalisms. This is because both processes require a different kind of tool support and therefore also produce different kinds of results. The system architecture of a prototype (which is iteratively evolved during interwoven prototyping and exploratory programming processes) therefore consists of two different but cooperating kinds of parts: *specification prototypes* (e.g., user interface prototypes) and *functional application parts*.

Specification prototypes are usually described with declarative formalisms which permit the specification of certain aspects of an application on a high abstraction level. For this reason we call them *high-level application parts*. Functional application parts are implemented in algorithmic programming languages. They result either from the exploratory programming process or they can be reused.

An architecture consisting of these kinds of parts is what we call a *hybrid* system architecture. A typical example of a hybrid system architecture is depicted in Figure 5.2. It consists of four high-level parts which could have been developed with different kinds of prototyping tools, and seven functional application parts in different states of development.

Besides the structure of a hybrid system architecture, Figure 5.2 illustrates also the three possible states of an executable functional application part. An application part can be implemented and tested (or reused without any modifications), it can be partially implemented, or it can be designed but not yet under implementation.

Conventional exploratory programming environments make it possible to execute application parts in two of these states: application parts under implementation and already finished and tested application parts. By providing a simulation mechanism, the exploratory programming environment of TOPOS also permits the execution of functional application parts that are only designed. This execution mode enhances exploratory programming in various ways, the most notable of which is the possibility to carry out a prototyping-oriented validation of a designed but not yet implemented system architecture.

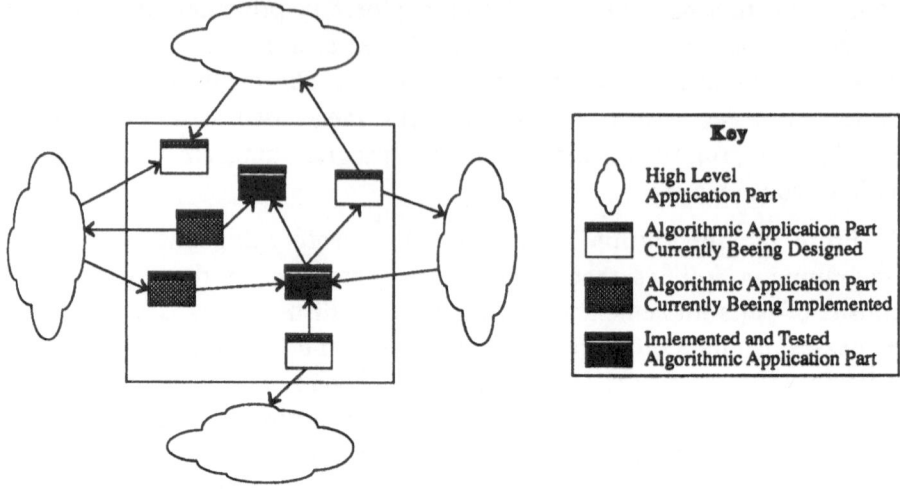

Figure 5.2. Example of a hybrid system architecture

In order to carry out a prototyping-oriented software life cycle—which means to incrementally evolve an application with a hybrid system architecture—we need a set of closely cooperating tools. These tools have to integrate a set of heterogeneous prototypes and functional application parts in a way which permits us to experiment with them as if they were one application.

There are two approaches to achieving such a closely cooperating tool set. The first approach is to write one single tool which provides support for the development of high-level *and* functional application parts. Examples of such tools are 4th Dimension and HyperCard, which were presented in Section 2.3. The second approach is to separate the development of high-level and functional application parts. This approach employs various tools to develop different kinds of application parts. A further tool is needed to manage the cooperation of the various tools. This approach makes it possible to use an environment for exploratory programming and to integrate it with a set of tools for the development of high-level application parts (high-level tools), depending on the kind of planned application.

The advantage of the second approach is its generality and flexibility. Its application is not restricted to a single area, because for every application area an appropriate set of tools can be selected and integrated. The importance of different tool sets for different application areas can be illustrated by the fact that a developer needs different tools for the development of a business application than for the development of a robot control system. In developing business applications, for example, tools for prototyping the data management as well as input/output masks and report forms are needed. Developing a robot control system, for example, requires support in prototyping the dynamic visualization of the work carried out by the robot and in prototyping the system architecture which defines how a set of distributed processes cooperates.

The more closely coupled environments obtained by taking the former approach, in comparison, usually provide closer coupling between the various constituent development tools. But it is much more difficult to extend their set of tools. The advantage of closely coupled environments is usually good integration of the various tools they provide, which makes them easy to apply. The disadvantages are their restricted application area and the fact that they frequently provide only rudimentary programming environments for the integrated algorithmic programming language (because too much effort has gone into the development of high-level tools).

Independent of the approach followed, it is decisive for the quality of an environment for prototyping-oriented software development that all available application parts can be executed as early as possible during their development, and that parts in different development stages can be executed together. From this follows that an exploratory programming environment has to provide different cooperating execution mechanisms for application parts in the different development stages.

Parts which are implemented and tested should be executed as efficiently as possible. Parts under implementation should be executed in a comfortable programming environment. Designed parts (for which implementation has not yet started) should be simulated in the context of the running application.

# 5.3 Overall Structure of TOPOS

According to the general discussion presented above, the following tool support needs to be provided by a prototyping-oriented software development environment:

- Requirements analysis and specification has to be supported by high-level tools allowing the fast declarative specification of prototypes for certain application parts such as the user interface and the data management.

- Exploratory architecture validation and system implementation have to be supported by an exploratory programming environment which permits the execution of software systems consisting of parts in the three different development stages discussed above.

- A software development environment has to provide further tools supporting project management, system documentation, and the management of all artifacts which are produced during software development and maintenance.

- The development environment should allow the incorporation of other kinds of tools depending on the application area. For example, it can be desirable to incorporate an expert system shell if the application under development contains knowledge-based parts.

TOPOS was designed with these requirements and the goal to obtain an open system in mind. It consists of an exploratory programming environment, the System Construction Tool (SCT), and an open set of high-level tools which communicate with each other and with SCT through a message dispatcher (see Figure 5.3).

SCT consists of a comfortable exploratory programming environment and a system architecture simulator. It closely cooperates with the Component Management Tool (CMT), which supports project management and administration, and DOgMA, which supports documentation and maintenance.

The Message Dispatcher permits the integration of a large number of different high-level tools into TOPOS. In order to keep Figure 5.3 easy to survey, only the Dynamic Interface Creation Environment (DICE), a user interface prototyping tool, is depicted explicitly. The box labeled with ??? stands as placeholder for any other tool which could be integrated, such as a relational database manager or a tool for the prototyping of distributed systems.

The rest of Part II describes the individual components of TOPOS and how they can be coordinated. Chapter 6 presents the component management system CMT. Chapter 7 discusses the user interface prototyping tool DICE. Chapter 8 describes the exploratory design and programming environment SCT. Chapter 9 presents the Message Dispatcher, the mechanism which TOPOS provides to integrate other tools into its execution system. Chapter 10 explains both generally and with a concrete scenario how TOPOS can be put to work. Chapter 11 discusses the experience we gained in applying TOPOS and the implications that can be drawn therefrom.

DOgMA is the tool TOPOS provides to support documentation and maintenance. It is not directly relevant during a prototyping-oriented development process. A presentation of its underlying concepts and of its application would therefore be out of place. Further information about DOgMA can be found in [Sam91].

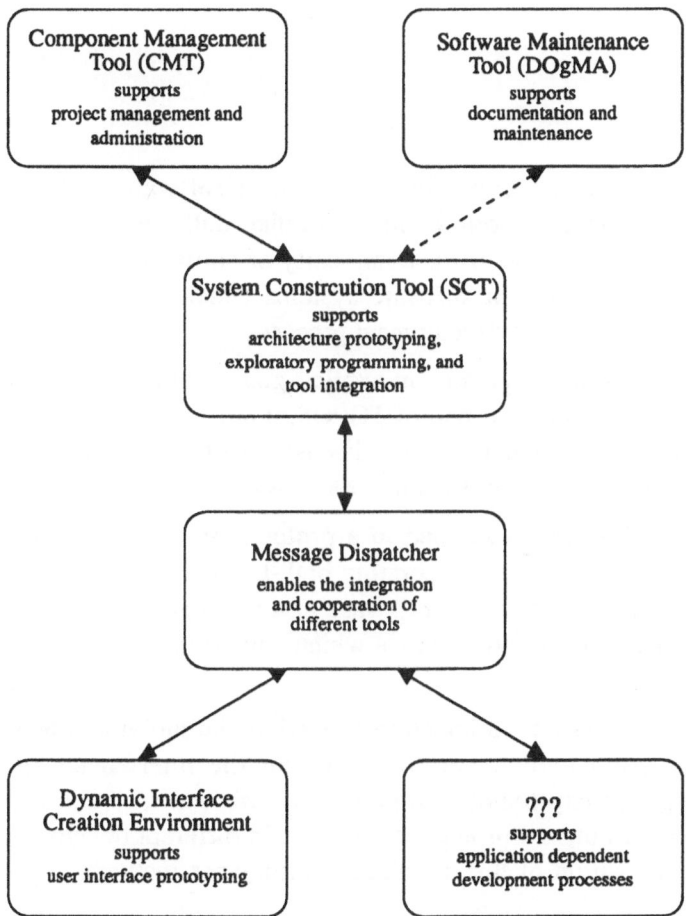

Figure 5.3. Overall Structure of TOPOS

# 6 The TOPOS Component Management Tool (CMT)

Compared to designing and implementing a software system, the management of its current configuration is a rather dull job. Nonetheless, many difficulties arise because of the complexity of software systems built today. This is especially true for software systems which are realized in a prototyping-oriented software development process.

While it was not originally an explicit goal to build a comfortable component management tool as part of TOPOS, it proved necessary. Two reasons for this can be derived from the discussion of the prototyping-oriented software development process in the previous chapter.

First, applications developed in a prototyping-oriented software development process consist of cooperating high-level and functional parts. This means that a developer has to keep track of a heterogeneous set of application parts and of the tools and methods which can be used to edit, browse, and execute them.

Second, the system architecture as well as the individual heterogeneous application parts evolve iteratively during the interwoven specification prototyping and exploratory programming processes. Such a proceeding results in a working set of application parts in different development stages, and the composition of this set directly influences methods and tools to be applied.

CMT, the Component Management Tool of TOPOS, was therefore designed to support a developer in coping with the kinds of complexity introduced by the application of the prototyping-oriented software development strategy. What kind of support it provides and how it can be put to work is the topic of this chapter. Section 6.1 describes the concepts underlying CMT, i.e., the kind of information which is managed and how this information can be structured.  Section 6.2 shows how the tool can be put to work by a developer.

# 6.1 Concepts Underlying CMT

CMT provides support by managing information about all artifacts (documents) which are produced during a software development process and by executing the system under development.  For this purpose it handles the following kinds of information:

- documents containing information about a software system (e.g., functional application parts, input formalisms for high-level prototyping tools, and any kind of documentation)

- attributes for classifying these documents

- paths indicating the location of the documents in a UNIX directory tree

- object code libraries needed to execute the software system

- information about available execution and editing tools

While documents managed by CMT are regular UNIX files, all unnecessary details about the file system are hidden from the user.  Instead of ordering the documents in a directory tree, *attributes* are assigned to the *documents*  This means that every document can be described by any number of attributes and every attribute can be assigned to any number of documents.  Based on these attributes, various kinds of selection mechanisms can be applied to obtain a subset of the managed documents.

The advantage of the attribute-based organization over a directory tree is that documents can be organized in more than two dimensions.  Projects, for example, can be logically organized into overlapping subprojects using the attribute mechanism, which is obviously not possible with a directory tree.

While the developer works without bothering about the underlying file system, CMT needs information to find the documents.  For this reason an ordered list of *paths* is maintained.  When system, user or project data are loaded into CMT, every document is located by sequentially searching all directories indicated in the path list until a file with the name of the document is found.

Working with such a path list has advantages compared to storing the absolute path of every document if whole libraries have to be replaced at once, or if a project has to be moved to another place in the directory tree. Replacing a library means, for example, inserting the path of the new library into the path list before the previously used library path. The disadvantage of working with a path list is that documents with the same name can only be managed as overlays.

UNIX applications frequently use functions provided by *object code libraries* and link compatible object code files generated from compilers for other programming languages. In order to execute such applications, CMT manages an ordered list of object code libraries and files which are dynamically linked and loaded before the execution of an application, the same way as the object code for directly executable modules.

Configuration information about projects using the same libraries and sharing reusable code corresponds to a sizable degree. In order to share configuration information between different projects and to avoid the tedious duplication of configuration data, information can be stored on one of three levels (e.g., Figure 6.1):

- Information stored on the *system level* is available to everybody working with SCT. (There may be differences between different installations of SCT). It is managed centrally and consists mainly of frequently used library documents and the corresponding attributes, paths and object code libraries.

- Information stored on the *user level* is available in every project belonging to a specific user. It consists mainly of library documents that are used frequently by this specific user, and the corresponding information.

- Information stored on *project level* makes up the biggest part of the configuration information and defines a concrete project.

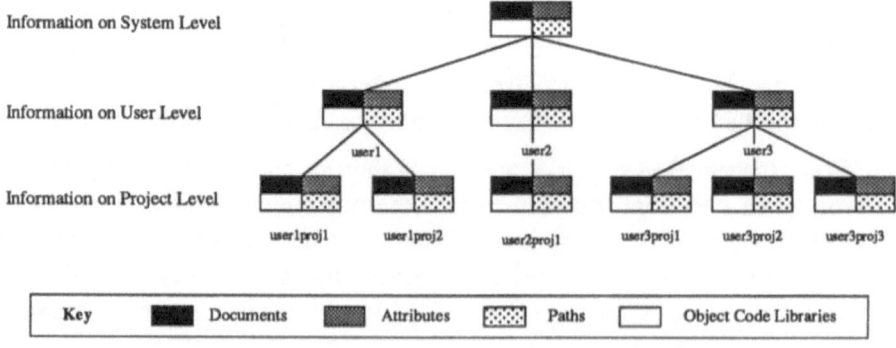

Figure 6.1. Hierarchy of configuration data stored by CMT

A good example of the advantage of this concept is the updating of all projects after a new compiler release was installed and the standard library had to be moved to another place in the file system. In this case it suffices to insert the path of the new standard library before the old one on system level, and all projects that used the standard library before automatically will use the new library afterwards.

If one of the users wants to continue using the old library for compatibility reasons in all his projects, the old path is inserted on the user level and CMT will find the old libraries before the new ones when searching the path list. If a new project is started by this user, who wants to use the new libraries in this project, the new path is inserted again on the project level.

CMT not only provides support for management and organization of information about application parts, but also builds the centerpiece of TOPOS from a developer's point of view. This is because CMT provides the possibility to trigger editing and execution of application parts without bothering a developer with the appropriate editing and execution tools. In order to provide this functionality, CMT stores information about available execution and editing tools as well as the attributes that serve to identify the documents to which these tools can be applied.

# 6.2 Application of CMT

At the beginning of a working session with TOPOS, CMT is usually the first tool that is invoked. Figure 6.2 shows CMT directly after startup. At this time only the data on system and user level is available. The scrollable list at the right side displays all attributes, and the scrollable list in the middle all documents defined on system and user level. The little boxes labeled $S$ (for system) and $U$ (for user) indicate on which level the attributes and modules are defined. (Notice that there is no information on project level at startup time, because no project has been opened yet.)

The buttons aligned along the left side serve to enter global commands which do not affect a selected document or attribute. The buttons below the scrollable lists serve to select documents and attributes as well as to issue commands referring to selected documents.

*Project Commands.* The first step after starting CMT is usually to open a project by pressing the *Open Project* button and selecting the project file in the file dialog box (Figure 6.3). There is no danger of opening a non-project file because CMT recognizes the type of a file and permits only the selection of the highlighted project files as shown in Figure 6.3. Pressing the *Save Project* button invokes the same file dialog box, which permits the specification of where the project should be saved. Pressing the *New Project* button (see Figure 6.2) creates an empty project, and pressing the *Delete Project* button discards the currently loaded project file.

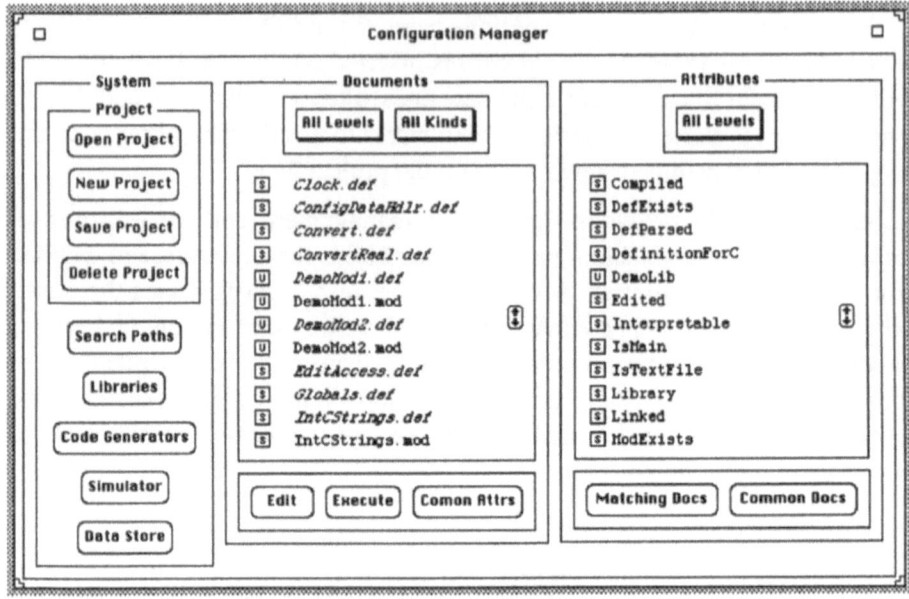

Figure 6.2. CMT's user interface

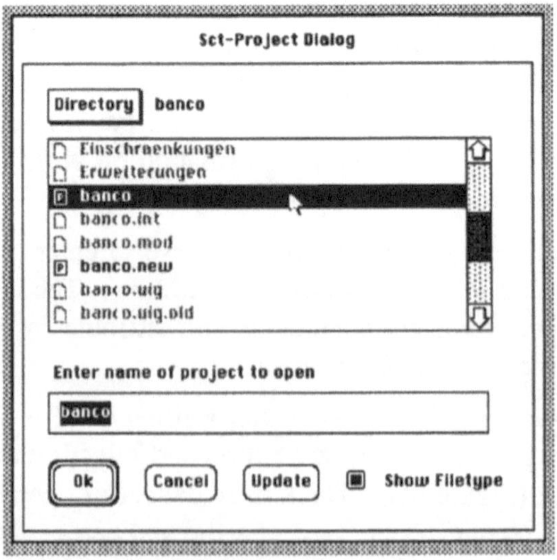

Figure 6.3. File dialog box for selecting a project file

*Selection Mechanisms.* After a project is opened, all documents of all levels are shown in the document list and all attributes are shown in the attribute list. The following selection mechanisms can be used to make subselections and to get information about which attribute was assigned to which document:

- Selecting a document causes its attributes to be displayed in the attribute list.

- Selecting one or more documents and pressing the *Common Attrs* button displays all attributes in the attribute list which were assigned to all selected documents.

- Selecting one or more attributes and pressing the *Common Docs* button causes all documents which have all the selected attributes assigned to be displayed in the document list.

- Selecting one or more attributes and pressing the *Matching Docs* button causes all documents which have at least one of the selected attributes assigned to be displayed in the document list.

- Pressing one of the two buttons displayed above the document or the attribute list (see Figure 6.2) causes a menu to be displayed. These menus permit a developer to restrict the amount of information to be displayed in the two lists. Possible restrictions are documents or attributes defined on a special level (All Levels, System, User or Project) and all documents of a certain kind (All Kinds, Modula-2, DICE, Prolog, ...).

*Editing Documents and Attributes.* The menus in the documents and attribute lists provide features for adding and deleting documents and attributes, and for assigning attributes to documents and removing them from documents.

## Management of Other Documents

CMT can be used to manage any kind of documents and to invoke the editing and execution tools corresponding to various kinds of documents, as described above. In order to provide functionality going beyond the attribute-based mechanism for organizing and selecting documents, CMT needs information about the different tools which are available. This information has to be entered by the developer who integrates a new tool into TOPOS.

Using the *Document Type Manager* depicted in Figure 6.4, it is possible to specify for each kind of document an attribute name identifying it, an edit tool which is started with the file name as command line argument when the *Edit* button is pressed, and an execution tool to which a message is sent when the *Execute* button is pressed.

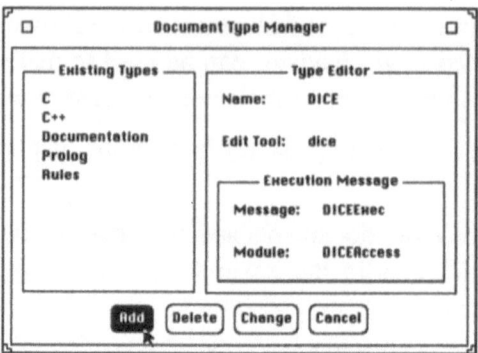

Figure 6.4. Document Type Manager

*Browsing and Editing the Path and Library Lists.* Pressing the *Search Paths* button or the *Libraries* button (see Figure 6.2) invokes a tool for browsing and editing the corresponding list (see Figure 6.5). Single lines of the lists can be added (*Add Path*), deleted (*Delete Path*), and moved (by direct manipulation). The *Search Path Manager* furthermore permits the selection of all documents stored in the directory indicated by the selected path (*Matching Docs*) and displays them in the document list.

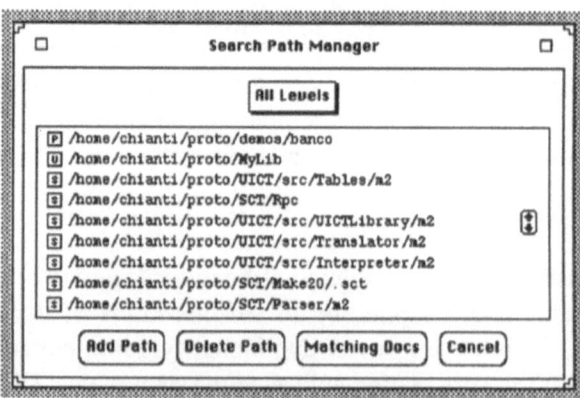

Figure 6.5. Search Path Manager

*Invoking Other Tools.* The *Edit* and *Execute* buttons in the *Documents* subwindow in Figure 6.2 serve to invoke the editing or execution tool for the currently selected document. Which tool is invoked depends on the type of the selected document. For user-defined document types, user-defined tools are started with the document name as command line argument. For functional application parts the exploratory programming environment described in Chapter 8 is invoked.

Each working session begins with the invocation of CMT (see Figure 6.2). Thus CMT provides two buttons for invoking further tools of the exploratory programming environment (i.e., the *Simulator* described in Section 8.6 and the Workspace Manager (*Data Store*) described Section 8.5).

The list on the left side of the *Document Type Manager* (see Figure 6.4) shows for which kinds of documents tool information is stored, and the box on the right side contains the fields for editing, browsing, and changing the effective information. The information which can be entered consists of:

- the *Attribute* which is used to identify the corresponding documents,

- the name of the *Edit Tool* that can be used to edit the documents which have the corresponding Attribute assigned

- the name of the *Message* (and its enclosing *Module*) which is sent with the name of the document as parameter to the corresponding execution tool after the execution of the document was triggered.

How tools can be integrated into TOPOS and how messages are passed among the different tools is discussed in Chapter 9.

Another feature of CMT is that it provides the names of all added document types in the menu which pops up when the *All Kinds* button (see Figure 6.2) is pressed. This makes it easy to select all documents of a kind. For an example, see Figure 6.6, where all documents of type Modula-2 were selected using this mechanism.

*Management of Functional Application Parts*

From a developer's point of view, CMT is a tool which cooperates with other tools for which it manages the input and output documents. These tools can be invoked directly from CMT. CMT also provides user interface services for and cooperates closely with the exploratory programming environment.

CMT provides two kinds of user interface services. First, CMT allows a developer to browse and edit the mode in which an functional application part should be executed and it illustrates how an application part currently could be executed. Second, it provides a user interface to initiate the generation of interprocess communication interfaces and of a makefile which allows automatic generation of a standalone application at the end of the development process.

*Management of Information about Execution Modes.* TOPOS provides three execution mechanisms for functional application parts in different development stages, as discussed in Chapter 5. Implemented and tested parts are compiled and directly executed for the sake of efficiency. Parts currently under implementation are interpreted to provide a comfortable programming environment. Parts which are designed but for which implementation has not yet started are simulated.

One effect of these three execution modes is that a developer has to be able to edit and browse the development stage of every functional application part and needs feedback in order to see how a part will be effectively executed. It is possible, for example, that a part which is under implementation, and should therefore be interpreted, has to be simulated because the code is currently being restructured and thus not executable.

Information about the intended execution mode for a functional application part is stored and manipulated in the form of ordinary system attributes, with the exception that CMT does some consistency checks. Parts with the attribute *edited* were just created and cannot be executed at all. Parts with the attributes *simulable* and *interpretable* are intended to be simulated and interpreted, respectively. Parts with the attributes *compiled*, *linked*, and *library* are intended to be directly executed. (The three different attributes affect only the way the object code to be executed is obtained).

If and how a functional application part currently can be executed is displayed by little black squares in the document list, as depicted in Figure 6.6. Depending on the letter inscribed in the square, a module is simulable (*S*), interpretable (*I*) or directly executable (*E*). These execution modes cannot be directly manipulated by a developer. They are determined by the exploratory programming environment.

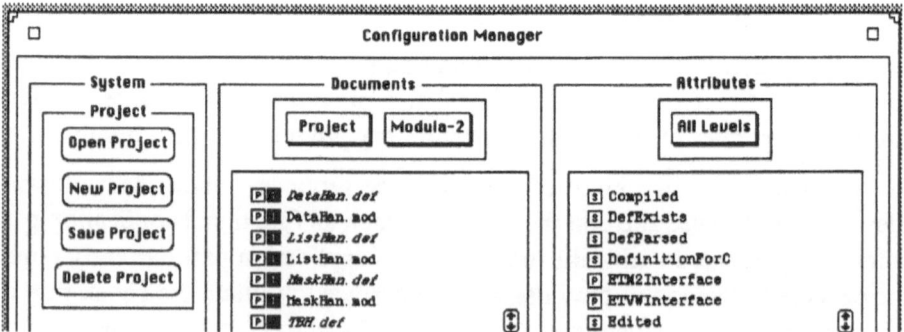

Figure 6.6. CMT displaying a document list with interpretable and simulable modules

Another feature which can be observed in Figure 6.6 is that the documents in the document list were restricted by the user to Modula-2 modules defined on the project level by using the two buttons above the document list and the menus invoked by them.

*Code Generation Interface.* In working with TOPOS there are two cases where code has to be generated: First, at the end of a development process, when an application has to be decoupled from TOPOS, a makefile can be generated which manages the compilation of a standalone version of the application. Second, if a part of an application should run as a server process in order to be shared by different running instances of the application, inter-process communication stubs as well as a main module and a makefile can be generated. The compilation and linking of the modules implementing the server are managed automatically by the UNIX make facility.

Figure 6.7 displays the Code Generation Manager, the tool used to control these two cases of code generation. The only information a developer has to enter in order to generate a standalone application is whether the application uses the Message Dispatcher for the purpose of dynamic binding (see Chapter 9), because in this case a library has to be bound to the final application.

If a developer wants to generate an interprocess communication interface for a set of modules, this set has to be defined by providing an attribute which designates all application parts to be decoupled.

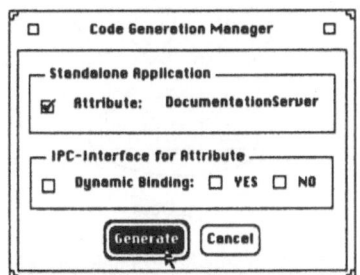

Figure 6.7. Code Generation Manager

*Support of Teamwork and Version Control*

Chapter 3 discussed requirements for an exploratory programming environment. Two of them were support of teamwork and version control.

*Teamwork* is supported by a mechanism similar to the transparent file systems of NSE (see Section 3.2). The basic idea underlying this approach is that all unchanged documents belonging to a project are shared, while every developer has a private copy of the documents he/she is currently working on.

This approach is efficiently supported by CMT's path mechanism. This path mechanism permits a developer to overlay modified private application parts over the application parts shared with other team members. This is done by inserting the name of the directory where the private copies are located before the project directory in the path list. Afterwards on editing and execution requests CMT selects the private version if there is one, otherwise the shared version. The only thing the developer has to take care of is to create a private copy of a document before changing it. This is easily enforceable by denying developers the write permission on shared documents.

Figure 6.8 shows an example of such an overlaid project organization. The three application parts shared by the team members are located in directory *ApplDocs*. Two users, Susan and George, are currently working on this application. Susan is working on *doc1* and George on *doc3*. Each of them has a private directory (*SusansDocs* and *GeorgesDocs*) where they keep their private versions of the document on which they are currently working. If they trigger editing or execution of a document, CMT selects the private version if there is one, otherwise the shared version.

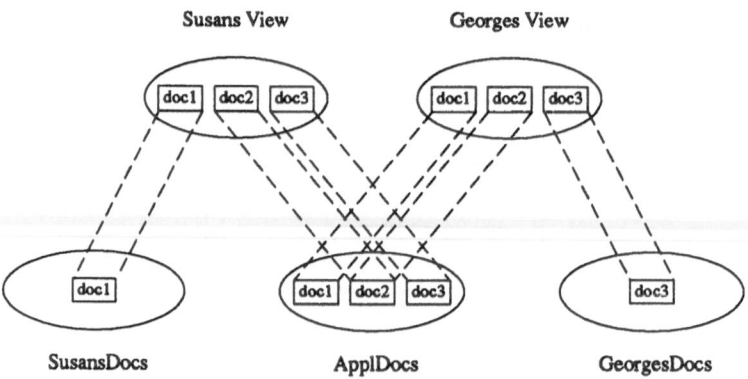

Figure 6.8. Teamwork example with CMT

CMT provides no support for version control on its own. This is not necessary because if TOPOS is applied in projects where currently available version control systems such as RCS [Tic88] and SCCS [Roc75] are appropriate, these tools can be used without any problems due to the fact that all documents managed by CMT are ordinary UNIX files.

# 7 The TOPOS User Interface Prototyping Environment DICE

According to the prototyping-oriented software development strategy described in Section 1.2, the first activity is the exploration of the requirements on a planned system. The user interface is considered to have an enormous impact on the functional requirements on a software system. Foley [Fol90] confirms this assumption: "It is important to follow the Bauhaus dictum, *form follows function*, lest the user interface style dictate the capabilities of the overall system." Thus the first step in the TOPOS project was the development of a user interface prototyping environment, which was called DICE, Dynamic Interface Creation Environment.

This section begins with an explanation of the concepts underlying DICE that have an influence on the way a user interface prototype is developed and on the supported user interface paradigm. Afterwards we show how DICE can be applied by presenting its user interface in some application examples.

## 7.1 Concepts Underlying DICE

Dialog-oriented software systems and their associated user interfaces can be described as *finite automata*; they are defined in terms of a set of states and possible state transitions. From the viewpoint of the user of a software system, these states are defined in terms of certain representations on the screen. The state transitions are triggered by the user's reaction to a particular state representation and/or by the software system itself, i.e., by its functional application parts.

DICE provides two kinds of tools for the creation of user interface prototypes:

- A tool to permit the convenient and flexible creation of state representations—the layout of the user interface—supports the specification of the
  *static aspects* of the user interface prototype.

- A tool to allow the specification of state transitions—the reaction of interface elements to user events—supports the specification of the *dynamic
  aspects* of the user interface prototype.

*Concepts for the specification of static aspects*

Every user interface created with DICE consists of one or more windows. A
direct-manipulation graphic editor (with WYSIWYG capabilities) enables the
user to define the screen layout. User interface elements of various types are
provided. Each user interface element's type defines its basic functionality.
The most important user interface elements afforded by DICE are the
following:

- *Text Subwindow* has the typical functionality of a modern text editor (text
  being selected by means of a mouse, cut/copy/paste being supported, etc.).
  The associated menus as well as the text document that is initially
  displayed in this subwindow can be specified.

- *Graphic Subwindow* has the typical functionality of a modern graphic
  editor. Various shapes like rectangles, ovals, lines, bitmaps, can be
  drawn, moved, resized, etc. The associated menus as well as the graphic
  document that is initially displayed in this subwindow can be specified.

- *List Subwindow* provides a scrollable list of text entries, one of which can
  be selected and associated with an action. Again, the initial list entries as
  well as the associated menu that is displayed in this subwindow can be
  specified.

- *Static* and *Editable Text Items* support the display/entry of text.

- *Enumeration Items* support the display/entry of numbers.

- *Buttons* (Pop-up, Action, Radio, Toggle) can be associated with any kind
  of action.

- *Sliders* can be used to adjust analog values.

- The *Cluster* is a building block which serves to group other building
  blocks, to align them, and to recalculate their sizes after the size of the
  enclosing window changed.

The set of user interface elements can be arbitrarily extended. The layout algorithms are adaptive; i.e., the layout of individual user interface elements can be changed easily. User interface elements can be collected in groups and are scaled when there is a change in the size of the group of which they are a part.

*Concepts for the specification of dynamic aspects*

The most important aspect during the development of a prototype for exploring the user's requirements is not the layout of the user interface but its *dynamic behavior*. Parts of the dynamic behavior are specified by the user interface elements themselves because each user interface element has a predefined functionality depending on its type (e.g., a *Text Subwindow* providing all usual editor commands). But that is, of course, in many cases insufficient to create a realistic prototype.

To enhance the possibilities to specify dynamic behavior, predefined messages have been associated with each user interface element. Messages can be sent from any user-activated user interface element (e.g., buttons, menus, lists) to any other user interface element of a prototype, e.g., *ChangeText* to a Text Subwindow, *Open/Close* to any window). A tool called *Message Editor* allows the definition of which message(s) should be sent on activation from a particular user interface element to other user interface elements. This is a further possibility to considerably enhance a prototype's functionality.

Predefined messages strongly depend on the particular application domain; hence it is important to be able to change and extend these predefined messages in a simple way. This goal is achieved by means of the object-oriented implementation of DICE, which makes it possible to change and extend predefined messages of all user interface elements without modifying DICE's source code. This is achieved by deriving subclasses from the user interface element classes already implemented in DICE and extending or overwriting the inherited methods.

The specified prototypes are always executable without a compile-link-go cycle. This enables the evaluation of the prototype parallel to its design. DICE also supports the simultaneous processing of several prototypes. This is particularly important if earlier prototypes are employed as a pattern in the development of a new prototype, or if parts of an existing prototype are to be transferred into a new prototype.

*Concepts for extending the functionality of a prototype beyond what can be expressed with DICE*

There are two ways to extend the functionality of a prototype beyond what can be expressed with DICE:

- DICE defines an expressive protocol together with an appropriate interface, so that any UNIX process can be connected with a user interface specified with DICE. Via this interface the functional part of an application obtains the high-level events from the user interface (e.g., which button was pressed or what text was entered into an editable field) and it can send events to the user interface (e.g., set the text in an editable field or enable a menu entry).

  This approach makes it possible to interpretively execute the user interface with DICE, while the functional parts are developed in a flexible exploratory programming environment such as SCT (see Chapter 8). The functional parts can be implemented in any available programming language (e.g., Cobol, Fortran, Pascal, Ada, C). DICE is therefore ideal for the prototyping and incremental development of applications as long as the functionality of DICE's basic building blocks suffices to build the user interface.

- If the functionality of DICE's basic building blocks has to be flexibly enhanced (e.g., instead of the standard text editor and editor with hypertext functionality is needed), it is possible to generate C++ classes which implement the user interface as specified. These classes can then be extended and modified by deriving subclasses. If the graphically specified part of the user interface has to be changed, the generated classes do not have to be modified.

Both approaches for extending the functionality of a prototype beyond what can be expressed with DICE can be taken to evolve a prototype into the final application.


# 7.2 Application of DICE

On startup, DICE displays its Control Panel and its User Interface Element Panel (see Figures 7.1 and 7.3).

The left part of DICE's Control Panel displays a list of currently loaded prototypes (①). When DICE is started, this list is empty. A system developer has two possibilities to load a prototype:

- A new empty prototype can be created by pressing the *New Prototype* button.

- A prototype that has been stored on an external device can be added to the list of loaded prototypes. After the *Add to List...* button is pressed, DICE opens a file dialog (see Figure 7.2) where the user selects the proper prototype.

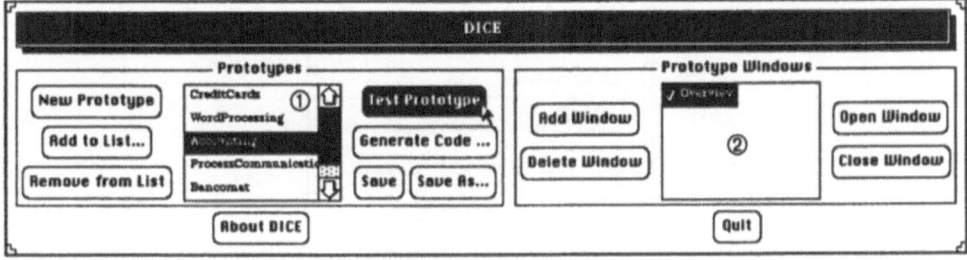

Figure 7.1. DICE's Control Panel

The other action buttons (*Remove from List, Test Prototype, Generate Code, Save,* and *Save As*) are enabled if a prototype is selected in the list of loaded prototypes:

- *Remove from List* removes the selected prototype from the list of loaded prototypes, but does not delete it.

- *Test Prototype* executes the prototype interpretively.

- *Generate Code* generates ET++ subclasses, which means C++ source code.

- *Save* stores the current version of the selected prototype on an external device. The name and location in the hierarchical file system are attributes of the prototype, determined either by a file dialog (see Figure 7.2) which is opened after pushing *Add to List...* or the *Save As...* button.

- *Save As* lets the user store the selected prototype on an external device. The file name is entered by means of a file dialog as depicted in Figure 7.2.

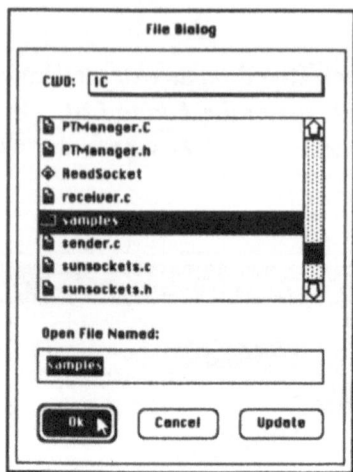

Figure 7.2. File Dialog

If a prototype is selected in the prototype list (① in Figure 7.1), all windows belonging to that prototype are displayed in the window list (②). The prototype *Accounting* (see Figure 7.1), for example, consists of only one window, *Overview*.

A prototype consists of a set of *windows* that are specified using a *window editor*. A window editor allows the developer to edit components of a window (e.g., to insert, move or resize constituent interface elements, to edit the window title, etc.).

For each window displayed in the window list (see ② in Figure 7.1), a checkmark at the left indicates that its corresponding window editor is open. The possibility to close window editors of a particular prototype helps to prevent the user from having a mess of open windows on the screen. Windows can be created, deleted, opened, and closed via the corresponding push buttons (*Add Window, Delete Window, Open Window, and Close Window*) in DICE's control panel (see Figure 7.1).

To insert user interface elements in a prototype's window, one simply chooses the proper element in DICE's User Interface Element Palette (see Figure 7.3) and marks the position where the item is to be placed.

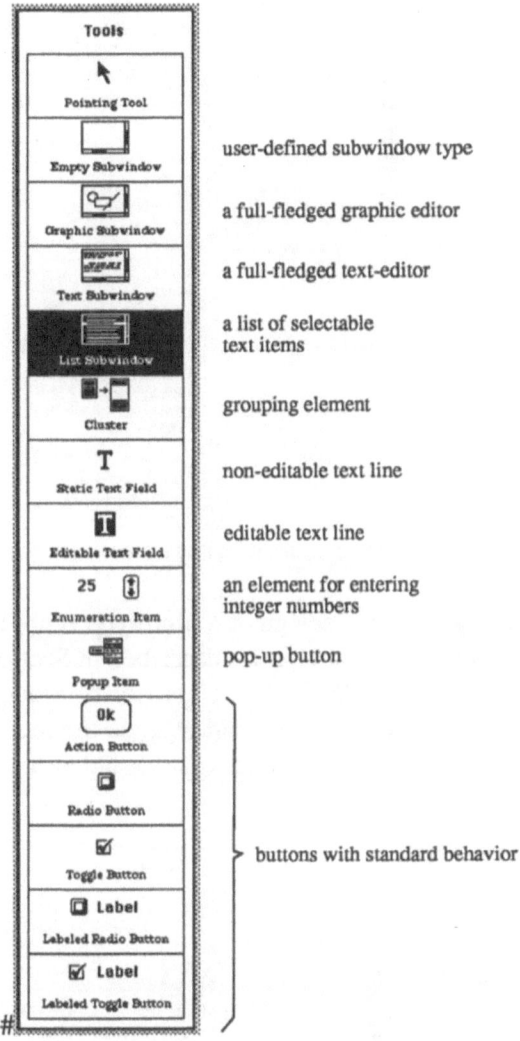

Figure 7.3. DICE's User Interface Element Panel

Attributes can be specified for each user interface element. Figure 7.4 shows an example in the specification of the attributes for the selected *List Subwindow* (see upper left part of Figure 7.4, where the selection is marked with small black squares).

We can specify, for example, the initially displayed text items. (In Figure 7.4 text stored in the file *AccFile* constitutes the initial list items.)

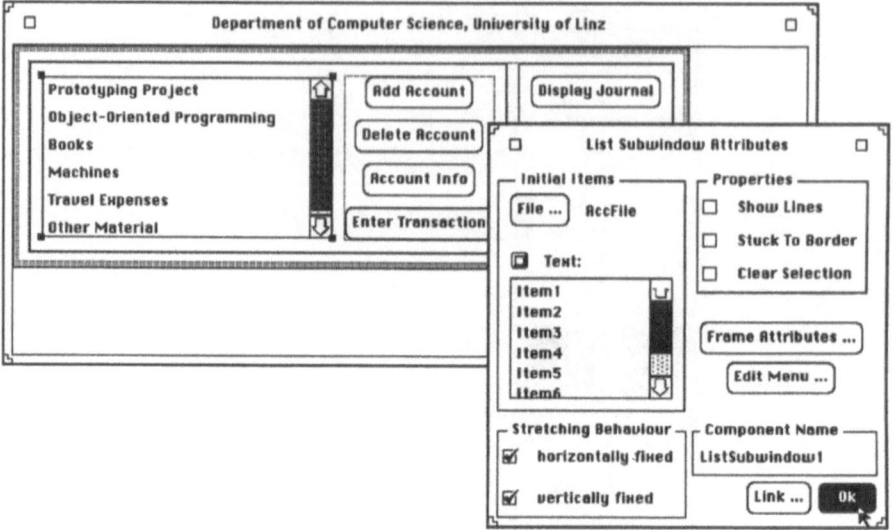

Figure 7.4. Specifying attributes of user interface elements

The most important aspect in the design of a prototype is not the layout of the user interface but its dynamic behavior. As described in Section 7.1, each user interface element created with DICE has a number of predefined messages assigned to it. For example, a window understands the messages *Open* and *Close* and a text field the messages *Enable, Disable* and *SetText(...)*, etc.

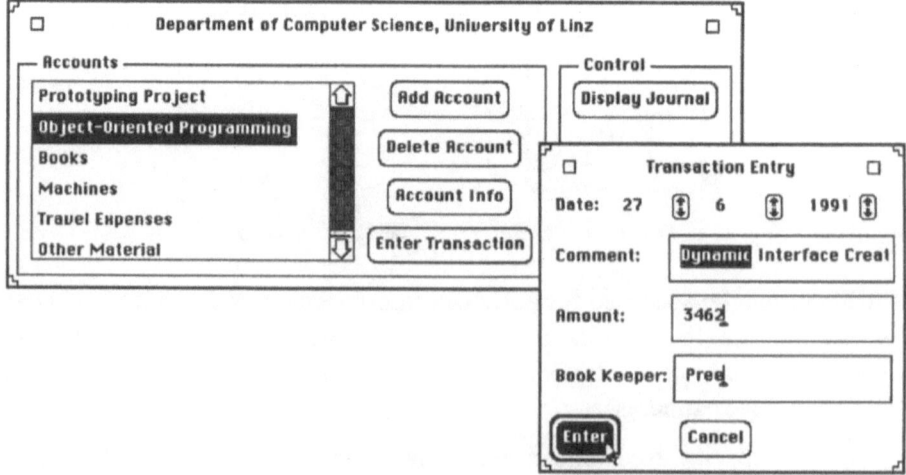

Figure 7.5. Example of a user interface simulated with DICE

Let us consider the interface of the simple account administrator system in Figure 7.5 as an example. Assume that a dialog for entering a transaction (*Transaction Entry* window in Figure 7.5) is to be displayed if the *Enter Transaction* button is activated. In order to specify this dynamic behavior, the *Enter Transaction* button has to be selected to specify its attributes (see Figure 7.6).

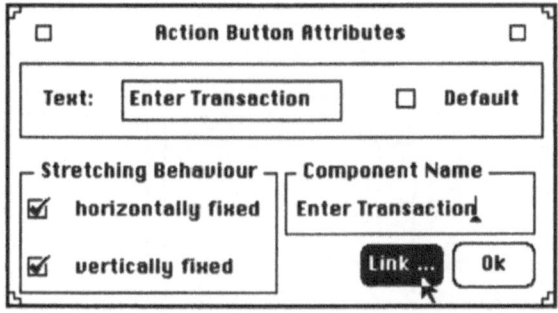

Figure 7.6. Attribute Sheet for the *Enter Transaction* button

Pressing the *Link* button in the Attribute Sheet (see Figure 7.6) causes the invocation of the Message Editor (see Figure 7.7), with which the required dynamic behavior can be specified. We have to determine that the message *Open* is sent to the *Transaction Entry* window if the *Enter Transaction* button is pressed. This is done by selecting the target object (in our case the name of the window, *Transaction Entry*) and the message *Open* among the messages this element understands. All possible messages of a user interface element selected in the target object list are shown in the list *Possible Messages* (see Figure 7.7). In this way we can define any number of (predefined) messages to be sent when an element is activated. Thus important parts of the dynamic behavior of the prototype can be specified without writing a single line of code. The execution of the specified prototype is triggered by pressing the *Test Prototype* button in the Control Panel (see Figure 7.1).

In this way DICE permits the specification and simulation of the static and dynamic behavior of a system. The correspondence of prototype functionality and the user's requirements can be verified by playing realistic examples without programming and without a compile/link/go cycle.

*From the Prototype to the Final Product*

As described in Section 7.1, there are two ways to evolve a user interface prototype created with DICE to a finished application:

- DICE's *source code generation facility* can be employed and the functional parts of the application can be implemented in an object-oriented way by deriving subclasses.

- The *interprocess communication interface* can be used and the functional application parts can be implemented in any programming language (e.g., with SCT, which is described in Chapter 8).

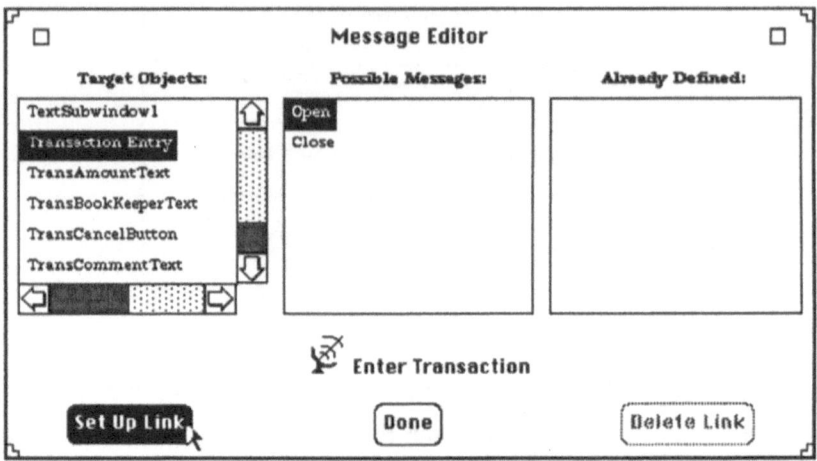

Figure 7.7. DICE's Message Editor

*Using the code generation facility*

Pressing the *Generate Code* button (see Figure 7.1) causes DICE to generate subclasses of the application framework ET++. Compilation of these classes results in a C++ application that is identical to the prototype specified with DICE.

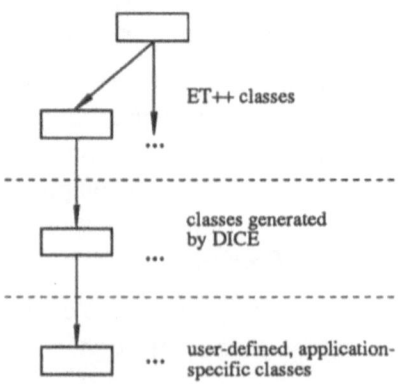

Figure 7.8. Code generation

DICE's code generation concept allows the separation of generated code and user-defined modifications (see Figure 7.8). C++ classes generated from DICE are designed in such a way that additional functionality can be implemented in (user-defined) subclasses of the generated classes by overriding or extending appropriate dynamically bound methods.

Let us consider the account administration prototype (Figure 7.5) as an example. When the *Enter* button in the window titled *Transaction Entry* is pressed, a check of the correctness of the entered amount should be done before storing the transaction in a database. This functionality cannot be provided by DICE's prototyping facilities. Therefore we need to add special code in order to implement this behavior.

DICE uses the component names of user interface elements in the generated code. Component names can be defined for each user interface element in the corresponding attribute sheet (e.g., Figure 7.6). We assume that the button labeled *Enter* (see Figure 7.5) has the component name *EnterTransButton*.

DICE generates the class *Transaction_Entry*. (The name is identical with the title of the prototype window for which code is generated; blanks are replaced by underscores.) DICE reuses behavior implemented in the ET++ class *Document* by generating *Transaction_Entry* as a subclass of it. *Document*, for example, manages a window where the appropriate contents are displayed. Furthermore, the ET++ class *Document* has a dynamically bound method *Control* which is called each time a user interface element is activated inside a window associated with a *Document* object. Thus the method *Control* is used in the generated code to implement the behavior of user interface elements specified by means of predefined messages. (Let us assume that we specified by means of DICE's Message Editor that the window *Transaction Entry* is to be closed if the button labeled *Enter* is pressed.) The code generated by DICE is the following:

```
class Transaction_Entry: public Document {
  ...
  void Control(int itemID) {
      ...
      case EnterTransButton:
          // statements for closing the window
          break; // no further action
          ...
  }
};
```

In order to check the correctness of the amount, we implement a class *ExtTransaction_Entry* (for extended transaction entry). We assume that

*AmountField* is the component name of the text field where the amount is edited in the *Transaction Entry* window (see Figure 7.5).

```
class ExtTransaction_Entry: public Transaction_Entry {
    ...
    void Control(int itemID) {
        ...
        case EnterTransButton:
            int amount= AmountField->GetVal();
            if (AmountOk(amount)) {
                // store transaction in database
                TransactionEntry::Control(id);
                // execute the behavior of the generated
                   class
                // (i.e.  close the window)
            }
            break;
            ...
```

The code fragment presented above is simplified in order to stress the essential idea of adding functionality in subclasses of generated classes. (E.g., a specific function has to be called that returns a pointer to an object with a specific component name.  It is impossible to just write the component name (*AmountField* in the statement *AmountField ->GetVal()*) instead of such a function call).  Furthermore, the names of subclasses (*ExtTransaction_Entry*) that are to be used instead of the originally generated class (*Transaction_Entry*) must be specified so that DICE's Code Generator knows which class is to be used for object generation.

To sum up, this kind of code generation isolates changes in the user interface from coded functionality as far as possible.  For instance, if the user interface layout is changed, code (i.e., ET++ subclasses) must be generated again.  The user-defined classes that have been derived from the classes originally generated are not involved.  Changes in these classes only become necessary if interface elements are renamed or switched between windows of the prototype.

*Using the interprocess communication interface*

Functional application parts of a DICE prototype can be implemented in any formalism and communicate with the user interface prototype specified with DICE by means of a simple protocol that is described below.  The integration requires *no code generation* and thus no compile-link-go cycles.  An arbitrary number of components implemented in various formalisms can be connected with a user interface prototype that is specified and tested within DICE.

Since DICE is implemented on UNIX systems, the *socket mechanism* is used for interprocess communication of independent processes (see Figure 7.9).  The interface specified with DICE and the process(es) interacting with the interface form a User Interface Management System with mixed control [Hay85], [Bet87]. This means that an application's "work" is accomplished by various loosely coupled parts of a software system. A DICE user interface prototype consists of all visible parts of the user interface and maybe some basic functionality specified by means of predefined messages. Other functionality may be implemented in functional application parts which are coupled with the user interface by a simple protocol.

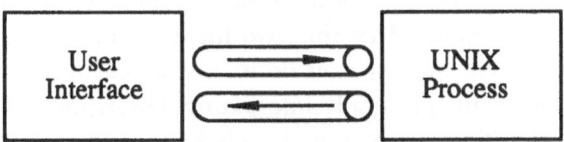

Figure 7.9. Connection between a user interface prototype and an arbitrary process

We illustrate this protocol as far as is necessary to understand DICE's interprocess communication concept:

*User Interface Prototype -> Connected Process*: If a user interface element of a prototype is activated in DICE's test mode (activatable user interface elements being all kinds of *buttons, Enumeration Items, text items* in a *List Subwindow*, and *menu items*), an element identifier and its associated value are sent to the connected process(es) in the following format: identifier=value. The identifier is usually the component name of the activated element. If a menu item is selected, the identifier is the component name of the user interface element the menu is part of (either a *Pop-up Item*, a *Text Subwindow*, or a *List Subwindow*) concatenated with a period (".") and the text of the selected menu item. If a text item in a *List Subwindow* is selected, the identifier consists of the component name of the *List Subwindow* concatenated with a period and the text of of the selected text item.

Activated *Action Buttons*, menu items, and text items in *List Subwindows* always send TRUE as their value. The value of an *Enumeration Item* is its current integer value; (Labeled) *Radio Buttons* and *Toggle Buttons* send either TRUE or FALSE as value (depending on their state).

*Connected Process -> User Interface Prototype*: A connected process can ask for the value of an interface element by sending identifier? to the user interface prototype. If a user interface element exists that matches identifier, it "answers" as if it had been activated using the format described above. The values of a user interface element can be changed from the connected process by sending identifier=value to it. This allows some special changes in the user interface, too: windows, for example, can be opened or closed using the value OPEN or CLOSE. A *List Subwindow* accepts EMPTY as value (to make the list empty). A text string sent to a *List Subwindow* as value means that this text is to be appended as a list item in the corresponding *List Subwindow*.

The communications protocol is the precondition that a user interface developed with DICE can be connected with any conventional or object-oriented software system.

Let us consider the interface of the simple account administrator system in Figure 7.5 as an example. This time we illustrate how a check of the correctness of the entered amount can be implemented in Modula-2. Due to DICE's communication protocol, integrating DICE and SCT is straightforward. When the "Enter" button in the window entitled "Transaction Entry" is pressed (Figure 7.5), the user interface prototype sends "Enter = TRUE" (assuming that the component name of the button is "Enter"). SCT provides a module named *DICEInterface* for UNIX process intercommunication; this module serves to open the connection and to handle data sent by DICE. Thus the Modula-2 code implemented with SCT takes the following form:

```
MODULE Accounting;
    FROM DICEInterface IMPORT        OpenConnectionToDICE,
    ...
    WaitForMessageFromDICE, SendMessageToDICE,
    ...;
    ...

    PROCEDURE CommunicateWithDICE();
    VAR
        identifier: ARRAY[0..max NameLen] OF CHAR;
        value:..........
        amount: REAL;
    BEGIN
        REPEAT
            WaitForMessageFromDICE(identifier,value);
            IF (StrEqual(identifier, "Enter") AND
                StrEqual (value, "TRUE") ) THEN
                Send MessageToDICE("Amount?"); (* supposed that a text
                    field that displays the amount is named "Amount" *)
                WaitForMessageFromDice(identifier,value);
                IF AmountOk(ConvertStringToReal(value)) THEN
                    ...........
                END;
            ELSIF
                ...........
            END;
        UNTIL (StrEqual(identifier,"Quit") AND
               StrEqual(value,"TRUE"));
    END CommunicateWithDICE;
    ...........
    BEGIN (*module body *)
```

```
    . . . . . . . . . . .
    IF (OpenConnectionToDICE()=0) THEN
        CommunicateWithDICE();
    . . . . . . . . . . . .
    END;
END Accounting.
```

DICE fulfills all the requirements placed on modern prototyping tools and supports *exploratory* and *evolutionary prototyping*. Not only the efficiency of the prototyping tool itself but also the efficiency and quality of the resultant prototype and the generated application are substantial. We have applied DICE in various medium-sized projects with very good results. Because of its object-oriented implementation, DICE can easily be extended and adapted to specialized requirements. The addition of new user interface elements and new methods for existing user interface elements is no problem.

# 8 The TOPOS Exploratory Programming Environment

While we consider a good programming environment an important factor for the success of a conventional software development project, it is of utmost importance during exploratory programming. For this reason much effort went into the development of the System Construction Tool (SCT), TOPOS's exploratory programming environment.

The goal in designing SCT was to take the best concepts and features of existing programming environments, to integrate them in an innovative way, and to improve them by developing new complementary concepts. There are two areas where this approach was especially successful.

First, SCT provides different execution mechanisms for program components in different states of development. This makes it possible to provide excellent browsing facilities, short turnaround times, and fast execution. Furthermore, the introduction of simulation as an execution mode makes it possible to combine exploratory programming with exploratory design.

Second, SCT supports programming in Modula-2[1], an excellent module-based programming language with strong type checking. This is remarkable because programming environments suitable for exploratory programming usually support development in interpretive programming languages without strong type checking, such as Smalltalk or Lisp. SCT therefore combines the advantages of known exploratory programming environments with the advantages of strong type checking and language support for modular design.

This chapter starts with a discussion of the concepts underlying SCT (Section 8.1). Section 8.2 gives an overview of the architecture of SCT. The

---

[1] The development of a second version of SCT, which supports object-oriented design and implementation in C++, is currently underway.

next four sections present the underlying concepts of each component of SCT
and how each component can be applied.

## 8.1  Concepts Underlying SCT

A central aspect of every programming environment is its underlying *exe-cution mechanism*. This is because the execution mechanism determines,
among other things, execution efficiency, the quality of information about
static and dynamic application aspects that can be provided, the efficiency of
resource allocation, and turnaround times.

In developing an exploratory programming environment that supports the
development of large software systems, all these aspects have to be consid-ered during the selection of an execution mechanism. In order to justify the
decisions that were made in the selection of SCT's execution mechanism, the
tradeoffs of interpretation and compilation (followed by direct execution) are
briefly outlined below.

Interpretation makes it possible to achieve very short turnaround times
because it makes the compile-link-go cycle obsolete. The tradeoff for this
short turnaround time is a loss in execution speed and an increased main
memory requirement (due to the fact that a lot of information about the
software system to be executed has to be held in main memory). It therefore
makes sense to use interpretation as the execution mode for an exploratory
programming environment as long as the requirements for execution speed
can be met and as long as the size of the software systems to be developed
does not exceed the limit imposed by the available main memory.

Compared with interpretation, compilation and subsequent direct exe-cution of object code results in longer turnaround times, faster execution
speed, and reduced run-time memory requirements. A drawback of a com-pilative approach is that, besides the object code, a lot of meta-information—information about the program under development—has to be kept in main
memory in order to build a comfortable programming environment.

Conventional compilative programming environments store the meta-information on files and load it on demand. This approach yields good results
if meta-information is only used for debugging purposes. Compilative pro-gramming environments that provide good browsing and cross-reference in-formation have to hold the whole meta-information in main memory, the
same way as interpretive environments do. The problem with this approach is
that the storage requirements for the development of large software systems
become immense. ObjectWorks for C++ [Par90] and Saber C++ [Sab90], for

example, are not able to manage an application framework such as ET++ (about 120,000 line of code) in 32 megabytes of RAM and still provide a reasonable interactive responsiveness.

SCT achieves a better mix of turnaround times, execution speed, and main memory requirements than programming environments relying on pure interpretation or compilation. This is achieved by providing different execution modes for components in different stages of development. We call this approach *hybrid execution.*

Hybrid execution permits a developer to selectively balance the advantages and disadvantages of interpretation and compilation by explicitly selecting the execution mode for every module. An adequate way to apply SCT is to interpret modules that are currently under implementation and to compile and directly execute modules that are already implemented and tested. The results of this approach are:

- good turnaround times because modules under development are interpreted

- fast execution speed because all implemented and tested application parts are directly executed

- a moderate main memory requirement because the complete meta-information is only held for interpreted modules, while meta-information for directly executed subsystems can be loaded on demand

Hybrid execution is especially suited for module-oriented languages because modules are well-isolated building blocks of a reasonable size. This makes it easy for a developer to identify logical subsystems to be interpreted or directly executed. SCT is not the only programming environment supporting hybrid execution. A widely know system is Saber C++, which was mentioned above.

Besides interpretation and direct execution, which were selected for practicability reasons, SCT provides a further execution mechanism for conceptual reasons. This execution mechanism is *simulation.* The motive for the introduction of simulation is that simulation makes it possible to execute software systems consisting of application parts that have been, designed but for which implementation has not yet started. This kind of simulation allows a developer to *validate* a system architecture in a prototyping-oriented way before it has to be implemented.

A simulative approach becomes especially interesting if it is possible to avoid manual simulation of the whole application under development. In an ideal scenario available high-level and functional application parts are in effect executed, while only the newly designed application parts have to be simulated. SCT makes this scenario possible, first, by providing its *hybrid execution mechanism*, which is able to simulate, interpret, or directly execute Modula-2 code, and second, by providing an interface which makes it possible to integrate high-level execution tools into SCT's hybrid execution mechanism. (The integration of other execution mechanisms is discussed in Chapter 9.)

The practical relevance of a simulative approach depends very much on the effort needed to simulate a software system. One mechanism SCT provides to keep this effort small is its hybrid execution system, which was discussed above. The other mechanism is the recording, visualization, and replay of simulations. The obvious advantage of recording simulations is that complex simulations can be quickly carried out again after the application under development was modified. Besides this obvious application, recorded simulations can be used for several other purposes. They can, e.g., be used as complementary specifications for the implementation of modules, as test beds for newly implemented application parts, and as documentation during maintenance. These aspects as well as how a simulation is carried out are discussed in Section 8.6.

## 8.2 The Architecture of the Exploratory Programming Environment

The intent of this section is to give the reader a brief overview of the architecture of SCT. In order to achieve this, two different views have to be discussed. They are the view a developer has when applying SCT (the user interface), and the structure of the internal building blocks (the technical view). Figure 8.1 illustrates both of them.

From the user's point of view, SCT consists of five closely integrated tools. One of them, the Component Management Tool (CMT) is, technically speaking, a tool on its own. It was described in Chapter 6 and will not be further discussed in this chapter. For this reason its connection to the other tools is represented by a dotted line in Figure 8.1.

The other four tools discussed in this chapter are:

- the Browser, for static and dynamic information about the software system under development

- the Implementor, a combined program editor and a run-time monitoring tool

- the Simulator, which permits a developer to simulate Modula-2 modules

- the Workspace Manager, which makes it possible to keep volatile run-time data between test runs

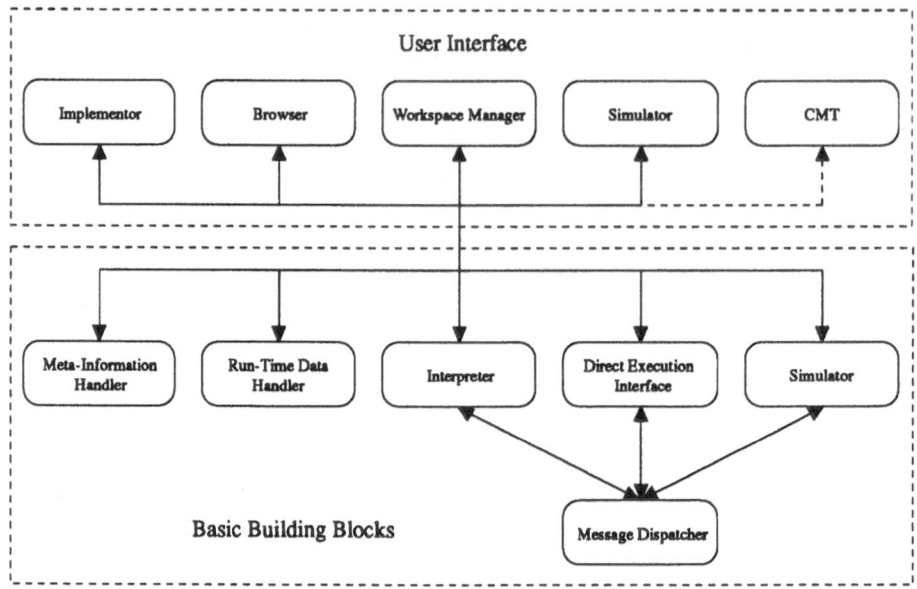

Figure 8.1. Architecture of SCT

The internal structure of SCT does not directly correspond to the tool structure a developer sees at the user interface level because different building blocks of SCT cooperate to effectively provide the services offered by the single tools.

On a high abstraction level the architecture of SCT consists of five parts besides the user interface. Two of them manage information about the software system under development and three of them serve to execute it.

The *data managers* are the *Meta-Information Handler*, which manages all information about the static aspects (the symbol tables and the parse trees) and the *Run-time Data Handler*, which manages the run-time data of the application under development as well as data that are made persistent by copying it into a workspace.

The three execution tools are the *Interpreter*, the *Simulator*, and the *Direct Execution Interface*, which handles all aspects of integrating object code into the hybrid execution process. They communicate via the *Message Dispatcher*, which also provides an interface to integrate other execution tools such as DICE into SCT's hybrid execution system. Because of its important role in tool integration, the Message Dispatcher is not considered to be part of SCT, but to be a building block of TOPOS (see Figures 8.1 and 5.3). The Message

Dispatcher is described in Chapter 9, which is entirely dedicated to the tool integration topic.

Because the user interface and the execution tools rely heavily on the information provided by the Meta-Information Handler and the Run-time Data Handler, all building blocks of SCT are closely integrated into one tool. From our point of view, this is a good organization for the closely cooperating kernel of a development environment. A separation into several tools running in different processes, in a way similar to the Fields environment ([Rei90a], [Rei90b]) would result in a flood of messages exchanged via interprocess communication without any obvious positive effects. The approach of integrating the various tools via a common relational data base would have even worse effects on SCT, because the interactive responsiveness—the most important feature of an exploratory programming environment—would be heavily reduced. This approach was taken in developing the Cadillac environment ([Gab90a], [Gab90b]), where more emphasis was laid on the support of concurrent updating of various application parts than on interactive responsiveness.

The purpose of this presentation of SCT is to describe the features of an advanced exploratory design and programming environment. For this reason the rest of this chapter is structured according to the four tools a developer sees at the user interface level, rather than according to the basic building blocks of SCT. One section is dedicated to each tool, its underlying concepts, and its application.

## 8.3  Implementor

The *Implementor* serves to edit Modula-2 modules, to check their syntactic correctness, to control their interpretive execution, and to invoke Browsers which provide information about static and dynamic system aspects.

This section starts by explaining the concepts underlying the Implementor that have an influence on how software is developed with SCT. Afterwards the Implementor's user interface is presented in order to show how the tool is used.

### 8.3.1  Concepts Underlying the Implementor

Every interpretive programming environment needs information about the software system under development in order to provide this information to the user and to execute the software system. Because it would take too much time to extract the information from the source code every time it is needed, it is usually extracted once and stored in RAM in the form of dynamic data structures called parse trees and symbol tables (see [Aho86]).

While the basic concepts used are very similar in most modern interpretive programming environments, they diverge in the following points:

- the amount of extracted data and run-time data which is stored permanently when a session is terminated

- the strategy which is applied when information has to be extracted again after a change was applied to the source code

- the optimization strategies applied to the parse trees

Two different approaches can be taken in storing extracted data and run-time data when a session is terminated. The first one is to write all data managed (source code, extracted data, and run-time data) into a file (image). The second approach is to store nothing but the configuration data describing the current project and to reextract all information at the start of the next session.

The advantage of the first approach is that it is possible to restart work in exactly the same environment in which the application was left. The disadvantage is that large amounts of disk space are needed, especially if different images are kept as backups. Furthermore, it becomes difficult to work in teams because libraries and common project documents cannot be shared, but have to be duplicated for every project member. This approach was taken in developing Smalltalk-80 and many interpretive programming environments for languages such as Lisp and Prolog.

SCT is intended to support exploratory programming as well as incremental development of large software systems. For this reason the image concept was rejected. Furthermore, it is no problem to reextract the information needed from the source code at start-up time because SCT's extraction tool analyzes up to 60,000 lines of code per minute and it does not take much more time to reextract the data than to load it from an image.

There are various strategies for reextracting information after the source code was changed. They range from incremental analysis on the statement level (i.e., every statement is analyzed after it is typed) to reanalyzing whole input files.

Incremental analysis was a concept realized frequently in research projects at the end of the 70s together with language-oriented editing tools. It was not very successful because its implementation frequently results in a rigid editing environment and contributes a lot to the complexity of a tool supporting it (e.g., [Pro84]).

Reanalyzing the whole input files, on the other hand, is usually slower and makes it difficult for the development system to find out if the run-time data of the currently active execution was outdated by a change in the source code.

SCT analyses source code on the module level and requires a developer to abort an execution if data definitions were changed. This decision was taken for two reasons. The first reason is that the analysis of entire Modula-2 modules makes it possible to apply simple, straightforward algorithms that are very fast because of their simplicity. In the case of SCT, a developer would not observe any difference in speed between in incremental solution and the analysis on the module level. The second reason is that a developer is usually able to decide without any problems if any changes were made to data definitions which could result in outdating the active run-time data. The developer would be more encumbered by using rigid syntax-oriented editing as a tradeoff for not having to decide whether an execution can continue.

In order to speed up interpretive execution, various optimizations are applied to the parse trees that are built during analysis. The optimizations implemented in different programming environments range from no optimization at all to transformation into intermediate code (e.g. Pascal P-code), and on to compilation into object code.

At the end of the Eighties there was a strong trend toward compilation even in environments which present themselves as interpretive (e.g., Object-Works for Smalltalk [Par89a]).

In realizing SCT, the solution without any optimization was chosen because this makes it possible to achieve a comfortable programming environment with a reasonable amount of implementation effort. SCT's parse trees and symbol tables therefore represent a one-to-one mapping of the source code into a format that is easier to manipulate. The loss of execution speed does not affect SCT's usefulness because most of the very time consuming application parts such as the user interface are usually executed directly or even by other execution tools.

One aspect not discussed until now is that SCT does not have to analyze the whole software system it is going to execute. Only interpretable modules have to be completely analyzed. For simulable and directly executable modules, only the interface has to be analyzed. In order to use the browsing tools on directly executable modules, their implementation parts have to be analyzed, too. SCT allows the user to decide to what extent the software system should be analyzed, allowing a choice between very short turnaround times and more information for browsing.

## 8.3.2   Application of the Implementor

An Implementor serves to edit and browse one module and to launch the execution of software systems which have this module as their root. Any number of Implementors may be active. The only restriction is that only one Implementor can be used at a time to start an execution. Implementors are created in the Component Management Tool by pressing the *Edit* or *Execute* buttons (see Section 6.2) or during browsing in a Browser (see next section). Figure 8.2 shows the user interface of an Implementor. It consists of a line of push buttons serving to control analysis, execution and debugging and a comfortable text editor. Besides editing, which is done in a WYSIWYG editor and is not discussed further, an Implementor can be used for analyzing and executing modules, as well as for execution monitoring and debugging, which are often used during exploratory programming.

*Analysis and Execution*

Modules are analyzed for three reasons:  to check their syntactical correctness, to extract data which can be used for browsing them, and to prepare them for execution.

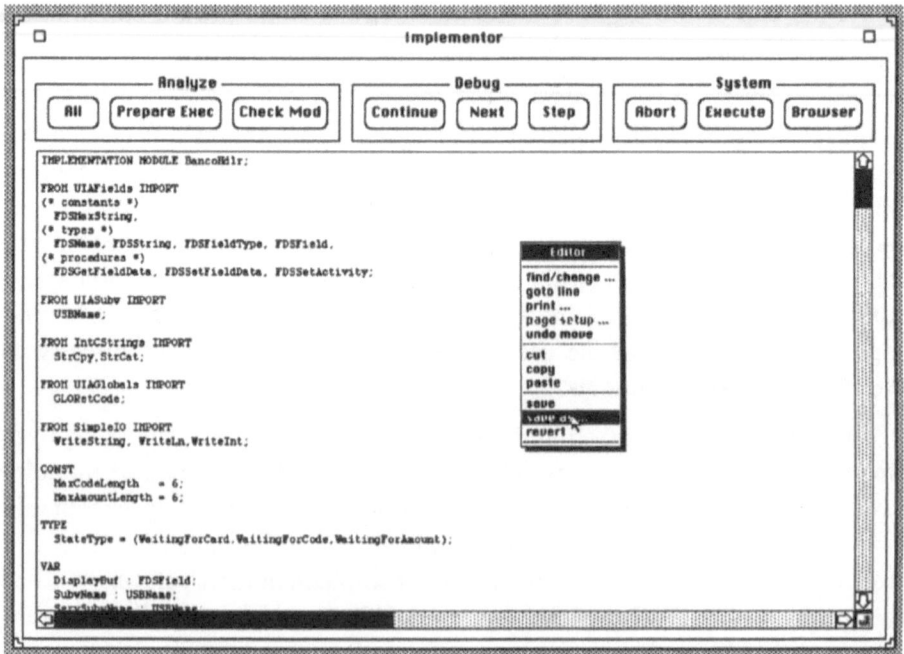

Figure 8.2.  Overview of an Implementor's user interface

Because of the explicit imports required in Modula-2, the analyzer can determine in which order the various modules of a software system have to be analyzed. A developer can select among three analysis functions, which can be triggered by pressing the buttons depicted in Figure 8.3.

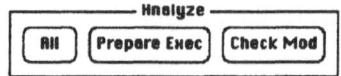

Figure 8.3. Buttons for management of the analysis process

- When the *Check Mod* button is pressed, the syntactic correctness of the current module is checked, which means that, besides the current module, only the definition modules from which something is imported are analyzed (only if they were not analyzed before).

- When the *Prepare Exec* button is pressed, the implementation parts of all interpretable modules from which something is imported are analyzed, enabling the execution of the current module.

- When the *All* button is pressed, the most extensive analysis process is carried out because all modules are analyzed to prepare them for browsing.

*Starting and Ending an Execution Process*

When the *Execute* button (see Figure 8.4) is pressed, the execution of the body of the displayed module is triggered. This feature completely blurs the difference between main and regular modules in the sense of Modula-2. The only remaining difference is that main modules cannot export anything. Before the execution is effectively started, the Implementor tests whether all modules needed for the execution have already been analyzed. If this is not the case, the analysis of the respective modules is triggered.

Pressing the *Abort* button aborts the current execution. The *Browser* button serves to invoke a Browser tool, which is described in the next section.

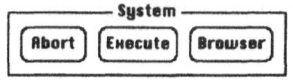

Figure 8.4. Buttons for starting and ending an execution process and for invoking a Browser

*Execution Monitoring*

There are various events after which the current execution is stopped: when a breakpoint in the source code is encountered, when a run-time exception is found, when the operating systems sends an interrupt, or when the developer sends an interrupt from the keyboard. In all these cases the current statement is displayed and highlighted in the editor of the corresponding implementor.

Once the execution is stopped, the run-time data can be browsed and edited as described in the next section, and changes can be applied to the source code. During these activities, execution can be resumed anytime by using one of the three buttons displayed in Figure 8.5.

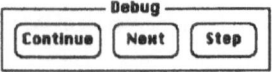

Figure 8.5. Buttons for controlling the execution process

By pressing the *Next* button, a developer triggers the execution of the next statement only. (If this statement is a procedure call, the execution of the whole procedure is considered to be one statement and the procedure is executed as a whole.) Pressing the *Step* button has almost the same effect as pressing the *Next* button. The only difference is that, in the case when the statement to be executed is a procedure call, execution stops before the first statement in the procedure to be called, making it possible to monitor the invoked procedure. After the *Continue* button is pressed, the execution is continued until a new breakpoint is encountered or until an exception arises.

## 8.4  Browser

This section describes the Browser, SCT's tool for browsing various aspects of the software system under development, for studying the current state of execution, and for editing the run-time data extracted during the analysis process described in the previous section.

The section starts with a discussion of the decisions which were made in implementing the Browser and which distinguish it from the browsers provided by the Smalltalk-80 environment. This discussion of basic concepts is followed by a description of how a browser can be applied.

### 8.4.1  Concepts Underlying the Browser

Tools for browsing software systems based on information extracted from the source code usually provide the possibility to get information about the static structure of a software system, to study the current state of execution, and to edit run-time data.

What kind of information is provided depends mostly on the supported programming language. Due to the similarities among existing programming languages, the kinds of information provided by various tools is quite similar. Most tools which are state of the art differ only in the comfort with which they allow a developer to extract the needed information.

Because of these similarities among tools, this subsection discusses only two aspects which distinguish the Browser from the Smalltalk-80 browsers described in Section 3.2 and which have a strong influence on the way the Browser is used.

The first aspect is how information can be refined and how reference data are displayed. Some environments always display refinement and reference information in new windows. The weak point of this approach is that during the inspection of complex data structures and long reference data chains, tens of windows are opened, which completely clutters the screen. For this reason it is almost impossible to examine various levels of refinement because the windows opened earlier during the browsing process can usually not be found anymore. In order to avoid this problem, the Browser makes a context switch, stacks the old level of refinement, and displays the new one in the same window. New windows are only created on request if the developer really wants to study different refinement levels at the same time.

The second aspect is how run-time data can be edited. Smalltalk-80 provides the possibility to type a Smalltalk expression, evaluate it, and assign it to a global or instance variable. In the Browser primitive data types are edited by selecting them and typing the new value. The Smalltalk-80 approach certainly has its advantages in an object-oriented environment because the typed expressions are used to create objects, which requires the determination of the constructor to be used. Editing of variables which does not involve the creation of objects, on the other hand, can be carried out much more comfortably by direct manipulation than by typing programming language statements.

### 8.4.2  Application of the Browser

A Browser as depicted in Figure 8.6 consists of two push buttons that serve to select the kind of data to be browsed, a text line that indicates what kind of data item is currently displayed on which refinement level, and a scrollable list of data items. Data items can represent constants, types, variables, procedures, or modules. Every data item consists of three descriptors: the name of the data item , the type of the data item, and *refinable* if the data object can be refined, or a possible run-time value.

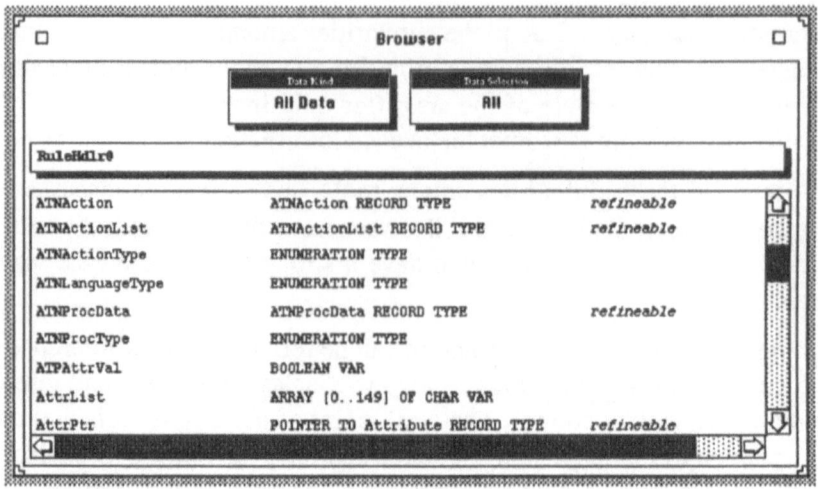

Figure 8.6. User interface of a Browser displaying the global data definitions of module *RuleHdlr*

*Browsing Commands*

Every Browser understands the following basic browsing commands independently of which kind of data items it currently displays. (The commands can be selected in the menu that pops up when the menu button of the mouse is pressed.)

- *Show Code.* This command can be used to display the source code which contains the currently selected data item in the corresponding Implementor.

- *Spawn.* This command results in the cloning of the current Browser. It is used if various refinement levels have to be studied at the same time.

- *Refine.* This command can be used to refine data items marked with the refinable flag. What kind of data is displayed after the triggered context switch depends on the currently selected data item. A double click on a refinable data item has the same effect.

- *One Level Up.* This command results in a context switch by undoing the last context switch and displaying the next higher refinement level.

- *Top Level.* This command results in a context switch by undoing all stacked context switches.

- *Importers.* This command results in a context switch and displays a list of all modules importing something from the current module.

- *Imported.* This command results in a context switch and displays a list of all modules imported by the current module (e.g., Figure 8.12).

- *Sort by Mod Names.* This command prefixes all identifier names with the name of the module in which they are defined and sorts them accordingly.

- *Sort by Ident Names.* This command undoes the effect of the *Sort by Mod Names* command.

*Selecting the Kind of Data to be Browsed*

By pressing on the two push buttons located along the top of each Browser, it is possible to select the kind of data to be displayed in the menu that pops up. This is always possible except when reference lists of imported or importing modules are displayed. The two menus which serve to make the selection are displayed in Figure 8.7.

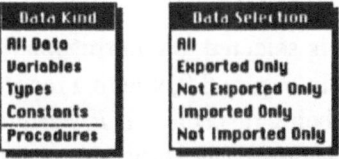

Figure 8.7.  Menus for selecting the kind of information to be browsed

*Browsing Data Definitions*

Data definitions are browsed using the general browsing commands described above. Figure 8.8 shows an example, a Browser displaying the refined data definition of a record type. The current state (context) was reached by first refining *AttrPtr* (a variable or type pointing to a record) and afterwards refining the *Object* field (a pointer to the record type whose fields are currently displayed).

*Browsing Run-Time Data*

In order to browse the currently active run-time data during an execution break, a Browser offers the possibility to edit and browse the global data and the procedure call chain. Which kind of run-time data are to be displayed can be selected in the menu that pops up when the *Data Kind* (Figure 8.7) button is pressed.

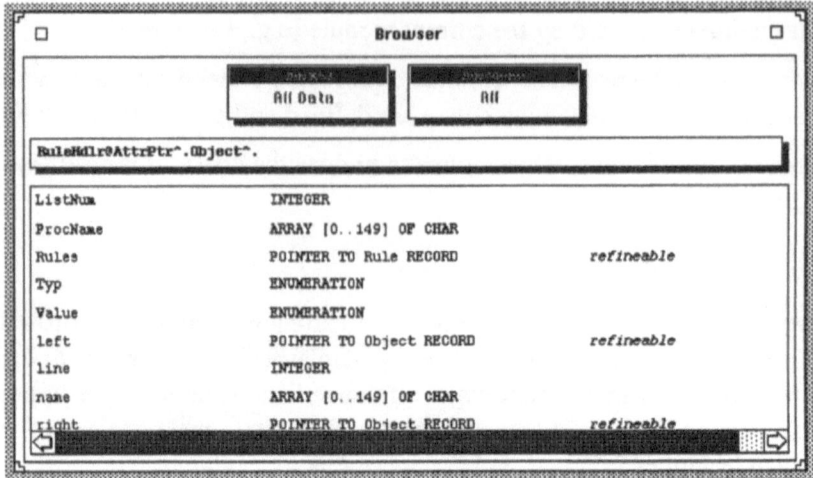

Figure 8.8. Browsing the refined type definition of *Object* defined in module *RuleHdlr*

If *All Data* or *Variables* is selected, the corresponding global run-time data are displayed as depicted in Figure 8.9, where a record (on the fourth level) of a binary tree is currently being inspected. If *Procedures* is selected, the list of the currently active procedures (the procedure call chain) is displayed as depicted in Figure 8.10.

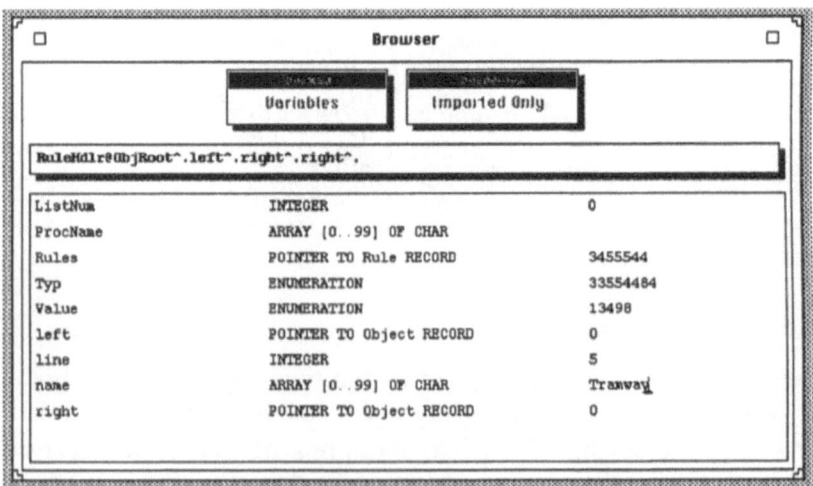

Figure 8.9. Refined global run-time data

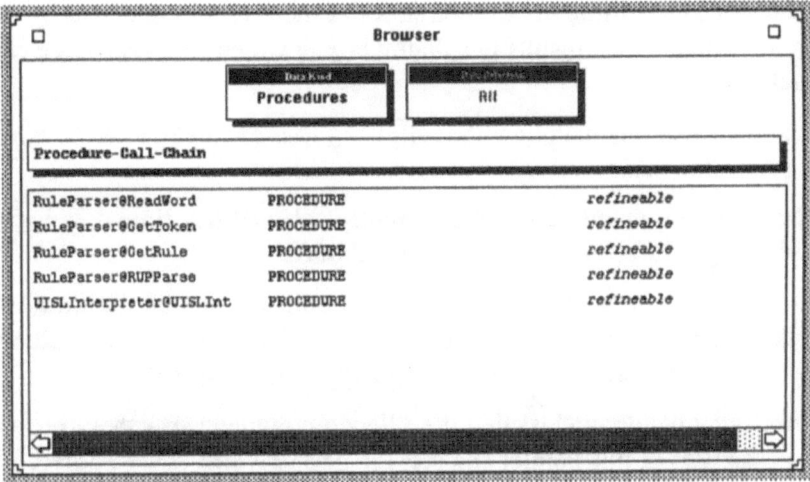

Figure 8.10.  Procedure call chain

When an active procedure in the procedure call chain is refined, the currently executed statement in this procedure instance is highlighted in the corresponding Implementor and a list of its local data (see Figure 8.11) is displayed.

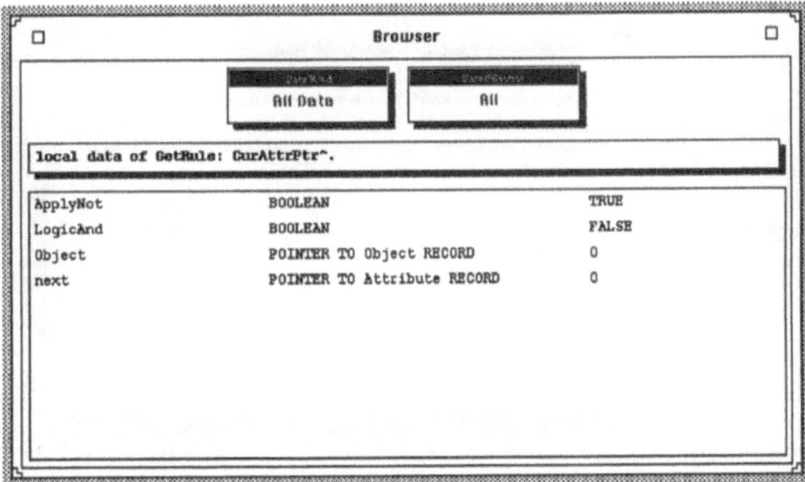

Figure 8.11.  Presentation of the current state of execution of an active procedure

*Editing Run-Time Data*

The Browser allows a developer to edit run-time data by direct manipulation, i.e., by selecting the value to be changed and by typing the new value.  Three

Modula-2 constructs—booleans, sets and enumerations—are handled in a more comfortable editing mode. Variables of these types are edited by clicking on the value, which results in a dialog box in which a correct value can be selected.

Besides direct manipulation, the following four commands can be used for editing run-time data:

- The *Copy* command copies the currently selected run-time data together with its type information into an internal buffer.

- The *Paste* command checks the type compatibility of the data in the buffer with the selected run-time data and replaces the selected value with the value from the internal buffer if the types are compatible.

- Selecting a pointer and issuing the *Allocate* command allocates a record of the base type of this pointer and sets the pointer value to the address of the created record. This mechanism therefore makes it possible to build dynamic data structures manually.

- The *Discard* command sets the value of the selected pointer variable to NIL.

### Browsing Module Dependencies

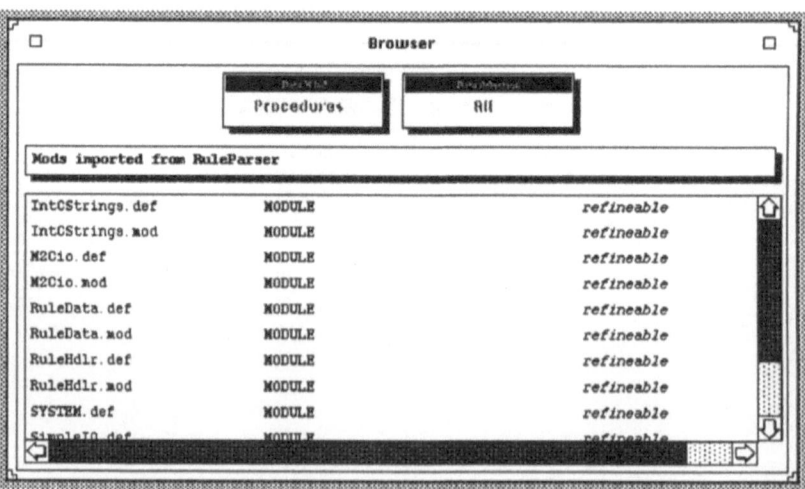

Figure 8.12. List of the modules imported by module RuleParser

Module dependencies are browsed using the *Importers* and *Imported* commands. The result of either command is a module list as depicted in Figure 8.12. Refining a module of such a list results in a context switch, after which the global data of the corresponding module is displayed in a list. By switching between the *Importers*, *Imported*, and *Refine* commands, it is therefore possible to follow whole import-export dependency chains.


# 8.5  Workspace Manager

This section describes the *Workspace Manager*, a tool for the management of persistent data structures. While the functionality it provides is similar to the functionality of the Browser, it is described in a separate section because a developer sees it as an autonomous tool which can only be invoked from the Component Management System.


## 8.5.1  Concepts Underlying the Workspace Manager

Interpretive programming environments for languages such as Smalltalk, Lisp, Prolog and APL usually provide a workspace. This means that they manage a pool of storage where all persistent global data are stored. This is an extremely useful feature for a developer applying exploratory programming and prototyping because it permits the execution of fragments of a software system, to browse and edit their output, and to use the output parameters as input for another application part. It is usually possible to store the whole workspace in the form of an image file at the end of a session and to restart a new session exactly in the same state in which the last one was terminated.

While the workspace concept is very useful for exploratory programming, it is not inherently suited for realization in a programming environment for Modula-2. This is because the module concept of Modula-2 results in a separation of the global data of the modules comprising an application. Furthermore, Modula-2 applications are closed systems which are not planned to receive input parameters and to return persistent output parameters.

SCT makes it possible to execute parts of an application, to provide them with input parameters, and to inspect the output parameters. (How this is done will be explained in the next subsection.) Furthermore, it is possible to edit complex data structures during a break of an active execution and to manipulate complex data structures with the *Copy, Paste, Allocate* and *Discard* commands, as described in the previous Section. In such an environment it would be useful to have some kind of a workspace into which data structures can be stored (pasted) if the developer is interested in keeping them after the current execution is terminated.

Most interpretive programming environments provide only one global workspace where all global data are stored. This is all a developer needs if he uses the workspace to store output parameters of application parts for later use. Besides one global workspace, SCT also provides one workspace for every simulated module. These workspaces are used to simulate the global data of the corresponding modules, and they can be accessed from the simulator as described in the next section.

### 8.5.2   Application of the Workspace Manager

The Workspace Manager and the Browser are very similar tools. The difference is that the Workspace Manager provides only the following four commands, which are needed for the management of data items:

- The *Cut* command serves to delete the selected data item and stores it (value and type information) in the buffer.

- The *Copy* command copies the selected data item (value and type information) into the buffer.

- The *Paste* command inserts the data item stored in the internal buffer into the list of data items. Before the insertion the user is prompted for a name because only value and type information, but no names, are transferred from and to the buffer.

- The *Spawn* command serves to instantiate a Browser for the selected data item.

Several Workspace Managers can be active at a time (a global one and one for every module currently being simulated). They can be distinguished by the text in their headers. The global Workspace Manager (e.g., Figure 8.13) is invoked from the Component Management System and the module-specific Workspace Managers are invoked from the Simulator.

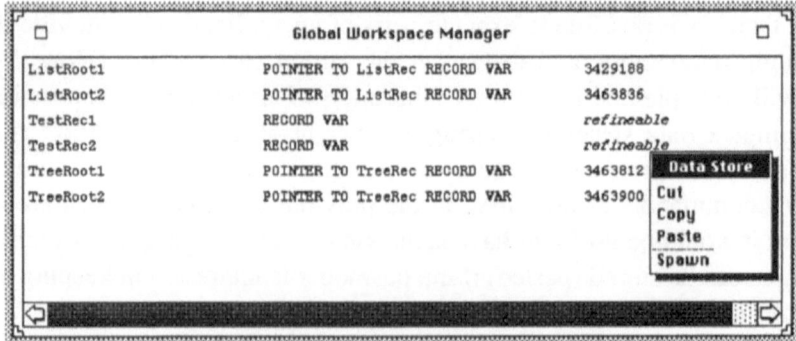

Figure 8.13. Global Workspace Manager

# 8.6 Simulator

The *Simulator* permits a developer to simulate Modula-2 modules that have been designed, but not yet implemented. The most obvious application of simulation is the prototyping-oriented validation of the architecture of a still incomplete software system. Besides prototyping there are a lot of other cases throughout the software life cycle where a simulative approach brings advantages. For example, simulation makes it possible to test newly implemented application parts in the context of a running application that is only partially implemented.

Section 8.6.1 describes what simulation of applications parts (to be) written in Modula-2 means and which activities can be supported by simulation. Section 8.6.2 presents the user interface of SCT's Simulator and explains how it can be put to work. In the following discussions the Simulator is treated as an isolated tool. How it cooperates with SCT's other tools and how it can be applied during a prototyping-oriented software development process will be described in Chapter 10.

## 8.6.1 Concepts Underlying the Simulator

For a developer simulating a software system with SCT means manually executing procedures that have been defined but not implemented, while all existing application parts (e.g., evolutionary prototypes and reusable modules) are really executed. A simulation run is started by triggering an execution which at some point involves the execution of a simulated procedure. This can be done in two ways. Either an entire application is launched or an application part is started by manually calling a procedure, as described in the next subsection.

As soon as an unimplemented procedure is called, the developer automatically obtains control in the Simulator, the simulation (manually execution) of this procedure can be carried out. During such a manual execution three tasks can be carried out, as depicted in Figure 8.14.

* Ongoing procedure calls can be triggered by selecting the procedure to be called, by setting its input parameters, and by dispatching the procedure call. If the procedure which is called has to be simulated, the developer obtains control again in order to manually execute it. Otherwise the procedure is executed normally and the developer obtains control again after its return or after another procedure is called which has to be simulated.

- Global data which represents the internal state of a module can be stored and manipulated in a workspace in order to mimic the behavior of hidden data types.

- The simulation of a procedure can be ended by setting its output parameters and by issuing the return command.

All activities related to the current simulation and/or testing activities are collected by the Simulator and visualized in the form of a procedure call tree. At the end of a simulation this information can be saved in a history file, which makes it possible to replay the simulation later.

If a simulation is replayed after changes were applied to the corresponding software architecture, consistency problems can arise. Procedures which were called in the recorded version could have vanished or their parameter list could have been changed. There are different strategies for dealing with such inconsistencies. The Simulator gives a developer the choice between either taking manual control and replaying the inconsistent simulation subtree again or discarding the inconsistent subtree.

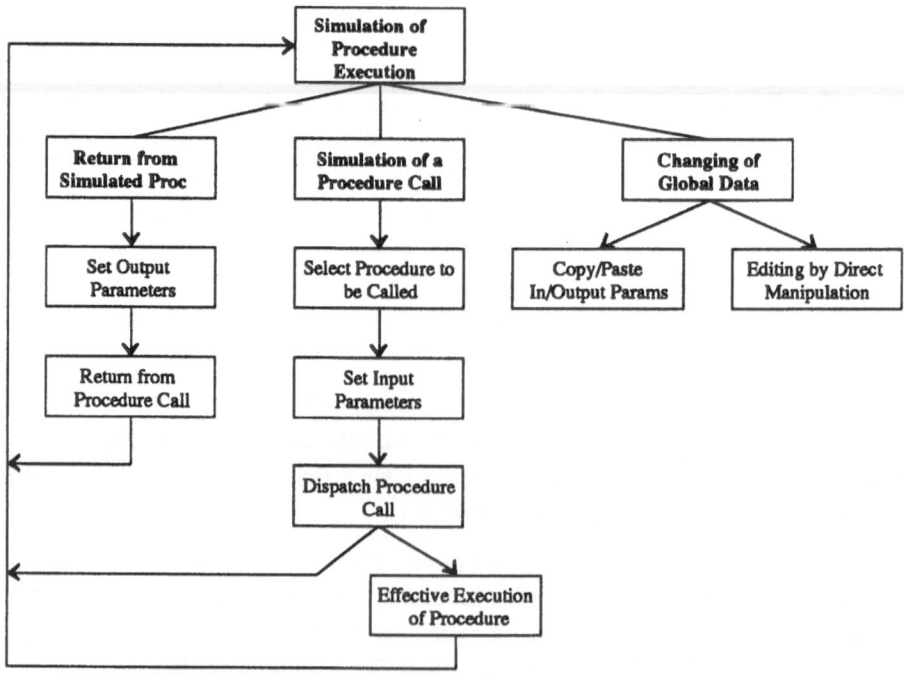

Figure 8.14. Activities carried out during simulation of a procedure

It is obvious that more sophisticated approaches to recovery could be taken. For example, a tool could try to rematch changed parameter lists and require a developer only to check if the rematch was successful and to provide the unmatched parameters. In the ideal case it would furthermore be possible to deal only with the inconsistent procedure calls, while everything else could be replayed. Research is going on in this direction and better strategies will be implemented in the next version of SCT.

The features provided by the Simulator support a developer not only in validating system architectures but also in carrying out many other tasks. A selection of these features is described below.

The scenarios played through during the validation of a system architecture can later be used as a *specification* for the programmers who implement the individual modules, and during maintenance they serve as *dynamic documentation*, exemplifying how the application was planned to work internally.

The Simulator makes it possible to start an execution by manually calling any executable procedure. This feature can be applied in *testing modules and application parts* of any degree of completion. In order to test a module, the developer calls its interface procedures repeatedly with different kinds of input parameters and checks the output parameters for correctness. All test cases for a module can then be stored in a history file and replayed after the module was changed. In the replay mode the Simulator compares the expected with the actual output parameters, making it possible to retest modules without much effort. During testing the Workspace Manager comes in handy because the complex data structures which are sometimes needed as test data can be managed and do not have to be reconstructed for every test run.

Another possible application of the Simulator is the experimentation with system libraries, reusable code, and interpretive high-level tools. This kind of experimentation is especially important during exploratory programming and the development of hybrid software systems. The Simulator supports such experimentation in two ways. First, it enables a developer to test any single feature immediately with the procedure call mechanism. Second, it supports the developer in connecting libraries, interpretive execution tools, and any other kind of existing code by simulating the connecting parts without having to write a single statement.

## 8.6.2  Application of the Simulator

The hybrid execution mechanism of SCT interrupts automatic execution as soon as a call to a unimplemented procedure is triggered. In this case control is transferred to the Simulator is displayed (see Figure 8.15). Figure 8.15 differs from previously shown user interfaces because it is not a single screen dump but a conglomerate of different screen dumps which illustrate all relevant features of the Simulator. For this reason the following description implicitly refers to Figure 8.15.

After control was transferred to the simulator, i.e., at the beginning of the manual execution of a procedure, the Simulator displays all relevant information about this procedure and the current state of execution. The *Local Data* subwindow shows the parameters of the currently simulated procedure. The *Called Procedures* subwindow displays a list of all procedures which have already been called from the current procedure during the current simulation, and the *Procedure Call Chain* subwindow displays the list of the currently active (simulated and interpreted) procedures. (Directly executed procedures can be active but are not displayed.)

Starting at this point the developer can carry out the three activities described above: triggering ongoing procedure calls, manipulating global data, and returning from the current procedure (ending its simulation).

In the Simulator a procedure call is triggered by selecting the procedure to be called in the *Procedures* subwindow, instantiating its local data with the *Activate* command, editing the input data, and dispatching the call with the *Execute* command. The input data can be edited in the same way that any kind of run-time data is edited in the Browser tool (see Section 8.4).

Once the local data of a procedure are instantiated, the procedure call has to be executed because otherwise the run-time stack becomes inconsistent. For this reason the Simulator window is inverted as a whole after the *Activate* command is issued and all but the data editing commands are disabled. This mode is sustained until the user issues either the *Execute* command, which dispatches the procedure call, or the *Deactivate* command, which undoes the effect of the *Activate* command.

One prerequisite for the fast triggering of procedure calls is the availability of browsing mechanisms which make it possible to quickly find the procedure to be called. The Simulator provides a list of modules and a list of procedures to support browsing. The *Modules* subwindow contains the list of all currently executable modules. If a module is selected, a list of all procedures defined in this module is displayed in the *Procedures* subwindow. Finally, the selection of a procedure results in the displaying of its parameters in the *Parameters* subwindow.

In order to provide a better overview of the modules displayed in the *Modules* subwindow, the *Select Level* and *Select Kind* submenus allow the restriction of the displayed modules either by the level on which they are defined (system, user or project) or by the mode in which the are executed (simulated, interpreted or directly executed).

There are various ways to manipulate global data of a simulated module during simulation. Exported global data can be manipulated in any available Browser tool as described in Section 8.4. Internal global data has to be simulated by storing all needed data in a separate Workspace Manager which is automatically provided for every simulated module and which is invoked by selecting the module and issuing the *Workspace* command in the *Modules* subwindow.

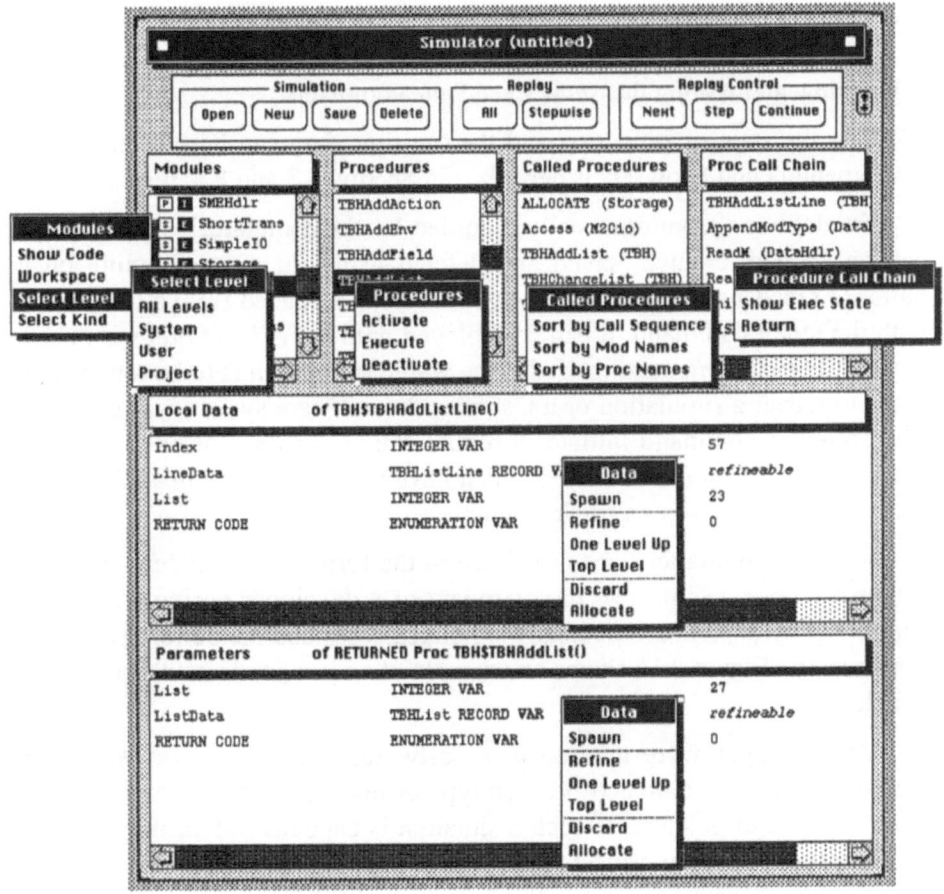

Figure 8.15. Active Simulator[1]

In order to return from the currently simulated procedure, its output parameters are edited in the *Local Data* subwindow and the *Return* command is triggered in the *Procedure Call Chain* subwindow.

---

[1] The background color of the active Simulator or Implementor is set to gray, which makes it much easier to keep track of complex execution courses where simulation and interpretation are intertwined.

Besides these three simulation activities, a developer frequently has to gather information about the current state of execution. One important aspect of this information is displayed in the *Procedure Call Chain* subwindow, which visualizes all active (simulated or interpreted) procedures.

In order to inspect the current state of execution of a simulated procedure, it suffices to select it in the *Procedure Call Chain* subwindow, whereupon its local data as well as all procedure calls which were executed from it are displayed in the corresponding subwindows of the Simulator. The state of execution of interpreted procedures can be visualized in an Implementor, which is invoked by selecting the procedure in the *Procedure Call Chain* subwindow and issuing the *Show Exec State* command.

How the state of execution and the run-time data can be browsed using Implementors and Browsers is described in Section 8.3 and 8.4, respectively.

Simulations are automatically recorded by the Simulator. A simulation can be opened, created, saved and deleted using the corresponding push buttons. Once a simulation has been carried out or loaded from a history file with the *Open* command, it can be replayed with the *All* and *Stepwise* commands. The *All* command is used if the whole simulation is to be replayed in order to repeat a simulation or a test after the software system was changed. The *Stepwise* command initiates a replay which can be controlled with the *Next*, *Step* and *Continue* buttons, which have the same meaning as the corresponding commands in an Implementor.

Recorded simulations are visualized in the form of a procedure call tree. This tree serves to improve the overview of a developer during simulation and replay by depicting the already simulated cases and the current state during a replay. Figure 8.16 shows an example of a visualized simulation during a replay.

After changes were applied to a software system, the corresponding history files can be outdated because type or procedure interface definitions were changed or deleted. If such a situation is encountered during a replay, the developer can choose between two actions to be taken. The current branch of the execution tree which has the incompatible procedure as its root can be discarded or resimulated.

If a new simulation is planned which starts the same way as an already existing one, it is possible to replay the existing simulation stepwise and to take over manual simulation control as soon as the new simulation deviates.

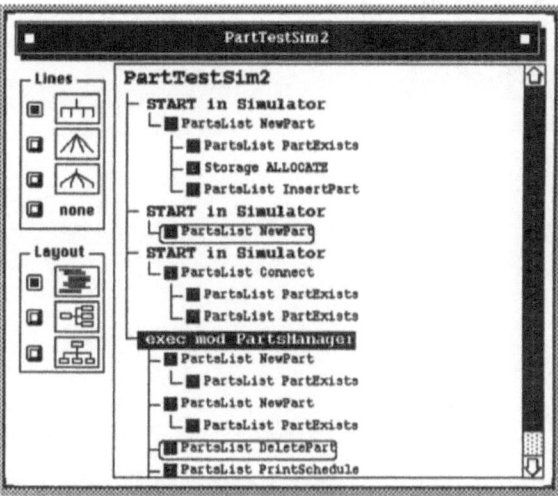

Figure 8.16.  Simulation tree window during replay

# 9 The TOPOS Tool Integration Mechanism

In Chapter 5 we argued that a general software development environment suited for prototyping-oriented software development has to be an open system because the set of suitable prototyping tools depends on the kind of application to be developed. In the ideal case it would be possible to select the best prototyping tools for every project and to integrate them into the kernel environment.

The overall structure of TOPOS (described in Section 5.3) reflects this rationale. In order to achieve the required extensibility, the kernel of TOPOS consists of three components. The first of them, the *Component Management Tool* (described in Chapter 6), supports a developer in basic housekeeping. It can be used for the management of input and output documents of the integrated tools as well as for the uniform invocation of the corresponding integrated editing and execution tools. The second component is the *System Construction Tool*, an exploratory programming and design environment (described in the previous chapter). The third component is the *integration mechanism*, which makes it possible to assimilate new execution mechanisms into the System Construction Tool's hybrid Modula-2 execution system.

Once various tools are integrated into TOPOS, it is possible to execute hybrid software systems written in Modula-2 and in the formalisms "understood" by the integrated tools. This brings multifold advantages during a prototyping-oriented software development process. For example, high-level prototypes written in different formalisms can cooperate immediately. Furthermore, integrating a prototyping tool automatically connects it with a comfortable exploratory programming environment. This greatly reduces the effort of extending the functionality of a prototype beyond what can be expressed in the formalism understood by the high-level tool.

This chapter explains how tools can be integrated into TOPOS's hybrid execution system. It starts with a discussion of the concepts underlying the integration of various tools in Section 9.1. It briefly outlines how tools can be integrated into the hybrid execution system of the System Construction Tool in Section 9.2. Section 9.3 presents some examples of tool integration.

# 9.1 Concepts for Tool Integration

A typical TOPOS hybrid execution system consists of a user interface prototyping tool, a relational database manager, and the hybrid Modula-2 execution system, as depicted in Figure 9.1. In discussing concepts for tool integration, the main question regards the contents of the black box that connects these tools.

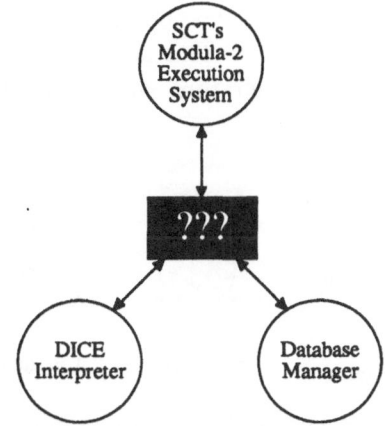

Figure 9.1. Sample structure of a hybrid execution system

Three aspects of this black box are of special interest in the context of integration of tools:

- How are messages forwarded between the various tools?

- Is there any kind of type checking, or are messages mere unstructured information blocks?

- How can good runtime efficiency be achieved?

*Message Forwarding Strategy*

There are three possibilities to fill the black box in the context of forwarding messages between various tools, as depicted in Figure 9.2.

- A proper communication mechanism can be implemented for every pair of tools that are to cooperate . This leads to a lot of point-to-point connections as depicted in Figure 9.2. Point-to-point solutions are feasible if there are only two or three tools to be integrated, if no generality is needed, and if it makes sense to implement different communication strategies for conceptual or efficiency reasons. Because of its lack of generality, this approach is certainly not an appropriate solution for a dynamically configurable open tool set like TOPOS.

- A central broadcaster can accept messages from all connected tools and forward them to all or a subset of the connected tools. This approach is appropriate for tool integration if one message can be used to trigger activities in various tools. It does not make sense, however, for the integration of tools as long as they are not planned to work in parallel, because during the sequential execution of a software systems messages always have one well-defined destination.

- A central dispatcher can accept messages from any tool and forward them to the corresponding target tool. This approach is a generalization of the function call concept and therefore well-suited for the integration of execution tools.

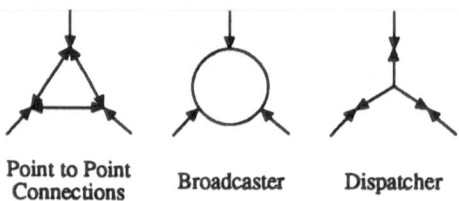

Point to Point          Broadcaster          Dispatcher
Connections

Figure 9.2. Message passing strategies

## Strong Type Checking

It is generally accepted that software systems implemented in formalisms allowing strong type checking are easier to test, contain less errors, and are more easily maintained than if they would have been implemented with a formalism not allowing strong type checking. The reason for this fact is obviously that strong type checking makes it possible to find a certain class of errors automatically at compile time instead of having to wait for their accidental occurrence at run time.

We are sure that the advantages of strong type checking hold not only for software systems implemented in one formalism but also for hybrid software systems. A general communication mechanism between different kinds of tools should therefore involve the passing of typed messages.

## *Run-Time Efficiency*

During the execution of a hybrid software system there are usually many more messages passed between functional application parts than between high-level components. This imposes special efficiency requirements on a message passing system if, for the sake of conceptual orthogonality, execution tools of the algorithmic programming language use the same message passing mechanisms as the high-level execution tools.

These efficiency restrictions certainly can best be met when the format of the messages closely corresponds to the information which has to be exchanged during a procedure call. Furthermore, it is very important that the component which dispatches the messages run in the same operating system process as the execution tools for the functional application parts.

## *Requirements on Tools to be Integrated*

In order to successfully build a hybrid execution system, not only a suitable message format and dispatcher are needed, but also a set of tools which fulfill the basic requirements for tool integration:

- The formalisms which can be executed by the tools to be integrated have to provide some means to define the cooperation with other formalisms.

- The tools to be integrated have to be open systems. They have to provide an interface which can be used to receive requests for certain services from other tools and to request services from other tools.

- The interfaces of the various tools must match semantically and the formalisms in which they are formulated must be compatible so that meaningful synchronization and exchange of data is possible.

Fortunately many prototyping tools supporting an evolutionary development approach provide the possibility to connect code written in an algorithmic programming language to their execution mechanism. The purpose of this connected code is to implement functionality which cannot be expressed in the high-level formalism which the tool can execute itself. Furthermore, these tools usually provide a procedural interface which makes it possible for the functional application parts to access the internal information managed by the tool. This possibility to add functional application parts, together with the procedural interface giving access to the internal information fulfill, the first two requirements described above.

DICE, the user interface prototyping tool (described in Chapter 7), is a typical representative of another class of tools which fulfill the first two basic requirements for integration. They provide an interprocess communication interface and a string-based message protocol which makes it possible to easily connect them with functional application parts. The advantage of this approach is that no link compatibility is required. It suffices that the programming language and the corresponding compiler or interpreter provide access to interprocess communication. The disadvantage is that it becomes necessary to implement a procedural interface which hides the string-based message protocol.

## The TOPOS Approach

Based on the concept of tool integration by message passing and on the fact that most prototyping tools provide interfaces to algorithmic programming languages it was decided to use Modula-2 procedure calls as the TOPOS message format. The message dispatcher was then implemented as a Modula-2 procedure call dispatcher which is closely integrated into the exploratory programming environment. This dispatcher is used to efficiently forward procedure calls between the Modula-2 execution tools provided by the System Construction Tool as well as between any two tools forming part of TOPOS.

The integration of a tool into the hybrid execution system of TOPOS means that a Modula-2 interface for its execution mechanism has to be written and integrated into TOPOS, and that the tool itself has to be connected to this interface either via interprocess communication or by linking it into TOPOS.

The integration approach of TOPOS has the following advantages:

- It provides a general, flexible, well-defined message format which lends itself to static type checking.

- It allows the efficient dispatching of messages between functional application parts executed by different tools.

- The abstraction level of a Modula-2 procedure call usually closely matches the abstraction level of the interfaces to functional application parts provided by high-level tools.

- It defines the message format but leaves a great degree of freedom to choose the best way to connect a tool to TOPOS.

# 9.2 Integration of Tools into TOPOS

The integration of tools is no trivial job. For this reason this section does not cover the process of tool integration in full depth. Instead, it provides an overview of the integration process by means of an outline of the various integration steps. Integrating an execution mechanism into TOPOS's hybrid execution system requires three steps:

- integration of the interface for receiving requests
- integration of the interface for sending requests
- integration of the tool with its interfaces

### *Integration of the Interface for Receiving Requests*

Interface modules for the procedural interface of an execution mechanism are added with the Component Management Tool the same way as any Modula-2 module is added to a project. While the addition itself is straightforward, the interfaces sometimes have to be written by the developer. If the tool provides a procedural interface written in Modula-2, its interface modules can be added without further preparations. If the tool provides a procedural interface for a language other than Modula-2, its interface has to be wrapped in a Modula-2 layer. If the tool provides a string-based communication protocol instead of a procedural interface—such as DICE does—an interface has to be designed and implemented which transforms Modula-2 procedure calls into the corresponding string sequences and sends them to the tool.

### *Integration of the Interface for Sending Requests*

While the integration of an interface for receiving requests is a straightforward process, the implementation of an interface which permits a tool to send requests requires some more understanding. The basic idea behind it is that the Modula-2 message dispatcher provides an interface for dynamic binding which is called with three parameters: two strings defining the procedure to be called and the module which exports it, and a list of parameter values to be passed. The job of the integrator is then to catch the requests sent by the tool to be integrated and to translate them into calls to the dynamic binding interface of the Modula-2 message dispatcher.

### *Integration of the Tool with SCT*

After the integration of the interfaces for sending and receiving requests, the the tool itself has to be connected to this interface. This can be achieved in various ways. Many tools provide a library which manages their connection to other tools via interprocess communication. If such a library is available, it suffices to link the library as directly executable code into TOPOS. If no standard interface is available, but the tool is to be run in a separate process, an interprocess communication interface can be automatically generated with the interface modules as input. If the tool is available in a linkable form, it is also possible to link it directly into TOPOS.

## 9.3 Examples of Tool Integration

Figure 9.3 shows a hybrid execution system of TOPOS with three integrated tools. These three integration examples are discussed briefly below.

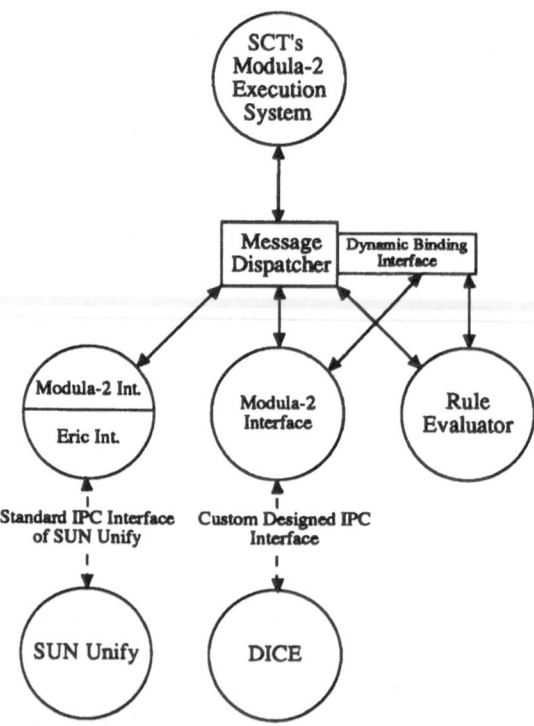

Figure 9.3. Tool integration examples

*Integration of SUN Unify*

SUN Unify [Uni86] is a relational database management system. It includes a database server which can be accessed from different applications and the ERIC interface, which can be linked to the applications and which manages the interprocess communication with the server process. Requests from an application are formulated in SQL and sent to the server across the ERIC interface, where they are evaluated. Afterwards the results can be extracted record-wise using the ERIC interface again.

The integration of SUN Unify was straightforward. First, a Modula-2 layer giving access to the ERIC interface was written. Then these modules were integrated into the application and, finally, the ERIC library was linked to SCT. Both integration of the interface modules and the linking of the library was done using the Component Management Tool. The whole integration process took a few hours.

*Integration of DICE*

In order to connect DICE, a Modula-2 interface was written which allows an application to send requests to DICE on Modula-2 language level and which translates these requests into the string-based message protocol understood by DICE. Then it was defined which Modula-2 procedures are to be called on which events sent from DICE, and an interface was implemented which receives the events and dispatches the corresponding procedure calls via the dynamic binding interface. Both interfaces were implemented in Modula-2 and integrated using the Component Management Tool. The whole integration process took us a few hours (less than the integration of SUN Unify because the interprocess communication interface of DICE is less complex).

*Integration of the Rule Evaluator*

During the development of TOPOS a simple expert system shell was implemented as a test project. Its functional application parts were written in Modula-2 and the user interface was implemented with UICT [Pom88], a predecessor of DICE. The Rule Evaluator was developed with TOPOS. For this reason it never had to be integrated at all because its interface could always be called from an application or from SCT's Simulator, and its requests were designed to be dynamically bound Modula-2 procedure calls from the beginning.

An interesting effect of the development of the Rule Evaluator was the possibility to execute hybrid software systems containing rule-based subsystems with TOPOS, while the functional application parts of the tool executing these rule bases were partially simulated, partially interpreted, and partially directly executed.

# 10  How to Use TOPOS for Prototyping-Oriented Software Development

Chapters 5 to 9 discussed the concepts underlying TOPOS and the set of tools which comprise its kernel. This chapter complements the last five by presenting a framework describing how TOPOS can be applied during a prototyping-oriented software development process. The first section outlines the framework in an abstract, schematic way; the second section presents a scenario which exemplifies how it can be put to work.

## 10.1  General Aspects

Figure 10.1 schematically depicts how TOPOS is applied during a prototyping-oriented software development process. The upper level shows the subprocesses that have to be carried out and the lower level depicts every subprocess in further detail. On the upper level two different kinds of arrows connect the processes. The thin arrows indicate the logical sequence of the processes and the bold arrows represent the cycles inherent in the model, which include several processes.

For the sake of clarity, cycles are not depicted which sometimes have to be carried out because errors in the results of preceding processes are found. These cycles have to be carried out in applying any method and exist for any group of processes. The goal of prototyping and exploratory programming is to reduce these costly, involuntary cycles by deliberately carrying out cycles during which critical decisions are verified. The deliberate cycles consist of the cyclical processes depicted on the lower level and of the two cycles represented by the two bold arrows on the upper level.

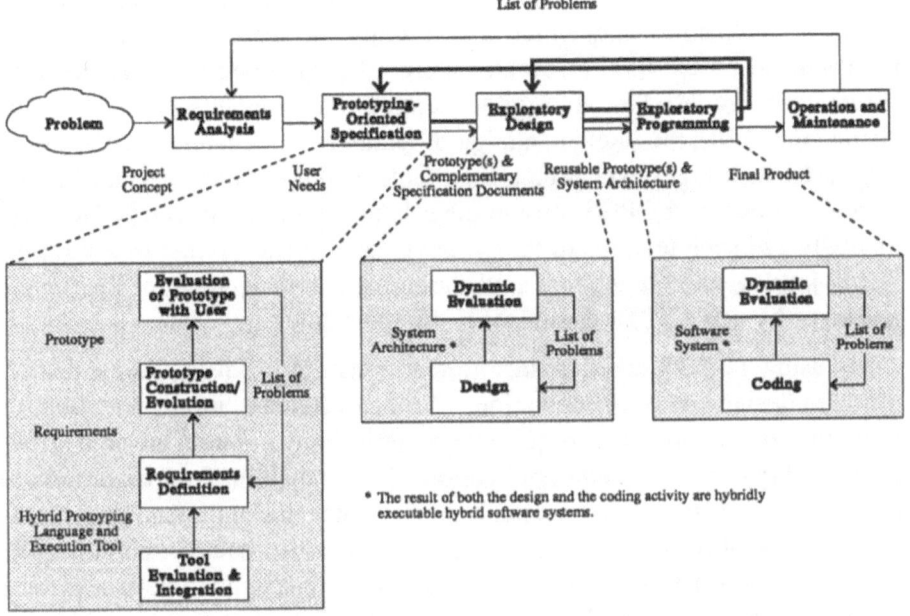

Figure 10.1 Prototyping-oriented software development as carried out with TOPOS

## *Prototyping-Oriented Requirements Definition (Specification)*

When TOPOS is applied, the prototyping-oriented requirements definition process is carried out as described in Section 2.1. It consists of an iterative refinement process on a prototype (e.g., a user interface prototype) which builds the base of the requirements definition. This iterative process—construction, evaluation, adaptation, reevaluation, etc.—allows the client to gain a deeper understanding of her/his own needs and wishes, as well as of what is technically feasible, and the application developer becomes better acquainted with the needs and wishes of the client. This process is continued until the requirements definition is acceptable for both the client and the developer.

In parallel to the iterative refinement of the prototype, various documents have to be written in order to describe the requirements which cannot be represented (with reasonable effort) in the prototype(s). The nature of these documents depends on the kind of application under development. For an information system, for example, such documents could include an entity/relationship diagram, information about the amount of data to be managed, and the frequency of data manipulations and queries.

The advantage in applying TOPOS is that the developer selects the prototyping tools (which best suit the specific needs) and integrates these tools into TOPOS before the cyclical process is started. During the prototyping process it can become necessary to check the feasibility and/or run-time efficiency of application parts which are currently specified. This kind of check is visualized by the bold arrow in Figure 10.1 which connects the requirements definition, design and implementation processes into one large cycle. Using other tools, the implementation of features which cannot be completely expressed with high-level prototyping tools would required the starting of a different process. TOPOS, on the other hand, enables a developer to incrementally add such features to the prototype and to execute the new designed and/or implemented functional application parts in the context of the running prototype by using SCT's Simulator and Implementor.

In using TOPOS, there is thus no real transition from requirements definition to design and implementation. During design and implementation, the prototype developed as a requirements definition is extended and grows incrementally into the final application. The transition from requirements definition to system construction happens when the understanding of the functionality of the later application is satisfactory for both the client and the developer and the functionality of the prototype is extended beyond what is needed for mere specification.

The results of a prototyping-oriented requirements definition process are:

- a requirements definition consisting of prototypes and complementary documents

- reusable prototypes (depending on the kind of application to be developed and on the high-level tools which were applied)

- reusable prototypes of application parts which were developed in order to check their feasibility and efficiency

*Exploratory Design*

The design activity distinguishes the prototyping-oriented software development as embodied in TOPOS from currently used approaches. To date the design of a system architecture has frequently been a monolithic process during which a whole new system architecture is designed. One way such a process could be supported was with tools permitting the static description of the planned architecture, and one way to validate an emerging system architecture was to review its description.

TOPOS permits a developer to improve this design process in three ways:

- TOPOS makes it possible to reuse the prototypes resulting from the requirements definition process, such as user interface components. Thus the goal of the architecture design process becomes more and more to find a system architecture which optimally integrates the reusable prototypes, other reusable application parts, and the applications parts which have yet to be implemented, into a working software system.

- TOPOS permits the simulative execution of the planned system architecture, while all prototypes and reusable application parts are interpreted or directly executed. This means that the planned system architecture can be dynamically validated in the context of all existing application parts. The validation of a system architecture, which was previously a paper-based task, therefore becomes a dynamic, exploratory design process.

- TOPOS allows the recording and replay of simulations of the execution of designed but not yet implemented application parts. We consider this a prerequisite for a simulative approach to system architecture validation because it is not possible to iteratively simulate large architectures if the whole simulation process has to be carried out manually again and again.

During an exploratory design process it may be necessary to implement certain application parts to check that they are feasible and that they will run with the required efficiency (which is depicted in Figure 10.1 by the bold arrow that connects the design and implementation processes). These application parts can be realized with SCT's exploratory programming environment and tested in the context of the architecture simulation.

The results of an exploratory design process are:

- a hybridly executable hybrid software system with a dynamically validated system architecture

- a set of recorded simulations which can be used as specifications for the programmers who implement the individual modules, as system documentation during maintenance, and as test cases for module and system tests

*Exploratory Programming*

The application parts which have to be newly written can be implemented with the Implementor, a comfortable exploratory programming environment. They can be tested on their own using SCT's Simulator as testbed, and they can be tested in the context of the hybridly executable application using the simulations which were recorded during the design validation process.

The result of the exploratory programming process is the implemented and tested final application.

*Operation and Maintenance*

The features provided by TOPOS not only support the development of applications but also their maintenance. This is especially true for adaptations due to changing user requirements. Such changing requirements usually lead to a new prototyping-oriented software development process, where all unaffected application parts can be considered to be reusable.

The main problem of starting a new software development process during maintenance is that the existing application has to be understood by the maintenance personnel, who frequently are not the developers of the application. SCT helps to ease this problem in two ways. First, it provides a set of browsing features which make it possible to investigate the static structure of the software system to be maintained. Second, it permits a developer to gain an understanding of the inner workings of the application by replaying a set of exemplary recorded simulations.

Even with recorded simulations as dynamic documentation, it is usually difficult to understand all the consequences which could result from a changes in a large, complex software system. For this reason it becomes especially important that changes in the system architecture can be validated by simulating the new and changed application parts instead of implementing them directly.

# 10.2 Application Scenario

This section outlines how a distributed project planning and control tool for a medium-sized company was developed with TOPOS. The scenario simply reflects in concise form a wealth of experience in working with TOPOS that would otherwise require many pages to present.

*Requirements Analysis*

The starting point for this scenario was that the projects carried out in Company X were becoming more and more complex. This growing complexity affected the planning and control of the individual projects as well as the coordination of the resources shared by the various project teams. For this reason Company X decided to develop an application for the planning and control of such projects. The first informal requirements called for an application which provides a comfortable user interface for editing, browsing, and graphically visualizing project information and for regularly entering the current status of projects. Furthermore, it was planned that the application would have to enable a user to automatically simulate different conflict resolution strategies in the case of conflicts over shared resources.

After the problem had been analyzed by developers and clients, they decided to take a prototyping-oriented approach, and TOPOS was chosen as the supporting tool set. This choice was made because the requirements were still unclear and because no other tool was available which would have supported the integrative evolutionary application of different prototyping strategies such as user interface, architecture, and algorithm prototyping.

*Prototyping-Oriented Requirements Definition*

The requirements definition process was divided into three prototyping-oriented subprocesses: a user interface prototyping process to learn more about the basic requirements, a performance prototyping process to test whether the implementation of the final application was possible with a standard database management system, and an algorithm prototyping process to learn more about the appropriate planning and conflict resolution strategies.

Before the cyclical prototyping process was initiated, the developers had to select the high-level formalisms to be used.

DICE (see Section 7) was chosen as the user interface prototyping tool for three reasons. First, DICE makes it easy to graphically specify and execute modern user interfaces which consist of DICE's basic building blocks. Second, DICE makes it possible to simulate functionality going beyond the standard functionality of its basic building blocks by making it possible to show arbitrary graphics in graphic subwindows. Third, DICE supports an evolutionary approach by giving a developer the possibility to either reuse a user interface prototype in the final application (in the case where the functionality of the basic building blocks suffices) or to generate C++ code, which completely implements the specified functionality and which serves as a base for the realization of complex components with the power of an advanced application framework (see Section 3.3).

A standard relational database management system (SUN Unify) was to be used for the final application. For this reason the feasibility of the final implementation was to be tested in a performance prototyping process with the same data base management system.

Prolog was chosen for the prototyping of the planning and conflict resolution strategies because it was more important to implement different kinds of algorithms than to reuse them later.

After the requirements definition process was planned, the next step was to integrate the selected tools into TOPOS. DICE, an integral part of TOPOS, was already assimilated. The integration of the database management system proved easy because it provided a standard C interface, which only had to be wrapped in a Modula-2 layer and linked to SCT.

The integration of Prolog was more challenging. The interface for starting the evaluation of Prolog rules from Modula-2 was integrated without changes. This was not the case for the interface for calling rules implemented as Modula-2 procedures from Prolog, which had to be adapted to call the interface of SCT's dynamic binding mechanism. In order to be able to use SCT's development monitoring tools as well as the Prolog programming environment, an interprocess communication interface was generated with CMT. The interface of the Prolog server was then adapted to start listening for rule evaluation requests from SCT after the developer manually switched into listening mode. This way it became possible to set breakpoints in the Prolog program before the execution of the hybrid application was started and to monitor the execution of the Prolog parts with the Prolog programming environment.

After tool integration, the user interface prototyping process was started. In this process a team of developers and clients implemented and evolved a user interface prototype to determine the functional behavior of the application at the user interface. During this prototyping process it was possible to show the later users the exact user interface of the final application, with the exception of the graphic visualizations. These graphic visualizations were simulated by drawing various scenarios using DICE's graphic subwindow building block. Parallel to the user interface prototyping process, the data model was designed and evaluated.

Once an agreement about the user interface and the data model was reached between the developers and the later users, the developers implemented a simple database and some Modula-2 test procedures to make sure that the final application would meet the users' efficiency requirements. It was not necessary to write a testbed in order to carry out the experiments with the database because the test runs where managed with the SCT's Simulator.

The next step was to prototype various planning and conflict resolution algorithms. This was done by implementing the database and the algorithms in Prolog. The application parts written in Prolog were then connected with the user interface and presented to the client as an almost complete prototype of the later application.

The result of the specification prototyping process was a requirements definition of the application to be built consisting of:

- a running prototype specifying the functionality of the application to be built

- a data model

- estimations of the size of the data to be stored

- a set of evaluated planning and conflict resolution algorithms

- estimations of the frequency of planning, control, and conflict resolution activities (based on the experiments carried out with the prototypes)

A further result of the the prototyping-oriented approach was the security that it was feasible to realize the application with the required efficiency using the selected database management system.

*Exploratory Design*

The design process for the system architecture consisted of two tasks. First, the logical data model was transformed into a physical data model. Second, the Modula-2 modules connecting the database and the user interface as well as the modules containing the planning and conflict resolution algorithms were planned.

During this planning process, design and validation steps were carried out iteratively. The validation steps consisted of the simulation of the planned Modula-2 modules in the context of the running user interface and the data management system. During this cyclical process different alternatives were evaluated. SCT's simulation replay mechanism made such an iterative proceeding possible by significantly facilitating the validation of the system architecture after changes were applied.

*Implementation*

The implementation process carried out at the end of the project was a conventional implementation process because most problems which would have required an exploratory strategy had already been solved during the requirements definition and design processes.

During the implementation process only the designed Modula-2 modules and the user interface components for graphic visualization had to be implemented, while the database and the user interface were reused. The designed Modula-2 modules were implemented by programmers who had not been part of the design team. This kind of teamwork proved unproblematic because the inner workings of the single modules were well-defined by the definition modules, the recorded simulations, and the Prolog prototype.

After the Modula-2 modules were implemented and tested in the context of the simulations recorded during the exploratory design process, C++ code was generated for the user interface. This made it possible to implement the application parts dealing with graphic visualization by simply overriding all graphic subwindows which were used for simulation purposes during the requirements definition process. The implementation of these C++ classes was straightforward because of the power of the underlying ET++ application framework discussed in Section 3.3.2.

*Operation and Maintenance*

Due to the fact that the later users were involved in the requirements definition process, they had no problem in putting the application to work. During the first three months the users found some errors in the realization and specified various possible improvements in the functionality as well as the user interface.

Coding errors were quickly corrected in SCT's interpretive programming environment and minor improvements were applied with the corresponding high-level tool. Ergonomic improvements in the user interface, for example, were implemented by drawing them with DICE.

The new requirements, on the other hand, led to a further prototyping-oriented software development process during which all unaffected application parts were considered reusable. In this process SCT's Simulator proved useful because it allowed the developers to check whether the changes and extensions they planned fit into the existing architecture.

During the succeeding maintenance process it became more and more difficult to correct errors because the details about the inner working of the application were forgotten and because more and more of the developers left the maintenance team. In this phase an understanding of the existing application parts was facilitated by the recorded simulations, which dynamically demonstrated how the various application parts cooperate.

# 11 Experience with and Implications of TOPOS

*Experience*

The most important experience which all users of TOPOS share is that the way software is developed has changed since they began using TOPOS. All of them had already been applying prototyping without such a development environment. The difference is that without TOPOS the prototypes had consisted almost exclusively of high-level parts, mainly of user interface and database prototypes. The lack of expressive power of the prototyping tools had been compensated by building mock-ups and by telling the client about what would be occurring if the functionality were already implemented.

Since they have been using TOPOS, they still build user interface and database prototypes, but the functionality of the prototypes is enhanced with small chunks of Modula-2 code right from the beginning of the prototyping process. Once requirements definition prototyping is terminated, the prototypes grow incrementally into the final applications without the disruption which was experienced before, when the mock-up parts had to be discarded at the end of the requirements definition process.

Various tools were successfully integrated into TOPOS. Examples are SUN Unify (a relational database management system), a Prolog interpreter, and a simple rule interpreter that was developed with SCT itself. The integration of all these tools has shown that a tool which does not send requests but acts as a mere server (such as a database management system) can be added effortlessly by any developer. The integration of tools using SCT's dynamic binding mechanism, on the other hand, requires experienced developers.

*Implications*

The development of SCT has proven that it is possible to implement programming environments for compilative programming languages with strong type checking which are almost as comfortable as environments for exploratory programming and still are open systems. The requirement that a programming environment be an open system is especially important because it makes it possible to develop realistic applications under UNIX. This is because an open system permits access to existing libraries and reusable application parts written in different formalisms without the need to carry out horrible hacks on the system level.

The realization and application of SCT made it possible to practically test the concept of simulation of module-oriented software systems. The advantages of a simulative approach can certainly be obtained by writing similar tools for other module-oriented languages such as Ada. The application of simulators for object-oriented software development is also possible.

The answer to the question of whether architecture validation by simulation is practical for large object-oriented software systems, on the other hand, is not so obvious. This is because object-oriented architectures consist of smaller entities (classes) which are related in much more complicated and dynamic ways.

Execution of hybrid software systems will become a common feature provided by many development environments. The reason is obvious. A great rationalization effect for software engineering can be obtained by increasing the abstraction level on which software systems are described. Unfortunately, formalisms and tools which allow a significant increase in the abstraction level can be built only for standardizable application parts. For this reason it is important to be able to integrate such formalisms with algorithmic languages to obtain hybrid languages which allow the development of entire applications.

Today some tools are commercially available which allow comfortable development of hybrid software systems with a predefined set of formalisms. The development of SCT, on the other hand, has shown that it is possible to implement a mechanism permitting a developer to configure the hybrid formalism which best suits specific needs. Commercial development environments providing an integration mechanism similar to SCT's would therefore certainly meet a market demand.

Prototyping-oriented software development is not a theoretically developed approach. It grew out of a lot of practical experience, and its usefulness was validated in many practical projects. This is also true for the integrative evolutionary prototyping-oriented approach supported by TOPOS. For this reason we believe that prototyping-oriented software development—supported by tools permitting the combination of prototyping and exploratory programming—is *a natural way* to develop software.

# Bibliography

[Aci90a]  Acius Inc.: *Documentation of 4th Dimension.* Acius Inc., 1990

[Aci90b]  Acius Inc.: *Documentation of the 4th Dimension Compiler.* Acius Inc., 1990

[Aho86]  Aho AV, Sethi R, Ullman JD: Compilers: Principles, Techniques and Tools. Addison-Wesley, 1986

[Alg88]  Algayres B, Encontre V: GEODE: A Graphic Environment for Real-Time Software Design. Actes de la 4ème Conférence de Génie Logiciel, AFCET, Paris, 1988

[App85]  Apple Computer Inc.: Inside Macintosh I-V. Addison-Wesley, 1985 and later

[App91]  Apple Computer Inc.: Documentation of Macintosh Programmer's Workshop and Utilities Volume 1. Apple Computer Inc., Cupertino CA, 1991

[Asp78]  Asprin R: Another Fine Myth. ACE Books, 1978

[Bal85]  Balzer R: A 15-Year Perspective on Automatic Programming. IEEE Transactions on Software Engineering, Vol. 11, No. 11, Nov. 1985

[Ber87]  Berliner EF, Zave P: An Experiment in Technology Transfer: PAISLey Specification of Requirements for an Undersea Lightwave Cable System. Proc. Ninth Int. Conf. on Software Engineering, IEEE Computer Society Press, March 1987

[Bes86]  Best E, Fernández C: Notations and Terminology of Petri Net Theory. Petri Net Newsletter 23, April 1986

[Bet87]  Betts B, et al.: Goals and Objectives for User Interface Software. Computer Graphics, Vol. 21, No. 2, April 1987

[Bia88]  Bianchi C, Goldsmith D: MacApp 2.0 Display Specification. Apple Computer Inc. Cupertino, CA, 1988

[Bis89]   Bischofberger WR, Pomberger G: SCT: a Tool for Hybrid Execution of Hybrid Software Systems. Proceedings of the First International Conference on Modula-2, Bled, 1989

[Bla89]   Blaschek G, Sametinger J: User Adaptable Pretty Printing. Software Practice & Experience, Vol. 19, No. 7, July 1989

[Boa83]   Boar BH: Application Prototyping—A Requirements Definition Strategy for the 80s. John Wiley & Sons, 1984

[Boc90]   Booch G: Object-Oriented Design. Benjamin/Cummings Publishing Company, 1990

[Boe76]   Boehm BW: Software Engineering. IEEE Transactions on Computers, Vol. 25, No. 12, Dec. 1976

[Boe81]   Boehm BW: Software Engineering Economics. Prentice-Hall, 1981

[Boe88]   Boehm BW: A Spiral Model of Software Development and Enhancement. IEEE Computer, Vol. 21, No. 5, May 1988

[Bra84]   Bransford JD, Stein BS: The IDEAL Problem Solver. W.H. Freeman and Company, New York, 1984

[Bro87]   Brooks FP: People Are Our Most Importand Product. In Gibbs E, Fairley RE (Eds.): Software Engineering Education. Springer-Verlag, 1987

[Bud91]   Budd T: An Introduction to Object-Oriented Programming. Addison-Wesley, 1991

[Cav88]   Cavalli AR, Paul E: Exhaustive Analysis and Simulation for Distributed Systems, Both Sides of the same Coin. In Actes de la 4ème Conférence de Génie Logiciel, AFCET, Paris, 1988

[CCI85]   CCITT Recommendations Z. 100-Z.104 Specification and Description Language. Red Book, ITU, Geneva, 1985

[Con87]   Conklin J: Hypertext: An Introduction and Survey. IEEE Computer, Vol. 29, No. 9, Sept. 1987

[Con89]   Connel JL, Shafer LB: Structured Rapid Prototyping. Yourdon Press, 1989

[Cox84]   Cox BJ: Message/Object Programming: An Evolutionary Change in Programming Technology. IEEE Software, Vol. 1, No. 1, Jan. 1984

[Däh87]   Dähler J, Gerber P, Gisiger HP, Kündig A: A Graphical Tool for the Design and Prototyping of Distributed Systems. Petri Net Newsletter, No. 27, Aug. 1987

[DeM78]   DeMarco T: Structured Analysis and System Specification. Yourdon Press, 1978

[Die87]    Diederich J, Milton J: Experimental Prototyping in Smalltalk.
           IEEE Software, Vol. 4, No. 3, May 1987.

[Fai85]    Fairley R: Software Engineering Concepts. McGraw-Hill, 1985

[Fel79]    Feldman SI: Make—A Program for Maintaining Computer
           Programs. Software Practice & Experience, Vol. 9., No. 4, April
           1979

[Fel87]    Feldbrugge F, Jensen K: Petri Net Tool Overview 1986. In Petri
           Nets: Applications and Relationships to Other Models of
           Concurrency, LNCS 255, Springer-Verlag, 1987

[Fic85]    Fickas SF: Automating the Transformational Development of
           Software. IEEE Transactions on Software Engineering, Vol. 11,
           No. 11, Nov. 1985

[Fli88]    Flint D: Hypertext. Butler Cox Foundation Research Report, 1988

[Flo84]    Floyd C: A Systematic Look at Prototyping. In Approaches to
           Prototyping, Springer-Verlag, 1984.

[Fol90]    Foley J, et al.: Computer Graphics: Principles & Practices.
           Addison-Wesley, 1990

[Fro89]    Fromherz MPJ: A Survey of Executable Specification
           Methodologies. Research Report Nr.89.05, Institut für Informatik,
           Universität Zürich, 1989

[Gab90a]   Gabriel RP, et al.: Foundation for a C++ Programming Environ-
           ment. Proceedings of C++ at Work-90, Secaucus, New Jersey,
           Sept. 1990

[Gab90b]   Gabriel RP, et al.: An Open Architecture for Programming
           Environments. Papers of the ECOOP/OOPSLA 90 Workshop,
           Ottawa, Oct. 1990

[Gam86a]   Gamma E, Marty R: ET—An Editor Toolkit for Bitmap-Oriented
           Workstations. Research Report Nr.86.01, Institut für Informatik,
           Universität Zürich, 1986

[Gam86b]   Gamma E, Marty R: Edit—An Extensible Text Editor. Research
           Report Nr.86.02, Institut für Informatik, Universität Zürich, 1986

[Gam89]    Gamma E, Weinand R, Marty R: Integration of a Programming
           Environment into ET++—A Case Study. Proceedings of the Third
           European Conference on Object-Oriented Programming, Univer-
           sity Press, Cambridge, 1989

[Gam91]    Gamma E.,: Object-Oriented Software Engineering: Class Li-
           braries, Design Techniques, and Tool Support (in German). Ph.D.
           Thesis University of Zürich, 1991

[GAN85]    Special Issue on the GANDALF Project. The journal of Systems
           and Software, Vol. 5, No. 2, May 1985

[Gar86]   Garett NL, Smith KE, Meyramiles N: Intermedia: Issues, Strategies and Tactics in the Design of a Hypermedia Document System. Proceedings of the Conference on Computer-Supported Cooperative Work, Austin Texas, Dec. 1986

[Gen81]   Genrich H, Lautenbach K: System Modelling with High-Level Petri Nets. Theorethical Computer Science 13, North-Holland, 1981

[Ghe87]   Ghezzi C, Jazayeri M: Programming Language Concepts. John Wiley & Sons, 1987

[Gol84]   Goldberg A: Smalltalk-80—The Interactive Programming Environment. Addison-Wesley, 1984

[Gol85]   Goldberg A: Smalltalk-80—The Language and its Implementation. Addison-Wesley, 1985

[Goo88]   Goodman D: Danny Goodman's HyperCard Developer's Guide. Bantam Books, 1988

[Gre88]   Gresse C, Raffinat P: PROGRAIS: An Experimental Programming Environment to Support Transformational Development of Software. in Software Engineering Environments, Ellis Horwood, 1988

[Hay85]   Hayes PL, et al.: Design Alternatives for User Interface Management Systems Based on Experience with COUSIN. CHI 85 Conference Proc., Boston, April 1985

[Hol86]   Holloway S: Background to Fourth Generation. in Fourth Generation Languages and Application Generators, The Technical Press, 1986

[Ich79]   Ichbiah JD, et al.: Rationale for the Design of the Ada Programming Language. ACM Sigplan Notices, Vol. 10, No. 6, 1979

[Ige86]   Igel B: Net-Tools. Petri Net Newsletter, No. 25, 1986

[Jon84]   Jones TC: Reusability in Programming: A Survey of the State of the Art. IEEE Transaction on Software Engineering, Vol. 10, No. 5, May 1984

[Kau88]   Kaufer S, Lopez R, Pratap S: Saber-C, An Interpreter-Based Programming Environment for the C Language. Proceedings of USENIX, San Francisco, June 1988

[Kel89]   Keller RK: Prototyping-Oriented System Specification—Concepts, Methods, Tools and Implications (in German). Verlag Dr. Kovac, 1989

[Kra84]   Krasner G: Smalltalk-80—Bits of History, Words of Advice. Addison-Wesley, 1984

[LaL90]   LaLonde WR, Pugh JR: Inside Smalltalk, Volumes 1 & 2. Prentice-Hall, 1990

[Leb84]   Leblang DB, Chase RP: Computer-Aided Software Engineering in
          a Distributed Workstation Environment. Proceedings of the ACM
          SIGSOFT/SIGPLAN Software Engineering Symposium and
          Practical Software Development Environments, Pittsburgh, 1984

[Lis86]   Liskov BH, Guttag J: Abstraction and Specification in Program
          Development. MIT Press, 1986

[Löw87]   Löwgren J: Applying a Rapid Prototyping System to Control Panel
          Dialogues. Research Report ASLAB University Linköping,
          Sweden, Dec. 1987

[Mac86]   MacMETH: A Fast Modula-2 Lanugage System For the Apple
          Macintosh (User Manual). Instiut für Informatik, ETH Zürich,
          Aug. 1986

[Mar85]   Martin J: Fourth-Generation Languages—Volume I Principles.
          Prentice-Hall, 1985

[Mar86a]  Martin J: Fourth-Generation Languages—Volume II Represen-
          tative 4GLs. Prentice-Hall, 1986

[Mar86b]  Martland D, Holloway S, Bhabuta L: Fourth-Generation Lan-
          guages and Application Generators. The Technical Press, 1986

[Mar89]   Martin J: Information Engineering: Introduction. Prentice-Hall,
          1989

[Mat81]   Matsumoto Y: SBW System: A Software Factory. in Software
          Engineering Environments, H. Hünke, Ed., North-Holland, 1981

[Mey87]   Meyer B: Reusability: The Case for Object-Oriented Design. IEEE
          Software, March 1987

[Mey88]   Meyer B: Object-Oriented Software Construction. Prentice-Hall,
          1988

[Mey90]   Meyer B: Introduction to the Theory of Programming Languages.
          Prentice-Hall, 1990

[Mos85b]  Mostow J: What is AI? And What Does It Have to Do with Soft-
          ware Engineering. IEEE Transactions on Software Engineering,
          Vol. 11, No. 11, 1985

[Nie88]   Nielsen J: Trip Report: Hypertext 87. SIGCHI Bulletin, Vol. 19,
          No. 4, April 1988

[NSE89]   The Network Software Environment. Sun Technical Report Part
          No: 800-3295-10, Sun Microsystems, 1989

[Par83]   Partsch H, Steinbrüggen R: Program Transformation Systems.
          ACM Computing Surveys, Vol. 15, No. 3, Sept. 1983

[Par86]   Partridge D: Artificial Intelligence: Applications in the Future of
          Software Engineering. Ellis Horwood, 1986

[Par89a]  ParcPlace Systems: Objectworks for Smalltalk-80: User Documentation. ParcPlace Systems, 1989

[Par89b]  Parsaye K, Chignell M, Khoshafian S, Wong H: Intelligent Databases: Object-Oriented, Deductive Hypermedia Technologies. John Wiley & Sons, 1989

[Par90]  ParcPlace Systems: Objectworks for C++: User Documentation. ParcPlace Systems, 1990

[Pet88]  Peters LJ: Advanced Structured Analysis and Design. Prentice-Hall, 1988

[Pom86]  Pomberger G: Software Engineering and Modula-2. Prentice-Hall, 1986

[Pom88]  Pomberger G, Bischofberger WR, Keller R, Schmidt D: TOPOS—A Toolset for Prototyping-Oriented Software Development. Actes de la 4ème Conférence de Génie Logiciel, AFCET, Paris, Oct. 1988

[Pre87]  Pressman RS: Software Engineering. McGraw-Hill, 1987

[Pre90]  Pree W: DICE—An Object-Oriented Tool for Rapid Prototpying. Procs. TOOLS Pacific 90 Conference on Object-Oriented Programming, Sidney, 1990

[Pro84]  Proceedings of the ACM SIGFSOFT/SIGPLAN Software Engineering Symposium on Practical Software Development Environments. Software Engineering Notes, Vol. 9, No.3, 1984.

[Rei87]  Reisig W: Petri Nets in Software Engineering. in Petri Nets: Applications and Relationships to Other Models of Concurrency, LNCS 255, Springer-Verlag, 1987

[Rei89]  Reichenberger C: Orthogonal Version Management. Proc. 2nd Int. Workshop on Software Configuration Management, Princeton, 1989

[Rei90a]  Reiss SP: Interacting with the FIELD Environment. Software Practice & Experience, Vol. 20, June 1990

[Rei90b]  Reiss SP: Connecting Tools Using Message Passing in the FIELD Environment. IEEE Software, July 1990

[Rei91]  Reiser M: The Oberon Systems: User Guide and Programmer's Manual. ACM Press, 1991

[Rep84]  Reps T, Teitelbaum T: The Synthesizer Generator. Software Engineering Notes, Vol. 9, No.3, 1984

[Roc75]  Rochkind M: The Source Code Control System (SCCS). IEEE Transactions on Software Engineering, Vol. 1, No. 4, 1975

[Ros85]   Ross DT: Applications and Extensions of SADT. IEEE Computer,
          Vol. 18, No. 4, April 1985

[Sab88]   Saber-C Enhances Development for C Programmers. The Sun
          Observer, Vol. 1, No.4, 1988

[Sab90]   Saber C++ Documentation. Saber Software Inc., Cambridge MA,
          1990

[Sam91]   Sametinger J: DOgMA: A Tool for the Documentation & Main-
          tenance of Software Systems. Report des Institut für Wirtschafts-
          informatik, Johannes Kepler Universität, 1991

[San87]   Sandberg DW: Smalltalk and Exploratory Programming. ACM
          SIGPLAN Notices, Vol.22, No.10, Oct. 1987

[Sch86]   Schmucker KJ: Object-Oriented Programming for the Macintosh.
          Hayden Book Company, 1986

[Sch89]   Schönthaler F: Rapid Prototyping Supporting the Conceptual
          Design of Information Systems (in German). PhD. Thesis, Uni-
          versität Karlsruhe, 1989

[Sei90]   Seisel N: Comparison of Four 4GS Running on the Apple
          Macintosh (in German). Diplomarbeit Johannes-Kepler Universität
          Linz, 1990

[Set89]   Sethi R: Programming Language Concepts and Constructs.
          Addison-Wesley, 1989

[She83]   Sheil BA: Environments for Exploratory Programming. Data-
          mation, Feb. 1983

[Shn86]   Shneidermann B: Designing the User Interface—Strategies for
          Effective Human-Computer Interaction. Addison-Wesley, 1986

[Shn89]   Shneiderman B, Kearsley G: HYPERTEXT HANDS-ON! An
          Introduction to a New Way of Organizing and Accessing Infor-
          mation. Addison-Wesley, 1989

[Som85]   Sommerville I: Software Engineering. Addison-Wesley, 1985

[Spi89]   Spitta T: Software Engineering and Prototyping (in German).
          Springer-Verlag, 1989

[Squ82]   Squires SL: Working Papers from the ACM SIGSOFT Rapid
          Prototyping Workshop, Columbia, Md., April 1982. ACM Soft-
          ware Engineering Notes, Vol. 7, No. 5, Dec. 1982

[Sta81]   Stallman R: Emacs the Extensible, Customizable, Self-Docu-
          menting Display Editor. Proceedings of the ACM SIGPLAN/
          SIGOA Symposium on Text Manipulation, ACM SIGPLAN
          Notices, Vol. 16, No. 6, 1981

[Str91]    Stritzinger A: Reusable Software Components and Application
           Frameworks—Concepts, Design Principles and Implications.
           Report Departement of Software Engineering, Johannes Kepler
           University Linz, 1991

[Swi86]    Swinehart DC, Zellweger PT, Beach RJ, Hagman B: A Structural
           View of the Cedar Programming Environment. ACM Transactions
           on Programming Languages and Systems, Vol.8, No.4, 1986

[Sym89]    Lightspeed Pascal 2.0 Documentation. Symantec Inc., 1989

[Tar87]    Tare RS: UNIX Utilities: A Programmer's Reference. McGraw-
           Hill, 1987

[Tei84]    Teitelman W, Masinter L: The Interlisp Programming Environ-
           ment. In Interactive Programming Environments, McGraw-Hill,
           1984

[Tei85]    Teitelman W: A Tour Through Cedar. IEEE Transactions on
           Software Engineering, Vol. 11, No. 3, 1983

[Tho89]    Thompson T: The Next Step. Byte, Vol. 14, No. 3, 1989

[Tic85]    Tichy WF: RCS—A System for Version Control. Software Prac-
           tice & Experience, Vol. 15, July 1985

[Tic88]    Tichy WF: Tools for Software Configuration Management. in
           [Win88]

[Uni86]    SUN Unify Documentation. SUN, 1986.

[Wal87]    Walker JH, Moon DA, Weinreb LD, McMahon M: The Symbolics
           Genera Programming Environment. IEEE Software, Nov. 1987

[Was86]    Wasserman AI, Pircher PA, Shewmake DT, Kersten ML: Devel-
           oping Interactive Information Systems with the User Software
           Engineering Methodolgy. IEEE Transactions on Software Engi-
           neering, Vol. 12, No. 2, Feb. 1986

[Wei88]    Weinand A, Gamma E, Marty R: ET++—An Object Oriented
           Application Framework in C++. OOPSLA 88, Special Issue of
           SIGPLAN Notices, Vol. 23, No. 11, 1988

[Wei89a]   Weinand A, Gamma E, Marty R: Design and Implementation of
           ET++, a Seamless Object-Oriented Application Framework. Struc-
           tured Programming, Vol. 10, No. 2, 1989

[Win88]    Winkler JFH (Ed.): Proceedings of the International Workshop on
           Software Version and Configuration Control, Grassasu, 1988

[Wir85]    Wirth N: Programming in Modula-2. Springer-Verlag, 1985

[Wir88]    Wirth N, Gutknecht J: The Oberon System. Report ETH Zürich,
           1988

[Zav84]   Zave P: The Operational Versus the Conventional Approach to
          Software Development. Communications of the ACM, Feb. 1984

# Index

# Texts and Monographs in Computer Science

# Texts and Monographs in Computer Science